Scheler's Ethical Personalism

Perspectives in Continental Philosophy
John D. Caputo, series editor

1. John D. Caputo, ed., *Deconstruction in a Nutshell: A Conversation with Jacques Derrida.*
2. Michael Strawser, *Both/And: Reading Kierkegaard—From Irony to Edification.*
3. Michael Barber, *Ethical Hermeneutics: Rationality in Enrique Dussel's Philosophy of Liberation.*
4. James H. Olthuis, ed., *Knowing* Other-*wise: Philosophy at the Threshold of Spirituality.*
5. James Swindal, *Reflection Revisited: Jürgen Habermas's Discursive Theory of Truth.*
6. Richard Kearney, *Poetics of Imagining: Modern and Postmodern.* Second edition.
7. Thomas W. Busch, *Circulating Being: From Embodiment to Incorporation—Essays on Late Existentialism.*
8. Edith Wyschogrod, *Emmanuel Levinas: The Problem of Ethical Metaphysics.* Second edition.
9. Francis J. Ambrosio, ed., *The Question of Christian Philosophy Today.*
10. Jeffrey Bloechl, ed., *The Face of the Other and the Trace of God: Essays on the Philosophy of Emmanuel Levinas.*
11. Ilse N. Bulhof and Laurens ten Kate, eds, *Flight of the Gods: Philosophical Perspectives on Negative Theology.*
12. Trish Glazebrook, *Heidegger's Philosophy of Science.*
13. Kevin Hart, *The Trespass of the Sign.* Second edition.
14. Mark C. Taylor, *Journeys to Selfhood: Hegel and Kierkegaard.* Second edition.
15. Dominique Janicaud, Jean-François Courtine, Jean-Louis Chrétien, Michel Henry, Jean-Luc Marion, and Paul Ricoeur, *Phenemenology and the "Theological Turn": The French Debate.*
16. Karl Jaspers, *The Question of German Guilt.* Introduction by Joseph W. Koterski, S.J.
17. Jean-Luc Marion, *The Idol and Distance: Five Studies.* Translated with an introduction by Thomas A. Carlson.
18. Jeffrey Dudiak, *The Intrigue of Ethics: A Reading of the Idea of Discourse in the Thought of Emmanuel Levinas.*
19. Robyn Horner, *Rethinking God As Gift: Marion, Derrida, and the Limits of Phenomenology.*
20. Mark Dooley, *The Politics of Exodus: Søren Kierkegaard's Ethic of Responsibility.*
21. Merold E. Westphal, Jr., *Overcoming Onto-theology: Toward a Postmodern Christian Faith.*
22. Stanislas Breton, *The Word and the Cross.* Translated with an introduction by Jacquelyn Porter.
23. Edith Wyschogrod, Jean-Joseph Goux, and Eric Boynton, eds., *The Enigma of Gift and Sacrifice.*
24. Jean-Luc Marion, *Prolegomena to Charity.* Translated by Stephen Lewis.

Scheler's Ethical Personalism

ITS LOGIC, DEVELOPMENT, AND PROMISE

PETER H. SPADER

Fordham University Press
New York
2002

For permissions, see pages 319–321.

Perspectives in Continental Philosophy No. 25
ISSN 1089-3938

Library of Congress Cataloging-in-Publication Data

Spader, Peter H.
Scheler's ethical personalism : its logic, development, and promise / Peter H. Spader.– 1st ed.
p. cm. – (Perspectives in continental philosophy ; no. 25)
Includes bibliographical references.
ISBN 0-8232-2177-6 (hc.) – ISBN 0-8232-2178-4 (pbk.)
1. Scheler, Max, 1874–1928. I. Title. II. Series.
B3329.S484 S73 2002
193–dc21 2001007381

Printed in the United States of America
02 03 04 05 06 5 4 3 2 1
First Edition

For my wife, Nancy Skidmore Spader

CONTENTS

PART 3: THE CHALLENGE OF SCHELER'S NEW ETHICS

ACKNOWLEDGMENTS

The time-honored tradition of thanking those who have helped in the creation of a book is most appropriate. I did not create this book alone. I have been helped and encouraged by many people since that day at Columbia University when I first encountered the works of Scheler, down to the present time as Jack Caputo, Anthony Chiffolo, and others at Fordham University Press shepherd this manuscript to you (with special thanks to the copy editor, Jonathan Lawrence, and to an anonymous reviewer). Indeed, so many people have helped me over the years that it is impossible to name them all individually, though I here give thanks to them all. I will, however, now give the reader a sense of the scope of my indebtedness.

First, I am indebted to my colleagues here at Marywood and at the other schools where I have taught. Second are the people who responded to my essays at conferences and in articles. There is nothing quite like a fresh insight to help the development of ideas. Third are those who read the manuscript of this book as it grew and changed over the years. These people provided the kind of specific criticisms so necessary to the development of a manuscript. Fourth are the Scheler scholars I have met both in print and in live dialogues. Here I must name three who are especially close. Philip Blosser and Eugene Kelly have walked the path with me for some time now, and are most welcome companions. Above us all, however, is Manfred Frings, the editor of the Scheler's *Gesammelte Werke.* From the day I first read his book on Scheler (in 1965) I have drawn inspiration and support first from his works and later from the person. His encouragement and gentle mentoring have meant much to me, as they have to many Scheler scholars over the years.

Finally, I owe a very special debt to two others. The first is Erázim Kohak, late of Boston University and the woods of New Hampshire, now back in his beloved Prague. Erázim came to

Bowling Green University as a visiting professor when I was a young and green teacher there. At a very crucial point in my development as a scholar and person he lifted me up, lent a helpful hand, and taught me much about writing as he read drafts of many of my articles and early versions of this book. Finally, this book is dedicated to my wife, Nancy Skidmore Spader, whose love, wit, wisdom, and joy (not to mention her practical skills as a proofreader and editor) have sustained and illuminated me for more than forty years. In the light of her love I have seen Scheler's words take life.

Beyond all the individuals who have helped me, I thank Marywood University for its support, especially for a sabbatical leave in the fall 1999 semester that allowed me to finally finish the first complete draft of my manuscript. I thank also the publishers of the books I have drawn quotes from and the publishers of the articles I have woven into this book; these are listed in the Permissions section at the end of this book. Finally, the last traditional task of an acknowledgment is especially appropriate in my case. Despite the best efforts of all of these people, the errors that remain are all mine.

ABBREVIATIONS

Scheler's Collected Works in German

GW1 *Frühe Schriften*. Vol. 1, *Gesammelte Werke*. Bonn: Bouvier Verlag, 1971.

GW2 *Der Formalismus in der Ethik und die materiale Wertethik: Neuer Versuch der Grundlegung eines ethischen Personalismus*. Vol. 2, *Gesammelte Werke*. Bonn: Bouvier Verlag, 1980.

GW3 *Vom Umsturz der Werte: Abhandlungen und Aufsätze*. Vol. 3, *Gesammelte Werke*. Bonn: Bouvier Verlag, 1972.

GW4 *Politisch-pädagogische Schriften*. Vol. 4, *Gesammelte Werke*. Bonn: Bouvier Verlag, 1982.

GW5 *Vom Ewigen im Menschen*. Vol. 5, *Gesammelte Werke*. Bonn: Bouvier Verlag, 1954.

GW6 *Schriften zur Soziologie und Weltanschauungslehre*. Vol. 6, *Gesammelte Werke*. Bonn: Bouvier Verlag, 1963.

GW7 *Wesen und Formen der Sympathie*. Vol. 7, *Gesammelte Werke*. Bonn: Bouvier Verlag, 1973.

GW8 *Die Wissensformen und die Gesellschaft*. Vol. 8, *Gesammelte Werke*. Bonn: Bouvier Verlag, 1980.

GW9 *Späte Schriften*. Vol. 9, *Gesammelte Werke*. Bonn: Bouvier Verlag, 1976.

GW10 *Schriften aus dem Nachlass, Band I. Zur Ethik und Erkenntnislehre*. Vol. 10, *Gesammelte Werke*. Bonn: Bouvier Verlag, 1957.

GW11 *Schriften aus dem Nachlass, Band II. Erkenntnislehre und Metaphysik*. Vol. 11, *Gesammelte Werke*. Bonn: Bouvier Verlag, 1979.

GW12 *Schriften aus dem Nachlass, Band III. Philosophische Anthropologie*. Vol. 12, *Gesammelte Werke*. Bonn: Bouvier Verlag, 1987.

GW13 *Schriften aus dem Nachlass, Band IV. Philosophie und Ge-*

schichte. Vol. 13, *Gesammelte Werke*. Bonn: Bouvier Verlag, 1990.

GW14 *Schriften aus dem Nachlass, Band V. Varia I*. Vol. 14, *Gesammelte Werke*. Bonn: Bouvier Verlag, 1993.

GW15 *Schriften aus dem Nachlass, Band V. Varia II*. Vol. 15, *Gesammelte Werke*. Bonn: Bouvier Verlag, 1993.

Books and Collections of Essays by Scheler (English Translation)

E *On the Eternal in Man*. Translated by Bernard Noble. Hamden, Conn.: Archon Books by The Shoe String Press, 1972.

ER *Ressentiment*. Translated by Lewis B. Coser and William A. Holdheim. Milwaukee: Marquette University Press, 1998.

F *Formalism in Ethics and Non-Formal Ethics of Values: A New Attempt toward the Foundation of an Ethical Personalism*. Translated by Manfred S. Frings and Roger L. Funk, Northwestern University Studies in Phenomenology and Existential Philosophy. Evanston: Northwestern University Press, 1973.

MP *Man's Place in Nature*. Translated by Hans Meyerhof. New York: Noonday Press, 1971.

NS *The Nature of Sympathy*. Translated by Peter Heath. London: Routledge & Kegan Paul, 1954.

PE *Selected Philosophical Essays*. Translated by David R. Lachterman. Northwestern University Studies in Phenomenology and Existential Philosophy. Evanston: Northwestern University Press, 1973.

PP *Philosophical Perspectives*. Translated by Oscar A. Haac. Boston: Beacon Press, 1958.

PSK *Problems of a Sociology of Knowledge*. Translated by Manfred S. Frings. International Library of Sociology. London: Routledge & K. Paul, 1980.

PV *Person and Self-Value: Three Essays*. Edited by Manfred S. Frings. Dordrecht: M. Nijhoff, 1987.

Individual Works by Scheler (English and German)

ARG "Absolutsphäre und Realsetzung der Gottesidee." GW10 179–253.
DIS "Die Idole der Selbsterkenntnis." GW3 215–92.
EIR "Idealism-Realism." PE 288–356.
EOA "*Ordo Amoris*." PE 98–135.
EPL "Exemplars of Persons and Leaders." PV 125–98.
EPR "Problems of Religion." E 105–356.
FKC "The Forms of Knowledge and Culture." PP 13–49.
FWB "Die Formen des Wissens und die Bildung." GW8 85–119.
GIR "Idealismus-Realismus." GW9 288–356.
GOA "*Ordo Amoris*." GW10 347–76.
GPR "Probleme der Religion." GW5 101–354.
GR "Das Ressentiment im Aufbau der Moralen." GW3 33–149.
ISK "The Idols of Self-Knowledge." PE 3–97.
LDT "Lehre von den drei Tatsachen." GW10 431–502.
MEA "Man in an Era of Adjustment." PP 94–126.
MG "Mensch und Geschichte." GW9 120–44.
MH "Man and History." PP 65–93.
MWA "Mensch im Weltalter des Ausgleiches." GW9 145–70.
PO "Philosopher's Outlook." PP 1–12.
PSW "Probleme einer Sociologie des Wissens." GW8 15–190.
PTC "Phenomenology and the Theory of Cognition." PE 136–201.
PUE "Phänomenologie und Erkenntnistheorie." GW10 377–430.
PW "Philosophische Weltanschauung." GW9 76–170.
RR "Repentance and Rebirth." E 35–65.
RW "Reue und Wiedergeburt." GW5 27–59.
SMK *Die Stellung des Menschen im Kosmos*. GW9 7–71.
TPM "Die transzendentale und die psychologische Methode: Eine grundsätzliche Erörterung zur philosophischen Methodik." GW1 197–335.
TTF "The Theory of the Three Facts." PE 202–75.
VF "Vorbilder und Führer." GW10 255–344.

Works by Kant

KDV *The Doctrine of Virtue.* Translated by Mary Gregor. New York: Harper and Row, 1964.

KFM *Foundations of the Metaphysics of Morals.* Translated by Lewis White Beck. Indianapolis: Bobbs-Merrill, 1959.

KGM *Grundlegung zur Metaphysik der Sitten.* Vol. 4, Preussische Akademie der Wissenschaften. Riga: Johann Friedrich Hartknoch, 1787.

KMS *Die Metaphysik der Sitten.* Vol. 6, Preussische Akademie der Wissenschaften. Riga: Johann Friedrich Hartknoch, 1797–98.

KPR *Immanuel Kant: Critique of Practical Reason and Other Writings in Moral Philosophy.* Translated by Lewis White Beck. Chicago: University of Chicago Press, 1949.

KPU *Critique of Pure Reason.* Translated by Norman Kemp Smith. New York: St. Martin's Press, 1965.

KPV *Kritik der praktischen Vernunft.* Vol. 5, Preussische Akademie der Wissenschaften. Riga: Johann Friedrich Hartknoch, 1788.

KRV *Kritik der reiner Vernunft.* Vol. 4, Preussische Akademie der Wissenschaften. Riga: Johann Friedrich Hartknoch, 1787.

1
INTRODUCTION

1
Introduction

Prelude

In the early years of the twentieth century, a new beginning in ethics took shape as a German philosopher named Max Scheler laid the foundations for an ethical personalism that would challenge the austere rational ethics of Immanuel Kant. Scheler's work opened new insights into values, feelings, and the person. Using the classic phenomenological approach, he presented a fresh view of the intricacy of the world of values, seeing not just values, but values arranged hierarchically in ranks. He rehabilitated the role of feelings in morals, distinguishing "cognitive" feelings from passions. Indeed, Scheler defended a logic of feeling, presenting an interrelated realm of intentional feelings, acts of preference that give us the rank of a value, and acts of love that open our hearts to whole new realms of higher values, enabling us to grow morally. He showed us how acts of hatred blind and distort our vision of values. Crowning his work on values and feelings, Scheler defended the autonomy and dignity of the whole, integrated person—a being centered in the heart, not the head. Finally, he began to forge a subtle ethics worthy of his view of values, feelings, and the person. In sum, Scheler began to shape a new ethical personalism.

This book will develop the systematic nature of Scheler's quest for an ethical personalism in order to show how the work he so admirably began can be completed. Scheler was a pioneering explorer, and as happens with many pioneers, he was so taken with what he saw that his notes are sometimes garbled, his maps sometimes poorly drawn and noted. By retracing his steps I hope to correct some of the misunderstandings that have grown up over the years due to the nature of Scheler's task and the writings he has left us, for only then can we begin to concentrate not just on what he said but also on what he was trying to get us to see.

Scheler had a great genius both for generating new insights and for grasping the problems presented by what he then saw. He also had a great desire to work on all of those problems at once. What he did not have was the patience to explain in sufficient detail the logic of what he was doing and why he was doing it, or the grace of years to complete the mission he set himself. Thus the task of developing his promising beginnings is now ours.

The Promise of Scheler

Scheler's work is so promising because he reintroduces what had been cast out of ethics by rationalism. In the face of the complexity of competing values and the apparently chaotic and overwhelming world of feelings, many thinkers have retreated to reason—to the head—as the road to moral wisdom. As admirable as reason is, however, it has not given us an ethics true to the felt complexity of moral experience. This is why Scheler's attempt at a new beginning in ethics is so exciting.

Yet to understand what Scheler was seeking and why, we must first understand why feelings and the heart have been rejected as the road to moral wisdom, why so many have turned to reason. To do so let us look at Immanuel Kant, perhaps the greatest champion of pure reason philosophy has ever seen. Kant retreated to reason because he believed experience was an unworthy basis for knowledge, including moral wisdom. He believed experience was unworthy because it could not supply a truly stable basis for morals that is free from the contingency, relativity, and uncertainty of the empirical. For Kant, experience is a combination of the contingent, unreliable, chaotic matter supplied by the senses, on the one side, and the stable, reliable form given by reason, on the other. Thus knowledge must be rooted in the formal side of his formal-material dichotomy. Since pure reason gives us pure form, to gain knowledge, to gain moral wisdom, we must reject all but pure reason and the pure form it gives us.

Kant's retreat to this rational formalism forced him to reject much of what we ordinarily take to be part of our moral lives. He abandoned the fullness of the world of values because he believed that all values except the purely formal value of lawfulness were rooted in the material side of his dichotomy. He abandoned "material" feelings and the heart as a reliable source of moral direction (though the feeling of respect for the law is still allowed) for the same reason. Finally, given the role of pure reason as our only access to pure form, all we are as persons had to be subordinated to that same pure reason. In Kant we see an ultimate and pure triumph of reason over everything else.

Kant's approach produces the neat formulas of his categorical imperative, but the moral world we inhabit as feeling beings resists reduction to Kant's rational formulas. Our moral choices occur within a complicated world of competing values, with each value and value-complex demanding its due. Furthermore, when material values come into conflict, the retreat to Kant's rational formulas fails to give us adequate direction. For example, the men and women who enter military service for the sake of their country, knowing they will be asked to kill other persons, or on the other side, the men and women who refuse to enter military service because they cannot so bring themselves to kill other persons—all face a heart-wrenching clash of values as they decide what to do. Unfortunately for Kant, such value dilemmas have at their lived, felt core a conflict that cannot be adequately resolved simply by attempting to obey a categorical imperative to rationally decide which "maxim" can both be willed as a universal law and treats all rational persons as ends in themselves. Kant's setting of the formal value of lawfulness (of "universalizability") above all other values does give us the neat rational formulas of the categorical imperative, but these formulas ignore the call of the nonformal[1] values in a moral dilemma (in our example, the call of the complex and compelling set of values of the lives of human persons on one side, and the complex and compelling set of values signaled by the phrase "my country" on the other—not to mention other values as well). The values in a live moral dilemma are not defined by reason, and only by turning away from the fullness and complexity of the felt value conflicts to the sim-

[1] There is a debate over how to translate the German word *material*. The English word "material" is not totally inaccurate, as long as you do not import Kant's dichotomy into the debate by using it. Since this is difficult to do, I prefer the less elegant "nonformal," since it more clearly signals Scheler's basic opposition to Kant's use of the formal-material dichotomy.

plicity of a rational formula can we follow Kant. Yet nonformal values are not lived as variables in a purely rational formula, and any attempt to place them in such a formula strips them of the felt weight of their essential nature.

Scheler did not believe we needed to retreat to the austerity of a formalism to achieve reliable moral direction. In a series of works, the most central of which is *Formalism in Ethics and Non-Formal Ethics of Values: A New Attempt toward the Foundation of an Ethical Personalism* (*Der Formalismus in der Ethik und die Materiale Wertethik: Neuer Versuch der Grundlegung eines Ethischen Personalismus*),[2] he began to reclaim what Kant had expelled from ethics. Using the classic phenomenological approach, Scheler showed nonformal values to be an "objective"[3] and reliable basis for moral judgment. He sketched a world of complex, multi-tiered ranks of nonformal values that allows moral dilemmas to be faced in their full value dimensions. Scheler rescued feelings as well, showing that feelings are not all tied to the world of the empirically contingent. Indeed, the word "feelings" covers a very diverse range of phenomena. For example, the uncontrollable passions that bind and blind us are called "feelings," yet so too are the special "cognitive" acts of "feeling" that allow us to "see" what reason is blind to. Scheler showed that such "cognitive" feelings give us access to "objective" values and their place in an "objective" ranking of values. He explored the levels of such "cognitive" feelings from the simplest of intentional feelings up to love and hate seen as acts that open and close the eyes of our hearts to whole

---

[2] *Der Formalismus in der Ethik und die Materiale Wertethik: Neuer Versuch der Grundlegung eines Ethischen Personalismus* was first published in the *Jahrbuch fur Philosophie und phänomenologische Forschung* in two parts, the first in 1913 and the second in 1916. It is reprinted as volume 2 of the *Gesammelte Werke*. Max Scheler, *Der Formalismus in der Ethik und die Materiale Wertethik: Neuer Versuch der Grundlegung eines Ethischen Personalismus* (1913–16; rpt. Bern: Franke Verlag, 1980 [now Bonn: Bouvier Verlag]). The English translation is *Formalism in Ethics and Non-Formal Ethics of Values: A New Attempt toward the Foundation of an Ethical Personalism,* translated by Manfred S. Frings and Roger L. Funk (Evanston: Northwestern University Press, 1973). This work will be referred to below using the *Gesammelte Werke* edition and this translation by means of the abbreviation GW2/F. All quotations from this translation are with the permission of Northwestern University Press. See the Permissions section for details.

[3] When Scheler calls values "objective" he does not mean object-like, but rather is pointing to their noncontingent and nonrelative status.

realms of values. Finally, Scheler began to explore what can go wrong with such cognitive feeling, and points to "disorders of the heart" that are at the deepest roots of evil.

Scheler's work on values and feelings is enough to suggest the fertile possibilities his insights opened in contrast to the austere rational ethics of Kant. But above all of Scheler's insights into values and the heart stands his view of the person, a view that rejects any reduction or subordination of the person to a single element such as reason. Put simply, Scheler's belief is that the person *is* what ties together all of the different acts that the person performs. To use his own stark equation, the person is "*the concrete and essential unity of being of acts of different essences*" (GW2 382/F 383), and perhaps more importantly, "the *whole person* is contained in *every* fully concrete act, and the whole person '*varies*' in and through every act—without being exhausted in his being in any of these acts, and without 'changing' like a thing in time. . . . Identity lies solely in the qualitative direction of this pure becoming different" (GW2 384–85/F 385).

For Scheler the person is essentially a *dynamic* being, and since the person, the unity of acts, varies in each act, we cannot reduce the person to a single act, for although we can see the person within each concrete act, the person is not just a single concrete act alone, but the qualitative direction of a pure "becoming different" that is contained in each act. It is this dynamic, qualitative direction of the pure "becoming different" that is of the greatest significance for ethics. For if the person is a dynamic, qualitative direction of unique concrete acts, then ethics cannot focus on single acts alone, but must rather look to the dynamic growth, or decay, of the qualitative direction the person is.

Nor did Scheler simply explore values, the heart, and the person. The ethical approach he begins to forge in the light of his insights into values, the heart, and the person is as novel as these insights that demand it. For example, despite his belief in a hierarchical ranking of separate tiers of "objective" values, Scheler does not reduce morality to norms or laws, for (among other reasons) norms and laws tend to focus more on individual acts than on the qualitative direction of the pure becoming different the person is. Thus, despite the "objective" ranking of values that Scheler sees, he rejects any ethics that is rooted in a "table of values" or set of laws. Indeed, he ultimately points us to "model" persons as the best road to moral wisdom.

Once again, we see Scheler exploring exciting insights of potentially great significance. After centuries of rational attempts to understand the complexity we experience in every moral choice, Scheler opened the possibility of an ethics true to the richness of both the full range of values and value conflicts we actually experience and the complex beings of heart (as well as head and will) we actually are.

The Problems of Scheler

Scheler's creative outpourings initially struck a responsive chord. Herbert Spiegelberg notes in *The Phenomenological Movement* that "in the early twenties before the advent of Martin Heidegger Max Scheler was in the eyes of the German public the number two phenomenologist" (1971, 228). Yet despite the exciting possibilities opened by Scheler's work, as well as the early acclaim attested to by Spiegelberg, there are relatively few philosophers today,[4] especially in the English-speaking world, who have read Scheler or taken him seriously. Indeed, Scheler's low visibility on today's philosophical scene led a recent translator of a number of Scheler's key essays to begin his introduction with a lengthy answer to the "unavoidable" question of whether it was "any longer worthwhile to read Scheler as a philosopher" (Scheler, *Selected Philosophical Essays,* xi ff.), and a recent short introduction to Scheler ends with a section entitled "Why Read Scheler Today?" (Dunlop 1991, 71–84). How could this happen?

There are always a number of reasons why a particular thinker or line of thought is left by the wayside, and many of them have little to do with the merits of the thinker or the line of thought. For example, both the complexity of Scheler's insights and the relative lack of popularity of the classic phenomenological approach he used in his explorations are barriers to understanding

[4] Though the biannual Internationales Max-Scheler-Kolloquium sponsored by the Max Scheler Gesellschaft, the completion of the *Gesammelte Werke,* and a growing number of studies and translations of Scheler's work (in a variety of languages) show that this may well change.

and appreciating his work.[5] In Scheler's case there is a more basic problem. So far, no one has clearly and fully presented the logic of the development of Scheler's thought. This has left three serious enigmas about his work unresolved, enigmas that have hindered the understanding and appreciation of both what Scheler was doing and why he was doing it.

The first enigma lies in the fact that Scheler does not always provide the kind of evidence for his basic claims that one would expect, and which, indeed, he promises. This is particularly serious because the classic phenomenological approach as practiced by Scheler[6] requires a careful attempt to bring the reader (through a special kind of "description") to the experience of whatever one is talking about, for it is in the experience of the "things themselves" that we find evidence for any claims made. Although Scheler does, at times, present detailed phenomenological descriptions and investigations (one example is his book-length investigation of *ressentiment*),[7] at key points in the development of

---

[5] There are, of course, other possible reasons. Philip Blosser, in *Scheler's Critique of Kant's Ethics,* suggests factors such as "the decline of widespread interest in Value Theory," "the rise of logical empiricism with its insistence that only two kinds of cognitive language are possible," and "the ascendancy of existential philosophy and waning interest in ethics in post-World-War II Germany" (1995, 14–16). Earlier, Wilfried Hartmann surveyed "Max Scheler and the English-Speaking World" (1968) and developed four reasons: first, the "bad press" Scheler received in both England and the United States; second, Scheler's relationship with the Catholic Church; third, his "complicated style"; and fourth, the fact that in the English-speaking world, interest in phenomenology was centered mostly on Husserl's theoretical studies. All quotations from Blosser's book are with the permission of Ohio University Press. See the Permissions section for details.

[6] Many people—even those who would still consider themselves phenomenologists—do not accept the classic phenomenological approach as practiced by Scheler as valid. Indeed, this is such an important issue that I develop and defend Scheler's phenomenological approach, especially in chapter 3.

[7] The study is Max Scheler, "Das Ressentiment im Aufbau der Moralen." It is a revised version of an essay entitled "Über Ressentiment und moralisches Werturteil," which originally appeared in 1912. In its present version this essay first appeared in 1915 in the collection *Abhandlungen und Aufsätze,* later retitled *Vom Umsturtz der Werte.* It is reprinted in volume 3 of the *Gesammelte Werke.* Max Scheler, *Vom Umsturtz der Werte* (1915; rpt. Bern: Franke Verlag, 1972 [now Bonn: Bouvier Verlag]), 33–147. The English translation is Max Scheler, *Ressentiment,* with an introduction by Manfred S. Frings and translated by Lewis B. Coser and William A. Holdheim (1961; rpt. Milwaukee: Marquette University Press, 1998). This work will be referred to using the abbreviation GR/ER.

his vision what he gives us is not a phenomenological description but rather a curt recitation of claims.[8]

The second, and more dramatic, enigma is presented by the path Scheler's quest for a new ethical personalism took. Although the *Formalism in Ethics and Non-Formal Ethics of Values* is Scheler's most important book in ethics, it is also a sprawling work in which he only begins to develop his vision of values, feelings, ethics, and the person, promising to provide a definitive completion to his ethics in later works under way.[9] Instead he presented studies in religion and metaphysics that seemed to have little or no direct connection to his studies of values and the person, or to his ethics.[10]

The third enigma arose when, after presenting a spirited defense of theism, Scheler suddenly adopted a "panentheism" which he only briefly sketched[11] before dying of a heart attack at the relatively young age of fifty-four, leaving behind what James

---

All quotations from this translation are with the permission of Marquette University Press. See the Permissions section for details.

[8] Perhaps the most important example is the fact that Scheler never fully develops, nor does he provide evidence for, the hierarchy of value ranks he sketches. This matter will be developed in detail in the chapters below, as will all my claims made in this introductory chapter about the problems Scheler's thought presents.

[9] The very first sentence of the "Introductory Remarks" in the *Formalism* states: "In a major work planned for the near future I will attempt to develop a non-formal ethics of values on the broadest possible basis of phenomenological experience" (GW2 29/F 5).

[10] With a key essay being Max Scheler, "Probleme der Religion," in *Vom Ewigen im Menschen,* which first appeared in 1921. It was reprinted in volume 5 of the *Gesammelte Werke.* Max Scheler, *Vom Ewigen im Menschen* (1921; rpt. Bern: Franke Verlag, 1954 [now Bonn: Bouvier Verlag]), 101–354. The English translation is "Problems of Religion," in *On the Eternal in Man,* translated by Bernard Noble (1960; rpt. Hamden, Conn.: Shoe String Press, 1972), 105–356. This work will be referred to using the abbreviation GPR/EPR. All quotations from this translation are with the permissions of HarperCollins Publishers and SCM Ltd. Press. See the Permissions section for details.

[11] Scheler presented the fullest initial statement of his new position in *Die Stellung des Menschen im Kosmos* (Darmstadt: Otto Reichl Verlag, 1928). This work is reprinted in volume 9 of the *Gesammelte Werke.* Max Scheler, *Die Stellung des Menschen im Kosmos* (1928; rpt. Bern: Franke Verlag, 1976 [now Bonn: Bouvier Verlag]), 7–71. The English translation is Max Scheler, *Man's Place in Nature,* translated with an introduction by Hans Meyerhoff (New York: Noonday Press, 1971). This work will be referred to using the abbreviation SMK/MP. All quotations from this translation are with the permission of Beacon Press. See the Permissions section for details.

Collins called "an enigma which scandalized so many people" (1962, 107). To make matters worse, Scheler's new panentheism seems so flawed that it is hard to understand the philosophical reasons why he embraced it. This seemingly inexplicable change in basic position and the apparent flaws in the new panentheism present obstacles to even the most sympathetic critics.[12]

Now the three enigmas I have just sketched need not have remained so puzzling for so long. Indeed, such difficulties ought to be expected in a thinker exploring new territory. The fact that Scheler was more interested in pursuing his quest for a new ethical personalism than he was in supplying detailed evidence for all of his claims should not be surprising. Furthermore, given the novelty of his insights and approach, there should be no surprise that Scheler undertook changes in direction and position and had difficulties with the new positions he forged. Indeed, since his untimely death cut off the possibility of his meeting the problems his work presented, one might expect that scholars would have long ago followed up on Scheler's pioneering efforts and made the logic of his quest more understandable.

What happened instead is, given the promise of Scheler's pioneering work, surprising. All too many people simply gave up on attempting to understand the development of his thought as having a philosophically understandable logic. Put simply, many critics turned away from the attempt to understand the problems presented by Scheler's thought as rooted in his wrestling with philosophical problems, seeing them instead as symptoms of psychological problems of Scheler the man, problems that undercut his philosophical abilities. As I show in chapter 8, this psychological approach to understanding problems in Scheler's thought, and

[12] This is shown by Eugene Kelly's new study of Scheler, entitled *Structure and Diversity: Studies in the Phenomenology of Max Scheler* (Dordrecht: Kluwer Academic, 1997) (this book is volume 141 in the Phaenomenologica series). Kelly develops many of Scheler's insights with great eloquence, clarity, and appreciation, and his book is an excellent introduction to much of Scheler's work. When he comes to Scheler's late metaphysics, however, he speaks of Scheler's contradictions as a reason for its failure (165) and says: "I have never forgiven Scheler for this late turn to metaphysics, which, however it may aim at integration and at a world culture, is itself too partial and too uncertain to advance that process" (195). The contradictions and incompleteness of Scheler's work must be rectified if judgments such as Kelly's are not to continue.

especially the development of it, has been so widely accepted that it became a feature of the introduction to many early translations of Scheler's work into English. Nor has its appeal abated. One of the more recent anthologies of English translations of Scheler's writings still embraces it (Bershady 1992).

Now an understanding of the personality and the personal problems of a thinker can add a new dimension to our appreciation of that thought and its genesis. But when it takes the place of philosophical understanding of a philosopher's insights and the development of those insights—when, instead of helping us to explain the philosophical problems the thinker was wrestling with, it explains away the need to do so—the psychological approach becomes a danger rather than a help. When, for example, the psychological approach to the problems of Scheler's thought and its development invades the introductions to translations and anthologies of his writings, you are warned even before reading Scheler's own words not to take these problems as philosophically significant.

This is unfortunate, because the philosophical work that *has* been done on Scheler reveals insights of potentially great value (some briefly sketched above). Indeed, despite Scheler's present relative obscurity there have been significant studies of specific elements of his insights. Furthermore, many scholars *have* attended to what Ernst Ranly called, in his study of *Scheler's Phenomenology of Community,* "the intrinsic merits of his thought" (1966, 8). And countering the introductions to the early English translations of Scheler's work, we had an excellent topical overview of Scheler's thought by Manfred Frings entitled *Max Scheler: A Concise Introduction into the World of a Great Thinker* (1965).[13] This pioneering study of Scheler in English has now been supplemented and expanded by Frings's most recent overview of Scheler's work, this time based upon Frings's extensive acquaintance with and study of the totality of the Scheler corpus achieved as he completed the Herculean task of editing the *Gesammelte Werke.* This new topical study, entitled *The Mind of Max Scheler: The First Comprehensive Guide Based on the Complete Works* (1997), is a

[13] This book was reissued as a "New Edition" (Milwaukee: Marquette University Press, 1996).

landmark in the integration and presentation of Scheler's thoughts, covering the topic areas of ethics, society, knowledge, religion, science, evolution, reality, love, resentment, capitalism, future, time, and death. Furthermore, beyond Frings's efforts, other scholars have worked to show elements of systematic unity in Scheler's thought, ranging from Ranly's short schema at the end of his study to the massive work in French by Maurice Dupuy entitled *La philosophie de Max Scheler: Son évolution et son unité* (1959), a study supplemented by his *La philosophie de la religion chez Max Scheler* (1959).

Such studies do show that incompleteness, dramatic change, and seemingly flawed new positions are not all we find in Scheler's thought and its development. But they still have not shown clearly enough the philosophical reasons why Scheler's quest for a new ethical personalism developed just the way it did, nor have they provided the detailed arguments needed to meet the problem of incompleteness or resolved core difficulties presented by his new panentheism. Nor have they answered the kind of serious criticism Scheler's work has suffered down through the years to the present time (see, for example, the criticisms presented throughout Blosser's book *Scheler's Critique of Kant's Ethics* [1995]). Accomplishing all of these tasks together requires a fuller presentation of the logic of what Scheler was doing than has yet been provided.

The Task of This Book

In this book I seek to illuminate, develop, and defend Scheler's insights through an understanding of the logic of the development of Scheler's quest for a new ethical personalism. Reconstructing the logic of the development of a pioneering line of thought is not easy. Scheler himself was well aware of the difficulties his writings would present, but he was also aware of the systematic nature of his quest. In the preface to the first edition of his key work in ethics, the *Formalism in Ethics and Non-Formal Ethics of Values,* he apologizes for his "long excursions" into "theories of knowledge and values" and states:

> The reader may at times find these painful to read from the viewpoint of style. Yet, given the present deficient status of the foundations of the discipline of ethics, they appeared to me urgently needed from both a theoretical and a philosophical viewpoint, because of the objective inseparability of the problems involved and because of the roots that ethics extends into the theory of knowledge and the theory of values. Without these excursions the specifically ethical parts of my work would have remained without ultimate foundations. In addition, the achievement of a *systematic* character, which, in my judgment, should belong to any philosophical foundation, including a phenomenological one, required that I demonstrate, throughout this work, interconnections with epistemological views of mine which have not yet been published together in a special volume.[14]

As noted above, Scheler wrote in haste, impatient to get to the problems he saw, but as this passage reveals, he was aware of the systematically interconnected nature of his quest. Furthermore, he does give us clues about what he is doing and why he is doing it, and if we consider philosophically meaningful both these clues and what he actually does, the logic of his quest can be understood.

Understanding the logic of Scheler's quest has a number of benefits. First of all, it reveals philosophical reasons for why he did not always provide the kind of detailed evidence he initially promised, why his quest took the turns it did, and why his new panentheism appeared to be so flawed. More importantly, a grasp of the logic of the development of Scheler's quest improves understanding of the individual insights that Scheler achieved, for they are seen not just as isolated insights, but as interactive elements in the dynamic context of his quest. Furthermore, such

[14] Scheler continues: "There may arise here and there a view according to which phenomenology deals only with isolated phenomena and essences, and according to which 'any will to system is a will to lies.' I am completely removed from such picture-book phenomenology. For inasmuch as discoverable *states of affairs* of this world *itself* form a systematic interconnective complex, a will to system would not be a 'will to lies'; it would, on the contrary, be a will not to notice the systematic character residing in *things* themselves, which is to be regarded as a consequence of a baseless 'will to anarchy.' To the objective reader this work will in other respects show that I have every reason to detach myself from such kinds of 'irrationalism,' which at times seek to attach themselves to my coattails" (GW2 10–11/F xviii–xix).

an approach allows the imbalances in presentation caused by the dynamics of the quest to be identified in ways that will account for apparent flaws and allow us to begin to "correct" them. Finally, understanding Scheler's thought as part of the totality of the quest also suggests possible further development of that thought, and allows me in the last section of this book to meet general criticisms of his personalistic ethics not yet countered in the earlier tracing of Scheler's quest.

An Abstract of This Book

The approach I will take in this book is rooted in the belief that to understand the philosophical work of a pioneer like Scheler we must understand as clearly as possible what philosophical problems he is wrestling with at each stage of the development of his insights. Furthermore, we must understand how these problems and their attempted solution create the framework for future development by setting new challenges.

This book is divided into four parts. Part 1 contains this introductory chapter. Part 2, "The Challenge of Kant," begins with chapter 2's development of the initial problems that challenged Scheler by showing how Kant was driven to a rationally formalistic ethics and how Kant's work presents formidable requirements for any nonformal ethics that would dare to rival it. Chapters 2, 3, 4, and 5 then explore Scheler's response to Kant, as I develop Scheler's defense of nonformal values, feelings, and the integrity of the full person.

Chapters 3, 4, and 5 also begin to unravel the first of the three enigmas that have so perplexed even sympathetic students of Scheler: his failure to provide key evidence for his claims. To see how the *Formalism in Ethics and Non-Formal Ethics of Values* answers the challenge of Kant is to see why Scheler undertook precisely the tasks he did in this work and why he did not attempt to provide there all the details of a phenomenology of values or the person, despite the importance of providing such evidence. Meeting the initial challenge of Kant requires Scheler to show the *possibility* that Kant was wrong to reject nonformal values and feelings and to reduce the person to a purely rational being; it does not require that he simultaneously provide all of the evidence for his insights. Thus, in the *Formalism* there is a logic both to what Scheler does and to what he does not do.

Yet showing why Scheler did not attempt to provide in the *Formalism* the full, detailed evidence needed to refute Kant does not show why he did not do so in later works, especially in the light of his promises to do so. To answer *this* question we must realize that although Kant's rationalism set the initial challenge with which Scheler wrestled, Scheler's insights into the nature of values, the heart, and the person presented him with a formidable set of new problems by the end of the *Formalism*. These problems presented such a basic challenge to the ethical personalism he had sketched in this book that meeting this challenge took precedence over providing the kind of phenomenological evidence he promised to supply as part of his "completion of his ethics." For as important as such evidence would be to finally refuting Kant's rationalism, Scheler could not achieve his ultimate goal of a new ethical personalism without an ethics adequate to the world of values and the person he had seen.

Thus, after the *Formalism,* Scheler's focus is no longer primarily on Kant, but rather on solving these new problems now standing in the way of the completion of his ethical personalism. Although Kant set the initial problems for Scheler, once Scheler had freed values, the heart, and the person from contingency he spent the rest of his life working on providing an ethics equal to the complex world of values and the full persons standing before these values.

The new set of problems Scheler's initial insights had created is explored in part 3 of this book, entitled "The Challenge of Scheler's New Ethics." Chapter 6 begins this part of the book with a development of the ethics Scheler sketched in the *Formalism* and of the new challenges it presented to Scheler in his attempt to complete his ethical personalism. One key problem grows out of the fact, as noted above, that Scheler's ethics is focused on the person. Put simply, moral values such as good and evil are values of the person and are realized along with the realization of nonmoral values. And, since the moral values are values of the dynamic, qualitative direction of unique acts the person is, Scheler ultimately points us to exemplars (model persons) for moral direction. Although this opens exciting new approaches to understanding the role of models in moral development, the fact that for Scheler *persons* are the best source of moral direction presented him with a serious challenge, which he develops at the end of the *Formalism*.

This challenge arises from the finite nature of the human person. Finite persons are quite limited in the range of values they can see and exemplify. Indeed, at one point Scheler calls this "*the essential tragic of all finite personal being* and its (essential) moral *imperfection*" (GW2 575/F 590). Given this serious limitation of finite persons, it is difficult to see how we could ever use such flawed finite persons as adequate moral models. Since all finite persons are limited in what they can see, do we not face the problem of the "blind leading the blind"? Scheler was aware of this difficulty presented by his new ethics. At the very end of the *Formalism* he indicates one possible solution when he suggests that the best source of moral direction would not be such limited finite persons, but rather the "infinite person," God.

This linking of God and ethics at the end of the *Formalism* not only suggests a way out of this immediate challenge but also provides a solution to the second enigma that Scheler's work has presented to even sympathetic critics, namely, the question of why Scheler, after the *Formalism,* turned to seemingly unrelated studies in religion and metaphysics rather than completing his ethics as he had promised. They are not unrelated studies. Since Scheler's ethics is radically rooted in the person, and the person who can best guide us in moral development is the infinite person, God, Scheler *had* to undertake religious/metaphysical investigations of God in order to complete his ethics.

Chapter 7 follows Scheler as he undertakes his search for God. Again, Scheler's investigations present serious new problems for both his ethics and his theism. Put simply, given his understanding of values, the person, and the realization of values, Scheler was faced with a particularly difficult version of the classic problem of evil (the problem of reconciling the existence of a good creator God with the presence of evil in the world).

This brings us to the third enigma, the one that scandalized so many: Scheler's abandonment of theism and the consequent difficulties presented by his new panentheism. Once the problems

Scheler's search for God created for his ethics and theism are seen, the philosophical reasons for his change from theism to panentheism become understandable. Furthermore, the reasons why Scheler's initial presentation of his panentheism seemed so flawed can also be seen, and the "flaws" can be corrected. Thus, chapters 8 and 9 develop the change in Scheler's religious/metaphysical position and correct the apparent defects created by the unbalanced presentation of his new panentheism.

With this I end my re-creation of the trajectory of Scheler's quest for a new ethical personalism. The last section of the book, part 4, uses the insights gained in this study to show that one can develop and defend Scheler's ethical personalism. Up to this point in the book I have been following the logic of the development of Scheler's thought. This approach allows me both to resolve the three enigmas and to better illuminate the insights Scheler achieved during his odyssey. It also allows me to begin correcting some of the imbalances in presentation and resulting misunderstandings that arose because of the dynamic of the development of these insights.

At the same time, however, this focus on the logic of the development of Scheler's thought, as illuminating as it is of the insights and as useful as it is in allowing me to meet problems that arose because of that development, is itself limiting. If we are to take Scheler's insights seriously, we must see the possibility that we can build upon what Scheler accomplished and complete his ethical personalism—that we can finish the task he began. Furthermore, we must see how we can answer the general criticisms of Scheler's work that have arisen. The last three chapters of this book undertake this new direction, these final tasks, and I signal this by adopting an overall title of "Defending a Schelerian Ethical Personalism" for this fourth part of the book.

Chapter 10, entitled "Defending the Central Role of the Person in Scheler's Ethics," shows how we can develop Scheler's ethical personalism by resolving the twin problems of how finite persons can be moral exemplars despite the "tragic limitation of finite persons" and how we can achieve the basic change of heart necessary if we are to grow morally. I then defend Scheler by meeting an attack by Husserlian phenomenologists on Scheler's approach to the knowing of other persons, the classic problem of intersubjectivity. Finally, I address the question of whether persons or values have primacy in Scheler's approach.

Chapter 11, entitled "Defending the Central Role of the Heart in Value-Ception," focuses on several key attacks on Scheler's *way* of knowing values, meeting a number of basic attacks on Scheler's belief that it is through the heart that we have access to values. Finally, chapter 12 defends Scheler's understanding of values and the nature of values, also returning again to the defense of Scheler's phenomenological approach. (This may seem an odd way to end a book on ethics, but meeting the radically skeptical attacks on Scheler's type of classic phenomenological approach is essential if we are to take seriously what he was trying to get us to see.)

A Note on Quotes

One last comment. Throughout this book I make use of frequent direct quotations from Scheler's writings. I do so for two reasons. First, many readers will not have ready access to Scheler's writings, either in the original German or in English translation. I believe it is important that the reader have an introduction not only to the abstracted and interpreted ideas of Scheler, but to the "very words" (albeit in translation!) he used. Second, as Ortega y Gasset said of Scheler: "Characteristic of his work is the most curious team of qualities: clarity and disorder" (quoted in Frings 1996, 5–6). I hope to make more manifest the order that was always there, but I also want you to experience the clarity firsthand.

Let us begin.

2

THE CHALLENGE OF KANT

2

Kant's Rational Formalism

Introduction

If you wish to understand a person's thought, you must see *why* he or she is thinking; if that person is a philosopher trying to solve philosophical problems, you must see what those problems are. The initial challenges Scheler was attempting to meet in his quest for a new ethical personalism were set by the rational, formal ethics of Immanuel Kant. As noted in chapter 1, Scheler's ethics is an ethics of nonformal values, values "seen" through special acts of "feeling," not reason, and the person seeing these values is not simply a rational being but a being with a heart. Thus to understand Scheler's quest we must first understand the Kant that created in Scheler such a fundamental rejection of formal, rational ethics.

Kant's "Copernican Turn"

The Kant to which Scheler reacted is the Kant of the *Critiques*. Kant was, in his "precritical" years, not the extreme formal rationalist whom Scheler so vehemently rejects. He was, for example, not unsympathetic to the role of feelings in morals. Indeed, as W. H. Werkmeister points out in his book on Kant, as late as 1763 Kant "was still holding that the faculty of perceiving the good (i.e., the material content) is feeling," and "still believed that Hutcheson and others had made important contributions to ethics in terms of moral feelings" (1980, 36). But after his "Co-

---

Sections of this chapter appeared in my essay "Scheler's Criticism of the Emptiness of Kant's Formal Ethics," in *Kritisches Jahrbuch der Philosophie Band 3: Denken des Ursprungs-Ursprung des Denkens: Schelers Philosophie und ihre Anfänge in Jena* (Wurzburg: Königshausen & Neuman, 1998), 121–36, and are reproduced here with permission.

pernican turn" Kant believed that it was *reason* and not feeling which gives us access to secure moral direction, that formal values supplied such direction, and that we are moral beings only as purely rational persons. Why Kant came to these judgments and how the position he came to was such a basic challenge to Scheler must now be explored.

To understand Kant's ethics we must understand his epistemology. We must do so not only because Kant's work is interrelated, but because a basic question that led to the Kant of the *Critiques* was not an ethical question but rather an epistemological one, specifically the question of the *validation* of knowledge. The problem that concerned Kant was not that of trying to decide whether something *is* true or not, but *why* we believe that some beliefs are not only true, but true with *certainty*. In the face of skepticism, especially that of Hume, Kant focused on seeking not just certain knowledge but the *roots* of that certainty.

Kant's most basic move in his search for the roots of what certainties he believed we had involved him in a "turn" he likened to that made by Copernicus. The nature of Kant's "Copernican turn" is so important I will quote Kant's own words concerning it (in the preface to the second edition of the *Critique of Pure Reason* where he is discussing the attempts to achieve certain [*a priori*] knowledge):

> Hitherto it has been assumed that all our knowledge must conform to objects. But all attempts to extend our knowledge of objects by establishing something in regard to them *a priori*, by means of concepts, have, on this assumption, ended in failure. We must therefore make trial whether we may not have more success in the tasks of metaphysics, if we suppose that objects must conform to our knowledge. . . . If intuition must conform to the constitution of the objects, I do not see how we could know anything of the latter *a priori;* but if the object (as object of the senses) must conform to the constitution of our faculty of intuition, I have no difficulty in conceiving such a possibility. Since I cannot rest in these intuitions if they are to become known, but must relate them as representations to something as their object, and determine this latter through them, either I must assume that the *concepts*, by means of which I obtain this determination, conform to the object, or else I assume that the objects, or what is the same thing, that the *experience* in

> which alone, as given objects, they can be known, conform to the concepts. In the former case, I am again in the same perplexity as to how I can know anything *a priori* in regard to the objects. In the latter case the outlook is more hopeful. For experience is itself a species of knowledge which involves understanding; and understanding has rules which I must presuppose as being in me prior to objects being given to me, and therefore as being *a priori*. They find expression in *a priori* concepts to which all objects of experience necessarily conform, and with which they must agree.[1]

The "turn" Kant makes here is of the greatest significance, for with it he comes to believe we *bring to experience* "rules" that structure and form experience, *a priori* rules that are prior in the sense that *what* we can experience is predefined by these rules. Thus, if we can discover what these rules are, we can see why we have certainty in knowledge. The certainty is afforded by these rules—it is, indeed, guaranteed by them. This certainty lies in the operation of our understanding and is not dependent upon anything "outside" of us. With this bold stroke Kant solves the problem of the roots of certainty, but he does so, as we will develop below, at a terrible diminution of values, feelings, and the person.

The implications of Kant's new position for epistemology are many, and many of them have been worked out by Kant and his followers. For our purposes we will look at only those most relevant to Scheler's work in ethics. The first and most relevant of these implications is that if Kant is correct, then all we *experience* is, from the standpoint of guaranteed certainty, of mixed value at best. This is because *experience* is a composite, half of which is provided by the rule-giving understanding, the other half by the senses. It is only the rules of the understanding that guarantee certainty, for only the rules of the understanding are stable, unchanging, and noncontingent. Thus they give form and order to the unordered "chaos" (the "matter") supplied by the senses. Yet only if we can somehow separate the form from the matter of any "object" we experience, only if we can somehow discover the

---

[1] Immanuel Kant, *Kritik der reiner Vernunft,* vol. 4, Preussische Akademie der Wissenschaften (Riga: Johann Friedrich Hartknoch, 1787), xvi–xviii. The English translation is *Critique of Pure Reason,* translated by Norman Kemp Smith (New York: St. Martin's Press, 1965), 22–23. This work will be referred to using the abbreviation KRV/KPU.

form-giving rules of the understanding, will we be sure that we have uncovered the roots of certain knowledge.

This turn is of such significance for ethics because it rules out all nonformal elements as possible bases for noncontingent ethical judgments. For Kant, the values we experience can be taken seriously as the basis for moral decisions only if they can be shown to be part of the realm of form, and not part of the realm of the senses, of the contingent. Furthermore, nonformal values are not the only thing put at risk. If Kant is correct, all feelings—unless they can be shown to be purely formal—are condemned as well. Finally, the moral person would be only pure reason, for it is pure reason that supplies the form, the guarantor of certainty *a priori*. It is this rejection by Kant of nonformal (material) values, the "feelings" that give us access to these values, and the whole person we are to which Scheler reacts so strongly.

Kant's Approach to Rational, Formal Ethics

Before we turn to Scheler's critique of Kant, however, we must first understand Kant's ethical position in some detail in order to see the formidable challenge it presents to Scheler or anyone else who wishes to champion nonformal values or feelings in ethics.

Kant's concern with the validation of moral knowledge is, as many have pointed out, as deep as his concern with the validation of knowledge of objects. Yet Kant's seeking of moral knowledge *a priori* is, if anything, more difficult than in the case of knowledge of objects. In seeking moral knowledge *a priori* we cannot simply show how we use *a priori* rules of understanding to order the "matter" supplied by the senses. We must show how the *will* can be given *a priori* direction. We are no longer dealing with "external" objects but rather with ourselves as willing beings. The problem is made particularly difficult for Kant because in solving the problem of *a priori* knowledge of objects, he had created within human being a fundamental split. As rational beings we inhabit a "world" of law, of *a priori* rules of the understanding. As sensual beings we inhabit a world of unordered "chaos." Our *experience*, including our experience of ourselves, is the experience of beings *bridging* these two worlds. It is experience of the matter of our senses now *ordered,* now "formed," by our understanding; it is experience of ourselves as "empirical" beings. Thus the question Kant faces in the moral realm is whether he can separate out from moral *experience* a purely formal and *a priori* direction for the will. As Kant says in the introduction to his *Critique of Practical Reason:* "This is, then, the first question: Is pure reason sufficient of itself to determine the will, or is it only as empirically conditioned that it can do so?"[2]

This brings us to another important question. What, in the moral sphere, is the "empirical" that we must avoid? And what is the "form" that will supply the *a priori* direction to the will? We see what Kant means by the "empirical" and by the nonformal (material) element in morals in Theorem I (in chapter 1 of "The Analytic of Pure Practical Reason") of the *Critique of Practical Reason:*

> All practical principles which presuppose an object (material) of the faculty of desire as the determining ground of the will are without exception empirical and can furnish no practical laws.
>
> By the term "material of the faculty of desire," I understand an object whose reality is desired. (KPV 21/KPR 132)

As we can see from this short passage, Kant ties all material or content of desire to objects. Now as Kant had argued in the *Critique of Pure Reason,* any "object" is a mixture of the form given by the understanding and the unordered matter given by sense. Thus Kant might be expected to simply argue that such a "composite" cannot give *a priori* grounds for morals. Thus all objects of desire are proscribed as the basis for the moral direction of the will. And this is true. But Kant here highlights a new element in his definition of the "empirical," arguing that all practical principles presupposing an object of the faculty of desire are empirical because in such cases

> the determining ground of choice consists in the conception of an object and its relation to the subject, whereby the faculty of desire

---

[2] Immanuel Kant, *Kritik der praktischen Vernunft,* vol. 5, Preussische Akademie der Wissenschaften (Riga: Johann Friedrich Hartknoch, 1788), 15. The English translation is *Critique of Practical Reason and Other Writings in Moral Philosophy,* translated by Lewis White Beck (Chicago: University of Chicago Press, 1949), 129. This work will be referred to using the abbreviation KPV/KPR.

> is determined to seek its realization. Such a relation to the subject is called pleasure in the reality of an object, and it must be presupposed as the condition of the possibility of the determination of choice. But we cannot know, *a priori,* of the idea of any object, whatever the nature of this idea, whether it will be associated with pleasure or displeasure or will be merely indifferent. Thus any such determining ground of choice must always be empirical. (KPV 21/ KPR 132)

Kant goes on to assert that since susceptibility to pleasure or pain varies from creature to creature and this can only be known empirically, a principle based upon "this subjective condition" lacks the "objective necessity which must be recognized *a priori*" (KPV 21–22/KPR 132). All values of all objects are thus proscribed as the basis for moral direction. With this relating of nonformal values to pleasure in such a way that they are all condemned to empirical contingency, Kant must reject all ethics based upon nonformal values of objects.

It is not just objects of value that Kant here condemns as contingent. He also specifically condemns feelings of pleasure as a way of achieving moral knowledge given *a priori.* Thus, for Kant, all such feelings are also part of the empirical realm, and not on the side of reason and the *a priori.*

Kant develops the condemnation of pleasure and feelings in Theorem II (in chapter 1 of "The Analytic of Pure Practical Reason"):

> All material practical principles are, as such, of one and the same kind and belong under the general principle of self-love or one's own happiness.
>
> Pleasure from the conception of the existence of a thing, in so far as it is a determining ground of the desire for this thing, is based upon the susceptibility of the subject because it depends upon the actual presence of an object. Thus it belongs to sense (feeling) and not to the understanding, which expresses a relation of a conception to an object by concepts and not the relation of an idea to the subject by feelings. (KPV 22/KPR 133)

In a corollary to this second theorem, Kant also argues that one cannot talk of higher or lower desires, higher or lower pleasures: "All practical rules relating to content place the determining principle of the will in the *lower desires*" (KPV 22/KPR 133). According to Kant, the important determining factor here is not the *idea* of the pleasing object, but rather how much that object will *please*. Pleasure is pleasure. Some "objects" are more in our power, for example, and the pleasures we find in them can be called "more refined" on this account: "But this is no reason to pass off such pleasures as a mode of determining the will different from that of the senses" (KPV 24/KPR 135).

Kant's rejection of feelings as a way to moral direction is not mitigated by his acceptance of a single feeling, the "respect for law," which forms Kant's definition of duty early in, for example, the *Foundations of the Metaphysics of Morals*,[3] where he says: "Duty is the necessity of an action executed from respect for law" (KGM 400/KFM 16). At that point Kant takes care to distinguish "respect for law" from other feelings and, in fact, adds a long footnote defending himself by claiming that this respect is not empirical in origin (see KGM 401/KFM 17–18).

Now that we have explored what Kant believes does *not* give us reliable moral knowledge (moral feelings and nonformal values), it is time to find out what he believes *does*. It is reason, a pure reason that spontaneously produces those forming categories which provide order to the chaotic, contingent matter supplied by the senses. As purely reasoning beings, we inhabit a world separate from the contingency and uncertainty of the empirical world of the senses. It is a world of freedom. As Kant puts it:

> As a rational being and thus as belonging to the intelligible world, man cannot think of the causality of his own will except under the idea of freedom, for independence from the determining causes of the world of sense (an independence which reason must always ascribe to itself) is freedom. The concept of autonomy is inseparably connected with the idea of freedom, and with the former there is inseparably bound the universal principle of morality, which ideally is the ground of all actions of rational beings, just as natural law is the ground of all appearances. (KGM 453/KFM 71)

---

[3] Immanuel Kant, *Grundlegung zur Metaphysik der Sitten,* vol. 4, Preussische Akademie der Wissenschaften (Riga: Johann Friedrich Hartknoch, 1787). The English translation is *Foundations of the Metaphysics of Morals,* translated by Lewis White Beck (Indianapolis: Bobbs-Merrill, 1959). This work will be referred to using the abbreviation KGM/KFM. All quotations from this translation are with the permission of Pearson Education, Inc. See the Permissions section for details.

The idea of freedom, the idea that to be moral we must freely choose, that we must be "autonomous," is an idea central to Kant. Kant *must* find a "world" in which the human person can have a free will, since the "natural world," the world of experience, is a world under sway of the contingency of efficient causality (KGM 446/KFM 65). For Kant it is only as inhabitants of the purely rational ("intelligible") world that we are free.

Indeed, Kant goes so far as to contrast the natural world and the intelligible world in such a way as to *define* will itself as free and rational. In the section subtitled "The Concept of Freedom Is the Key to the Explanation of the Autonomy of the Will," he says: "As will is a kind of causality of living beings so far as they are rational, freedom would be that property of this causality by which it can be effective independently of foreign causes determining it, just as natural necessity is the property of the causality of all irrational beings by which they are determined in their activity by the influence of foreign causes" (KGM 445–46/KFM 64). He then asks the rhetorical question, "What else, then, can the freedom of the will be but autonomy, i.e., the property of the will to be a law to itself?" (KGM 446–47/KFM 65). Thus we see that for Kant the moral person must be a purely rational being, for only as purely rational beings can we free ourselves from the contingency of the empirical.

Indeed, we are now at the moral principle arrived at *a priori:* the unconditional, categorical imperative. For immediately after the last sentence quoted above, Kant says: "The proposition that the will is a law to itself in all its actions, however, only expresses the principle that we should act according to no other maxim than that which can also have itself as a universal law for its object. And this is just the formula of the categorical imperative and the principle of morality. Therefore a free will and a will under moral laws are identical" (KGM 447/KFM 65). This is "the fundamental law of pure, practical reason," the "categorical imperative," which is stated in the *Critique of Practical Reason* as: "So act that the maxim of your will could always hold at the same time as a principle of a universal legislation"[4] (KPV 30/KPR

[4] Or as it is stated in the *Foundations of the Metaphysics of Morals:* "Act only according to that maxim by which you can at the same time will that it should become a universal law" (KGM 421/KFM 39).

142). Thus we have arrived at Kant's purely formal, purely rationally arrived at, *a priori* moral direction to the will. With this we see all nonformal "material" eliminated. But is it?

Kant's Kingdom of Ends

There is one ray of hope that Kant's categorical imperative may be rescued from absolute, rational formalism. The statement of the categorical imperative we have been considering is only *one* basic (albeit varying) articulation of it. Kant approaches the categorical imperative from another angle, one which yields an articulation of it that promises to give a fuller direction to the will than lawfulness alone affords. This occurs when Kant approaches rational beings as ends, specifically as ends in themselves. Thus we must, for the sake of fairness, look at Kant's idea of the rational being as an end in itself and at the moral directive this might yield to see if it can give a more nonformal content to the categorical imperative. Kant develops his idea of the end in itself in a passage in the *Foundations of the Metaphysics of Morals* where he identifies what is properly the determinant of a rational will by distinguishing between subjective and objective ends, one based upon incentives (*Triebfeder*), the other upon motives (*Bewegungsgrund*), noting that practical principles are formal only when they disregard all subjective ends that can give us only hypothetical imperatives. But is there an objective end? Kant ends the passage with the claim that there is:

> But suppose that there were something the existence of which in itself had absolute worth, something which, as an end in itself, could be a ground of definite laws. In it and only in it could lie the ground of a possible categorical imperative, i.e., of a practical law.
>
> Now, I say, man and, in general, every rational being exists as an end in himself and not merely as a means to be arbitrarily used by this or that will. In all his actions, whether they are directed to himself or to other rational beings, he must always be regarded at the same time as an end. (KGM 427–28/KFM 45–46)

The rational being itself then becomes, in a sense, the "content" of the good will. As Kant says later: "Rational nature is distinguished from others in that it proposes an end to itself. This end would be the material of every good will" (KGM 437/KFM 56).

The fact that Kant here explicitly calls an end the *material* of every good will gives us hope that he is on the verge of coming to an articulation of the categorical imperative that would allow the incorporation of more than lawfulness in its direction to the will. Unfortunately, these hopes are dashed in the very next sentence of this passage: "Since, however, in the idea of an absolutely good will without any limiting condition of the attainment of this or that end, every end to be effected must be completely abstracted (as any particular end would make each will only relatively good), the end here is not conceived as one to be effected but as an independent end, and thus merely negatively" (KGM 437/KFM 56). We ought not be too surprised. Kant *must* back off from any positive content other than lawfulness. Unless he wishes to abandon his basic position, he cannot allow any positive "matter."

Indeed, it is not just in the "formal" works we have quoted that the limits on "matter" are evident. Although, as Philip Blosser points out (1995, 69), the English-speaking world did not have easy access to *Die Metaphysik der Sitten* (*The Metaphysics of Morals*), in which Kant does expand on his position, until the 1964 English translation of the *Doctrine of Virtue* section,[5] and this may have led to some misunderstandings of Kant's "formalism," the *Doctrine of Virtue* does not change Kant's basic position. The end of man is to overcome one's "animality" and strive to be a purely rational being.[6]

All the power of Kant's ethics derives from his ability to forge a clear-cut distinction between the formal and rational (the seat of all stability and certainty), on the one hand, and all that is nonformal (the realm of the contingent and chaotic), on the other. And upon this foundation Kant constructed what Scheler called a "colossus of steel and bronze" (GW2 30/F 6).

[5] Immanuel Kant, *The Doctrine of Virtue,* translated by Mary Gregor (New York: Harper and Row, 1964). Mary Gregor also translated the entire *Metaphysics of Morals* (New York: Cambridge University Press, 1991).

[6] A number of Kant scholars have suggested that emotions may well have a role in Kantian ethics. For a recent survey see, for example, Sherman 1990. Yet even if this may be shown, Kant's rejection of the contingently empirical must be maintained, and for Kant this includes nonformal values and feelings.

Scheler's Initial Objection to Kant's Formal Ethics

Now that we have come to the end of Kant's quest and have arrived at his categorical imperative *a priori,* it is time to step back and ask why Scheler reacted to it so strongly. Only then can we see the roots of Scheler's quest for a nonformal ethics of value and a new beginning in ethical personalism.

In order to understand Scheler's reaction to Kant's ethics, we must remember that ethics is not simply a theoretical pursuit. Ethics must help us understand and resolve moral problems, moral dilemmas. To hark back to Kant's own initial question, for all of its neatness and rational appeal has Kant actually achieved a moral principle that can, indeed, supply adequate direction to the will?

Scheler did not believe so, and quite early in his career he indicated some of what he found wanting in it. Two years after the publication of his dissertation, he presented his *Habilitationsschrift,* entitled "The Transcendental and the Psychological Method: A Basic Discussion toward Philosophical Method" ("Die transzendentale und die psychologische Methode: Eine grundsätzliche Erörterung zur philosophischen Methodik").[7] In it, as one might expect, Scheler criticizes transcendental principles in general, but with special attention to Kant. Thus it gives us a valuable glimpse into Scheler's initial objections to Kant.

Scheler puts his criticisms in the form of two theses: the first is that if Kant's transcendental principles are to be considered as epistemological principles valid for all possible experience, these principles are *too rich* in content; the second is that in actual application, both in scientific work and (in the case of the categorical imperative) in the practical problems of human life, these principles are *too poor* in content (TPM 253). Now this may seem like an odd criticism of a "formalism," since it focuses on the inadequacy of the content. The apparent oddness occurs only if one thinks that Scheler, like others before him, is attacking Kant's formalism simply as a totally "empty" formalism. Indeed, as Blosser points out, many people have thought Scheler's criticism was just

[7] This essay was published in 1900 in Jena by Dürr Verlag. It is reprinted in volume 1 of the *Gesammelte Werke.* Max Scheler, *Frühe Schriften* (1900; rpt. Bern: Frank Verlag, 1971 [now Bonn: Bouvier Verlag]), 197–335. The English translation is mine. This work will be referred to using the abbreviation TPM.

that simple, and that Scheler thus displayed a basic misunderstanding of Kant (1995, 69 ff.). As I will develop below, however, Scheler's criticism of Kant's formalism is not so much that it is simply empty but rather that it is inadequate.

Since one of the key elements of the contrast between Scheler and Kant lies in their radically different understanding of the distinction between the formal and the nonformal (material), a good place to begin our explication of Scheler's criticism of the emptiness of Kant's formal ethics is to develop their quite different understandings of this distinction. We will do so for another reason as well. Scheler's vision is so at odds with Kant's that Ron Perrin, a scholar looking at Scheler through the eyes of Kant, accuses Scheler of a "materialist reduction" that "tends to dissolve the traditional distinction between form and matter" (1991, 62). Even Blosser, who defends Scheler against this charge, suggests that Scheler "is not as expressly clear about how the form/matter distinction is preserved in his phenomenology as he might have been" (1995, 53 n. 15). Thus, although the full meaning and force of Scheler's critique of Kant's formalism will emerge only gradually as we develop his own positive positions in the next three chapters, it is worthwhile developing Scheler's understanding of the form-matter distinction here so that we can understand why, even in his early work, Scheler claims that the categorical imperative is both too rich and too poor in content.

First of all, for Kant the distinction between the formal and the nonformal is also the distinction between the *a priori* and the *a posteriori,* between what is stable and certain on one side and what is uncertain, chaotic, variable, and relative (contingent) on the other. As noted above, Kant believed "experience" could not supply reliable grounds for moral judgments because, for him, experience is a combination of the reliable "form" given by reason on the one side and the contingent, unreliable, unordered "matter" (supplied by the senses) on the other. For Scheler, however, although the distinction between the *a priori* and the *a posteriori*[8] is still the distinction between the absolute and the contingent,

[8] I am here focusing on the elements of the distinction between the *a priori* and the *a posteriori* relevant to our present concerns. There are, for Scheler, other important ways in which he differs from Kant. For example, for Scheler the distinction is found within experience. As we will develop in chapter 3, it is the

it is not to be found in the difference between the formal and the nonformal. As he says in the *Formalism:*

> It is completely clear that the field of the "*a priori–evident*" has *nothing at all* to do with the "*formal.*" Nor has the opposition "*a priori*"–"*a posteriori*" anything to do with the opposition "*formal*"-"*nonformal*" [material]. Whereas this first distinction is an *absolute* one, founded in the variety of *contents* that fulfill concepts and propositions, the second one is completely *relative* and at the same time related only to *concepts* and *propositions* with respect to their *universality.* For instance, the propositions of pure logic and arithmetic are *equally* a priori (the axioms as well as the theorems that follow from them). But this does *not* preclude our saying that the former are "formal" in relation to the latter, or that the latter are nonformal in relation to the former. For a *plus* of intuitive content is necessary for the theorems to fulfill them. Moreover, the proposition that one of the two propositions, "A is B" and "A is not B," is a false proposition is true only on the basis of the phenomenological insight into the *fact* [Sach*einsicht*] *that* the being and the non-being of something are irreconcilable (in intuition). Taken in this sense, this proposition has a *content of intuition* for its basis, and the content is not diminished as content because it applies to *any* object. This proposition is "formal" only for the entirely different reason that *any* object can stand for A and B; it is formal with respect to two of any such objects. Likewise, $2 \times 2 = 4$ is "formal" for plums and pears alike. (GW2 72–73/F 53–54)

Now although Scheler is focused here on making the point that the *a priori* is not the same as the formal, this passage also reveals key elements of his understanding of the distinction between the formal and the material. As he had noted earlier in "The Transcendental and the Psychological Method," for Scheler what is form and what is content (matter) is relative and functional (TPM 254). Since forms (formulae) differ, each form *as form* can be said to have a different "content." This "content" (which I shall call formal content) is what differentiates one form (as form) from another, and it must be distinguished from the variable content

distinction between what is given immediately (phenomenological facts) and what is given through a series of observations and only mediately. Incidentally, Imtiaz Moosa (1995) also provides an interesting contrast of Scheler and Kant's understanding of the *a priori.*

(matter) that "fills" each form (this latter type of "material content" is what we usually think of when we think of content).

To see what Scheler is getting at here, let us develop a variation on his own example. The numerical formula "2 + 2 = 4" is a form relative to the different contents, or "matter" (say plums and pears), that may "fill" this equation. At the same time, however, this "2 + 2 = 4" can itself be a content filling the algebraic formula A + B = C. The formula "A + B = C" can be filled with a variety of numbers (2 + 2 = 4, 3 + 4 = 7, . . .) just as the form "2 + 2 = 4" can be filled by any number of fruit, and many other "matters" as well. Thus "2 + 2 = 4" functions as form (in relation to the fruits, etc.) or content (in relation to A + B = C), yet as a form (formula) it has the distinct identifying "content" of "2 + 2 = 4."[9]

This understanding of the form-content distinction allowed Scheler in "The Transcendental and the Psychological Method" to claim that the content of Kant's formalism is both too rich and too poor. As noted above, in that early work Scheler states his criticism in the form of two theses. Let us consider his first thesis, that the categorical imperative as an epistemological principle valid for all possible experience is *too rich* in content. In this early essay, when Scheler begins to defend this thesis, after stating that the distinction between form and content is relative he goes on to say that even a supporter of transcendental principles would have to admit that such principles are richer in content than the "laws of thought" (*Denkgesetzen*) of formal logic (TPM 254).

Yet how are they "richer"? The transcendental principles are richer in content in the sense that as forms they are not as abstract and general as the laws of formal logic. This is why they fail as epistemological principles, since for them to serve as universal principles making possible all experience, they would have to be

[9] Incidentally, we can now see that Perrin is wrong to claim that Scheler has destroyed the form-content distinction. There is still a functional difference between the two. For example, values still have the form "quale," and the formula "moral goodness is realized along with the realization of positive, higher nonmoral values" is true. It is just that such formal truths tell us precious little until we fill in the forms with nonformal values. It is only if you wish to identify the form-content distinction with the *a priori–a posteriori* distinction, as Kant and Perrin wish to do, that you would miss the fact that form and content are still distinguished by Scheler.

absolutely general. If they are not, if there are several "formal" principles (or several versions of the "same" principle), then "experience" would vary depending upon which "principle" was operating. Scheler believes there is historical evidence that this is so, pointing to basic differences in the understanding and function of key principles such as law (he points out that there is evidence that the Greeks did not have a conception of law as Kant understands it).

More relevant to our study is the fact that in ethics the same situation holds. We cannot take lawfulness as the road to understanding all morality for a number of reasons. First of all, although lawfulness can be abstracted from concrete laws and can then become the "form" of a formula (as it does in Kant's categorical imperative), for Scheler it is not the only possible "form" of all moral experience. Historically, the "good" or "virtue," for example, has as much claim to be taken as the "form" of moral experience as lawfulness (TPM 256).

This is, however, not the most important reason. Scheler's ethics is an ethics of nonformal values, an ethics where the moral value (good, for example) is realized along with the realization of higher, positive, nonmoral values. It is an ethics in which our heart sees both the values and their ranks. Scheler's moral world is a complex world of ranks of values that are both positive and negative, higher and lower, values seen through a complex set of "feelings." Thus, to take one element (lawfulness) out of the total complexity of our moral experience and make it alone the epistemic form of all moral experience gives Kant's categorical imperative too rich a content in the sense that in concentrating on this one element while ignoring the others, this one element is given unwarranted importance at the cost of the elements left out. The result is a truncated vision of the moral world.

Nor is it just values (and the "feelings" that allow us to see values) that are left out. Scheler also notes in "The Transcendental and the Psychological Method" that if we limit ourselves to the formal, we will never understand moral persons. Scheler's ethics is not simply an ethics of values. It is primarily an ethics of persons, as is indicated in the subtitle to the *Formalism:* "A New Attempt toward the Foundation of an Ethical Personalism." Scheler's understanding of the person is much richer than Kant's, and thus what we must be and do is more complex as well. To show this, in "The Transcendental and the Psychological Method" Scheler points to Jesus. We will never understand the nobility of Jesus or his moral experience if we look at him simply under the value of lawfulness (TPM 256). As Scheler develops later in the *Formalism,* Jesus is not only an example of the highest type of value person (the holy person) but also a moral genius (GW2 309/F 305), a pioneer whose *ordo amoris*[10] allowed him to see higher values than other persons could see, and whose love allowed him to help us see these new realms of higher values as well. Indeed, Jesus opened whole new realms of higher values to the entire world. All of this is lost if you look only at whether what Jesus intended could be a categorical imperative. What Jesus was, what Jesus did, was unique. Indeed, even looking at Jesus the model, the personal exemplar, cannot be understood in a purely formal way.

Thus Kant's formula is too rich in content because it is not general enough. Its formal content is too rich in the sense that it is not "empty" enough. Kant's categorical imperative has too much, if too narrow, a content to act as an adequate basis for ethical decisions. This does not mean, however, that if we "thin out" the content more we would eventually get to an abstraction that would suffice.

This is shown by Scheler's second thesis, that these principles in actual application both in scientific work and (in the case of the categorical imperative) in the practical problems of human life are already too poor in content. Again, after using historical examples giving evidence that the conceptual frameworks of understanding experience show unmistakable signs of being richer than the transcendental principles can account for, Scheler turns to the moral realm. This time he uses a specific moral situation to make his point. His example is a case of possible stealing. If we approach such a case using Kant's categorical imperative from the standpoint of a maxim describing stealing in general, we will come to a judgment condemning stealing. Yet consider the spe-

[10] For Scheler the *ordo amoris* is central to what we can see of values, and it varies from person to person. This basic idea will be developed below, especially in chapter 4.

cific case of an unemployed man with a number of young children contemplating "stealing" money from a rich "profiteer" (*Wucherer*) (TPM 258). As Scheler points out, there is no requirement in Kant to approach this case using a general maxim concerning stealing, and if we use a maxim that includes the particularity of the case we face an entirely new rational calculation. Yet why is this so, and what light does it throw on the poorness of the content of the categorical imperative?

Let us start with the fullness of the moral dimensions of this particular case from the standpoint of Scheler's ethics. The case contains a conflict of values and value complexes. For example, there are the values of property. There are the values of the lives of the children. There are even issues of the legitimacy of the property of the profiteer. All of these values and value complexes (and probably others as well) enter into the judgment of what value (or value complex) ought to be realized. Indeed, what values can enter will depend upon the values accessible to the person making the judgment (which depends upon the state of his or her heart [*ordo amoris*]). If you take a Schelerian approach, the judgment of what is the moral thing to do will not be an easy one, but what is needed to do justice to the fullness of the value conflict at the core of the moral situation will be fully present.

In contrast to this rich conflict of values, let us turn to what we can consider using Kant's categorical imperative. First of all, the judgment will be made solely on the basis of which intention is universalizable. Thus all of the other values that are present must appear on the side of what is being judged. They all stand under that single value of lawfulness. They all count the same, as the judged. Furthermore, for Kant, all nonformal values have the same rank. Even Scheler's example of using two different maxims when approaching the profiteer example shows this. In this situation, as already noted, property values, the value of the lives of the children, and so forth are all present and in conflict. Yet depending on which maxim you choose, only some of these values are present, and even if more than one is present, they all have the same weight. For example, if you use a general maxim concerning stealing, the value of property is present, but the value of the lives of the children is not. Even with the particularized maxim where both of these values are present, they have, for

Kant, the same weight. They are all nonformal values, and the only value that determines the outcome is the formal value of lawfulness.[11] Yet we sense this is not adequate, that nonformal values are not all of the same weight. There *is* a difference between property values and the value of the lives of the children, and these nonformal values, with their differing weights, need to be part of the basis of our moral judging. The single moral value of lawfulness, the universalizability of the intent, is not enough.[12]

For Scheler each nonmoral value (or value complex) is either positive or negative and appears in a rank of values that is either higher or lower than other ranks. Each value (and value complex) has a unique place in the realm of values. Thus, each situation presents us with a unique set of competing values or value complexes. In each case if we realize the highest possible positive nonmoral value (or value complex) we will co-realize the personal moral value (good, for example). Kant's reduction of moral judgment to a judgment based upon the single formal value of lawfulness creates a moral principle that is too poor in content, for it leaves out the nonmoral values at the core of moral judgment.

Neither Scheler nor I endorse stealing from rich profiteers even in this case. It may very well be that the highest positive values to be realized in this case are not to be found in stealing from this person (or "liberating unfairly gained profits"). The point is not the outcome of the judgment, but how it is reached. Because Kant has included only one element as relevant to moral life in creating his attempted formulation of a categorical imperative, his

---

[11] This is true even if you can use Kant's approach to justify the father's protecting the lives of his children by "stealing." I am not claiming that you cannot come to a judgment in this case using Kant's approach. Indeed, it may even be the "same" outcome. (Scheler's point is not that you cannot come to a judgment, but rather that the judgment will vary depending upon which nonmoral values are present, and that Kant's approach does not allow the differences between nonmoral values to have the role they ought to in moral judgment.) It is true that using Kant's approach we can justify any intention that passes the test of universalizability and respects persons as ends in themselves. Yet we cannot, using lawfulness alone, truly justify which competing intention to choose when there is a conflict between them. To do this one must recognize the validity of the essential differences between nonmoral values in a way Kant cannot.

[12] Incidentally, I personally believe that the value of the lives of the children outweighs the value of property, but even if someone with a different *ordo amoris* disagrees with me, my point is still valid. My point is that nonformal values are not all of the same rank, the same weight.

formula is not adequate as a basis for practical moral judgments. It is too poor in content, for it ignores factors that are as important as, or more important than, the formal value of lawfulness[13]—namely, nonformal values.

Having accepted a narrow, austere formula that rules out all the richness and variety given in experience by condemning all that is *given* as being nothing but unordered *Stoff* (and thus totally unreliable until "ordered" by the rules of the understanding), having ruled out all we are given in feeling as nothing but the pleasure given by an empirical object, Kant had to live with what was left. Not only is it not enough, but this route could never give us what would be adequate. Our heart tells us that the basis of moral judgment must include more than just the formality of lawfulness. Thus, when we see Scheler accusing Kant's categorical imperative of emptiness, as he does in the *Formalism* (GW2 30/F 6), the emptiness he decries is not a total emptiness but rather an emptiness seen from the perspective of the fullness of the realm of nonformal values (and the fullness of the person) that Scheler champions.

Kant's Challenge to All Nonformal Ethics

Despite his criticism of the inadequacy of Kant's rational formalism, Scheler was keenly aware of the challenge Kant's work represented to any attempt to develop a material (nonformal) ethics, especially one rooted in nonrational insight. Furthermore, he was most appreciative of what Kant had accomplished in showing the inadequacy of all prior attempts at nonformal ethics. Indeed, in the first preface to the *Formalism,* Scheler says of his criticism of Kant that

> even in these sections of criticism it was always my assumption that Kant's ethics, and not the ethics of any other modern philosopher,

---

[13] I say as important as, or more important than, lawfulness because lawfulness is itself a very important value. The need for order is a basic human need. Thus if you are going to base all morality on one value, lawfulness is as good a candidate as "the good" or "virtue." Indeed, this may well account for the continuing pull of Kant despite our sense that his approach is ultimately a failure. Again, however, Scheler's point is that you cannot reduce the basis of moral judgment to one value.

> represents the most *perfect* we have in the area of philosophical ethics—although not in the form of a *Weltanschauung* or a consciousness of faith, but rather in the form of strict scientific insight. It was also my assumption that Kant's ethics, although pointedly criticized, corrected, and supplemented on various occasions, had not yet been shaken to its foundations. The implied unconditional reverence for Kant's work in these assumptions was a matter of course to me. (GW2 9–10/F xviii)

It is of great importance for an understanding of Scheler's thought to see that his intent is not to destroy Kant's insight that all ethics rooted in the empirically contingent are ultimately inadequate. Scheler's attitude toward Kant was truly one of reverence for the power of his insights, and Scheler accepts the need to find a stable basis for moral judgment. As he puts it in the "Introductory Remarks":

> It would be a great error, in my judgment, to maintain that any of the post-Kantian versions of non-formal ethics have refuted the Kantian doctrine. . . . All post-Kantian ethics, much as they may have served to cast new light on special moral values and the details of the concrete situations of life, manage in their principal parts to provide only the background against which the greatness, strength, and terseness of Kant's work stands out all the more. (GW2 29/F 5–6)

This raises the question of how, exactly, Scheler intended to meet the challenge Kant's rational, formal ethics presents to any nonformal ethics. In the "Introductory Remarks" to *Formalism,* Scheler indicates that he intends to undertake this task not by "internal criticism" of the consistency of Kant's system but rather by detecting and refuting Kant's presuppositions, both explicit and implicit, since his target is not "every little flourish" of Kant's work but "the idea of a *formal ethics as such,* for which Kant's ethics is only an example" (GW2 30/F 6).

Since these "presuppositions" reveal Scheler's understanding of the challenge that Kant's work presented to him, I will now submit Scheler's articulation of them in their entirety. For Scheler, Kant's approach presupposes the following:

1. Every non-formal ethics must of necessity be an ethics of goods and purposes.

2. Every non-formal ethics is necessarily of only empirical-inductive and a posteriori validity.
3. Every non-formal ethics is of necessity an ethics of success. Only formal ethics can treat the basic moral tenor (*Gesinnung*) or willing based upon it as the original bearer of the values of good and evil.
4. Every non-formal ethics is of necessity a hedonism and so falls back on the existence of sensible states of pleasure, that is, pleasure taken in objects. Only formal ethics is in a position to avoid all reference to sensible pleasure-states through the exhibition of moral values and the proof of moral norms resting on such values.
5. Every non-formal ethics is of necessity heteronomous. Only formal ethics can found and establish the autonomy of the person.
6. Every non-formal ethics leads to a mere legalism with respect to actions. Only formal ethics can found the morality of willing.
7. Every non-formal ethics makes the person a servant to his own states or to alien goods. Only formal ethics is in a position to demonstrate and found the dignity of the person.
8. Every non-formal ethics must of necessity place the ground of all ethical value-estimations in the instinctive egoism of man's natural organization. Only formal ethics can lay the foundation for a moral law, valid in general for all rational beings, which is independent of all egoism and every special natural organization of man. (GW2 30–31/F 6–7)

The statement of these Kantian "presuppositions" which Scheler wishes to challenge seems to cast Scheler's task as a negative one of showing they are erroneous. It is, however, important to see the positive goals in what Scheler is attempting to accomplish here. Although he will be spending much of his time trying to show that Kant is wrong, he is doing so to show that the requirements Kant's ethics presents to any nonformal ethics *can* be met. If Scheler can show that the first three presuppositions are wrong, he will at the same time show that not all nonformal (material) values are empirically contingent. If the fourth presupposition is wrong, it is possible that not all feelings are rooted in contingent sensible states. If the last four presuppositions are wrong, we may not have to retreat to the formal to defend the dignity of the person.

Since Scheler's list of presuppositions is somewhat cryptic, and since what they meant to Scheler and how he countered them will become more intelligible only as we develop Scheler's quest in detail below, I will now highlight the challenge of Kant's rational, formal ethics to Scheler's quest by transforming the above into three general requirements that Scheler must meet.

The Requirement of Noncontingent Values

The first requirement is that any ethics based upon nonformal values—indeed, based upon anything other than lawfulness—must show that this "material" is noncontingent. By noncontingent I mean that Scheler must show that nonformal values are autonomous, stable, invariant grounds for moral judgment and are not tied, for example, to the contingency of the empirical.[14]

The Requirement of Noncontingent Feeling

This first requirement has to do with the nature of the "material" in any material ethics. Let us now turn to how we have access to such material, to Scheler's espousal of the heart. For Scheler the "heart" is the seat of the moral realm, and it is through special moral "feelings" that we have access to the "material" his ethics is based upon. Kant's work shows that any "feeling" that purports to be a means of access to a stable basis for an ethics must be shown to be *itself* not rooted in contingency. Such "feeling" must not, for example, vary with the variable and contingent makeup of the human being (or of any "perceiver" for that matter). And such "feeling" must be separate from the "passions" that over-

[14] In olden times I would have spoken of absolute grounds, but the term "absolute values" now grates on the ear, for it conjures up dogmatic claims of omnipotent vision that many philosophers have rightly rejected. Yet it is an appropriate phrase to use if we limit ourselves to its root sense of independent from any other source, not contingent upon anything else (*ab-solus*). It is precisely this independence, especially from the "empirical," that Kant demands as a basis for moral judgment. If Scheler is to seek a nonformal (material) ethics of value, he must show that there are such independent, nonformal values that will supply such "absolute" grounds.

come and destroy the autonomy and freedom of the will. This is the second requirement that Kant's work reveals.

Furthermore, although it is not a separate requirement (since it is implied in the above two), in the light of the history of the battle between the head and the heart it is worth noting that such "feeling" must be shown to be capable of giving us an effective basis for moral judgment. This is important because of the widespread belief that judgments rooted in feelings are especially unreliable. Thus I believe that anyone who wishes to use "feeling" as an "organ of comprehension" must take special care to explain the apparently extraordinary variance of judgments based on "feelings." As a recent critic of Scheler succinctly put it: "The reasons of the heart are often enough persuasive: they are not so often right" (Heath 1975, 166).

The Requirement of the Noncontingent Person

The first two requirements are, in a sense, obvious ones, and Kant's work only serves to focus and make vivid their need. The third requirement is more subtle but no less important. To develop this last requirement, however, we must go back for a moment to look at a feature of Kant's ethics not developed above, namely, Kant's idea of the dignity of the person, an idea rooted in his conception of the rational being as a free, autonomous end in itself.

Although Kant's idea of the rational being as an end in itself failed to yield positive content beyond lawfulness for the categorical imperative, it did lead Kant to what he himself called "a very fruitful concept, namely, that of *a realm of ends*" (KGM 443/KFM 51). This realm, or kingdom, of ends consists of the systemic union of all rational beings, "a whole of all ends in systematic connection, a whole of rational beings as ends in themselves as well as of the particular ends which each might set for himself" (KGM 443/KFM 51).

I want to turn to this idea of a kingdom of ends because, although it did not yield any new content for the categorical imperative, it did allow Kant to develop a feature of his ethics that is most attractive and which leads to the next requirement any material ethics must meet. I am referring to the "idea of the dignity of a rational being who obeys no law except that which he himself also gives" (KGM 434/KFM 53). Kant develops this idea in the following passages from the *Foundations of the Metaphysics of Morals:*

> In the realm of ends everything has either a *price* or a *dignity.* Whatever has a price can be replaced by something else as its equivalent; on the other hand, whatever is above all price, and therefore admits of no equivalent, has a dignity. . . .
>
> Now morality is the condition under which alone a rational being can be an end in itself, because only through it is it possible to be a legislative member in the realm of ends. Thus morality and humanity, so far as it is capable of morality, alone have dignity. . . .
>
> And what is it that justifies the morally good disposition or virtue in making such lofty claims? It is nothing less than the participation it affords the rational being in giving universal laws. He is thus fitted to be a member in a possible realm of ends to which his own nature already destined him. For, as an end in himself, he is destined to be legislative in the realm of ends, free from all laws of nature and obedient only to those which he himself gives. Accordingly, his maxims can belong to a universal legislation to which he is at the same time also subject. A thing has no worth other than that determined for it by the law. The legislation which determines all worth must therefore have a dignity, i.e., unconditional and incomparable worth. For the esteem which a rational being must have for it, only the word "respect" is a suitable expression. Autonomy is thus the basis of the dignity of both human nature and every rational nature. (KGM 434–35/KFM 53–54)

For all the "defects" Kant's purely rational categorical imperative suffers, his recognition that the noncontingency of the person is the grounds of a deeply and reverently grasped *dignity* in each and every person strikes a chord. Kant's position achieves this by defining the person in narrowly rational and formalistic terms. Yet any challenge to Kant's rational formalism must also be true to the noncontingency and dignity of the person. This is the third requirement Kant's ethics places upon any material ethics.

Summary

Because the requirements Kant's rational, formal ethics imposes upon any nonformal ethics are so important to our development of Scheler's work, let me restate them briefly. First, a material ethics that accepts a content other than lawfulness as part of the grounds of moral judgment must show that this material is noncontingent. Second, if feeling is to be the "organ of comprehension" of this noncontingent material, this feeling itself must not be rooted in the contingent but must rather be separable from the passions that destroy the freedom and the autonomy of the will. Furthermore, we must see both that feelings can give us "absolute" knowledge and why, despite this, feelings seem to be so unreliable as a basis for moral judgments. Third, any material ethics must show forth the noncontingency and dignity of the person.

It is my conviction that these requirements form the initial context within which Scheler attempted to develop his personalistic, nonformal ethics of value. He accepted the challenge represented by Kant's ethics and, I believe, began to meet it. In the next chapter we will focus on Scheler's defense of material values as noncontingent, on his defense of objective nonformal values.

3

Values and Phenomenology

Introduction

In order to have a nonformal ethics of value that can challenge Kant, one must have nonformal values autonomous enough to be the basis for an ethics, values free of the web of contingent "empirical" causality—and we must know what they are. Thus, Scheler's first task is to show how knowledge of autonomous, nonformal values is *possible*. For this reason, before we can develop his understanding of values we must first explore his phenomenological approach to the knowledge of values.

The task of showing how we can have knowledge of autonomous, nonformal values is not easy. In the *Formalism in Ethics and Non-Formal Ethics of Values,* Scheler agrees with Kant that all previous attempts to base an ethics upon empirically known "goods" had failed because "whenever we make the goodness or the moral depravity of a person, an act of will, a deed, etc. dependent on their relation to a realm of existing goods (or evils) posited as real, we make the goodness or depravity of the will dependent on the particular contingent existence of this realm of goods, as well as on its experiential knowability" (GW2 32/F 9).

Indeed, for many years Scheler himself had unsuccessfully sought a nonformal basis for ethics free from contingency. For example, his early study of "The Transcendental and the Psychological Method" concluded with a series of summary theses, the very first of which states: "There is (with the exception of the principle of formal logic) no absolute, stable, self-evident datum from which philosophy, be it metaphysics, theory of knowledge, ethics or aesthetics could start" (TPM 334).

It is only with his adoption of the phenomenological approach,

---

Sections of this chapter appeared in my essay "Scheler's Phenomenological Given," *JBSP: The Journal of the British Society for Phenomenology* 9, no. 3 (1978): 150–57, and are reproduced here with permission.

an act that marks the transition from his early work,[1] that Scheler repudiated this thesis. Thus we must turn to Scheler's mature work to see why he believed that there were accessible, autonomous, nonformal values and that Kant was wrong to retreat to formalism in his search for a stable basis for moral judgment. As we saw in our exploration of Kant's ethics, to understand Scheler's quest for a new ethical personalism we must begin by understanding Scheler's approach to knowledge.

Values and Phenomenology

Seeing phenomenology as a way to the knowledge of autonomous values will not be easy for many contemporary thinkers. We stand at the end of more than ninety years of the development and criticism of phenomenology (much of it work by thinkers other than Scheler), and what we now see as phenomenology we see from the perspective of the results of this work. Furthermore, we live in a philosophical environment that is, in many ways, quite hostile to the basic beliefs and possibilities of classic phenomenology, especially the belief that there is anything that is "autonomous" or that we can have direct knowledge of such a "thing itself."

Indeed, Kant's attack on the possible autonomy of the nonformal has been supplemented. Although Kant's transcendentalism is no longer in fashion, for many thinkers language has now taken center stage, and although there is disagreement over whether or not language provides a stable framework, many people believe that all we can know—indeed, all we can experience—is contingent upon language. Once again the idea that nonformal values

[1] Scheler's work is usually divided into three periods: the first period was his earliest work under the influence of Rudolph Euken; the shift to the second period was marked by his adoption of the phenomenological approach and his development of his ethics; the shift to the third period was marked by his rejection of theism and his adoption of panentheism. Since our focus in this book is on understanding Scheler's quest for an ethical personalism and the problems created by it (including the problematic shift from theism to panentheism), I will not deal with the thought of his first period in this book, except where it is relevant to our task.

(or anything at all) could be truly autonomous or known to be so is rejected, often out of hand.

The belief that all we know is hedged in by the limits and operations of language is hard to refute. This book itself is presented to you through marks on a page (or computer screen), and such marks can be taken in ever so many ways. Yet, as Erazim Kohák points out in his excellent example of a contemporary use of the classic phenomenological approach (entitled *The Embers and the Stars: A Philosophical Inquiry into the Moral Sense of Nature*), the trap of language is not yet completely sprung:

> We need not, to be sure, accept the extreme linguistic preoccupation of our time. Like the idealist assumption that seeing can only be a seeing of seeing, the linguistic assumption that speaking can only speak of speaking, though capable of making significant contributions to our understanding of language, seems a transient fashion. It may well be based on a mis-apprehension not uncommon in the history of philosophy, the confusion of the medium with the message. (1984, 50)

Yet given the skepticism of the current climate, I fear that many people have already adopted the language-trapped stance (or another equally blinding conviction) which precludes both truly autonomous nonformal values and access to them. Fortunately, the goal of this book does not require the full demonstration of autonomous values or how classic phenomenology can give us access to them. What must be accomplished are two more modest goals: first, I must help you to see why *Scheler* believed phenomenology gave him such access; and second, I must do so in such a way that you accept it as a philosophically understandable *possibility* (however skeptical you remain).[2] The power of the current skepticism makes it difficult to take phenomenology, especially the early "naive" forms of phenomenology (which I refer to as classic phenomenology), seriously. Yet you must do so to understand Scheler. Perhaps more importantly, this early work still has

---

[2] My limitation of the task of this book is not meant as a way of forever ducking the need to refute the language-trapped positions. It is just that the present book must focus on what Scheler believed phenomenology allowed him to see. Hence, as important as a full development and defense of classic phenomenology is, this task must take a secondary role in the present study.

much to tell us about the nature and possibility of phenomenology.

Scheler's Phenomenological Approach

Despite the obstacles, it is not impossible to learn what phenomenology was to Scheler at the time of the *Formalism,* or why he believed it gave him access to autonomous, nonformal values.[3] Although one cannot pinpoint the exact date when Scheler "discovered" phenomenology, we do have one indication that he may have already moved toward a key element of his phenomenology even before he first met Husserl in 1901. In his account of that first meeting, Scheler says that he had already become dissatisfied with the Kantian philosophy with which he had been close until then, so much so that he had just withdrawn from the printer a half-completed work on logic. The dissatisfaction arose, Scheler indicates, because he "had come to the conviction that what was given to our intuition was originally much richer in content than what could be accounted for by sensuous elements, by their derivations, and by logical patterns of unification."[4] This

[3] Although I will focus on what phenomenology meant to Scheler at the time of the *Formalism,* with the completion of the *Gesammelte Werke* we now have better access to Scheler's thought, including his later work relevant to the development of his understanding of phenomenology. Indeed, in *The Mind of Max Scheler: The First Comprehensive Guide Based on the Complete Works,* Manfred Frings draws upon the later work as he develops in detail the unique features of Scheler's approach to phenomenology, contrasting especially his understanding of phenomenology with Husserl's (see especially chapter 7, "Subliminal Phenomenology" [1997, 181–92]). Furthermore, Frings has also published an illuminating short description of Scheler's phenomenology in his "Max Scheler" entry in the *Encyclopedia of Phenomenology* (629–34). In that entry Frings summarizes the uniqueness of Scheler's phenomenology: "The Phenomenology of Scheler is distinct from those of other phenomenologists in several respects: Phenomenology is not to be based in a method; Phenomenology must suspend sensory data in intuition; time originates in the center of the self-activity of life; consciousness presupposes the being of the person; emotive intentionality is pregiven to all other acts; the ego is an object of internal perception; and reality is resistance" (630). Since much of what is unique in Scheler's phenomenology will be mostly of technical interest to phenomenologists and our concern is to develop the logic of the development of Scheler's ethical personalism, I will develop only the differences (and the later views) that are relevant to our study.

[4] Witkop 1922, 197–98. This translation is from Spiegelberg 1971, 1:229.

passage shows evidence of a questioning that may well have led to phenomenology, if not the presence already of a core element of phenomenology—namely, Scheler's suspicion that some thinkers have arbitrarily impoverished what is given to us because it does not fit in with their theoretical framework.

To show this suspicion developed into a new approach, I will now turn to one of Scheler's systematic statements concerning the nature of phenomenology in an essay entitled "Phenomenology and the Theory of Cognition" ("Phänomenologie und Erkenntnistheorie").[5] As this statement is dated around the time of the writing of the *Formalism,* we are reasonably safe in using it as representing his views at that time.[6] The statement appears in an invited paper in which Scheler was asked to comment about phenomenology. He begins the paper with introductory reservations in which he indicates that he is speaking for himself and states his belief that the value of phenomenological investigations does not depend on the adequacy of our ability to understand and articulate the essence of phenomenology (pointing out that, for example, we do not yet fully understand mathematics or the natural sciences yet are reaping benefits from them). He then states:

> In the first place, phenomenology is neither the name of a new science nor a substitute for the word "philosophy"; it is the name of an attitude of spiritual seeing in which one can see (*er-schauen*) or experience (*er-leben*) something which otherwise remains hidden, namely, a realm of facts of a particular kind. I say "attitude," not "method." A method is a goal-directed procedure of *thinking about* facts, for example, induction or deduction. In phenomenology, however, it is a matter, first, of new facts themselves, before they

---

[5] This essay first appeared in Scheler's *Schriften aus dem Nachlass, Band I: Zur Ethik und Erkenntnislehre* in 1933 and is reprinted in volume 10 of the *Gesammelte Werke.* Max Scheler, *Schriften aus dem Nachlass, Band I: Zur Ethik und Erkenntnislehre* (1913–14; rpt. Bern: Franke Verlag, 1957 [now Bonn: Bouvier Verlag]), 377–430. The English translation appears in Scheler, *Selected Philosophical Essays,* translated with an introduction by David R. Lachterman (Evanston: Northwestern University Press, 1973), 136–201. This work will be referred to using the abbreviation PUE/PTC. All quotations from this translation are with the permission of Northwestern University Press. See the Permissions section for details.

[6] Maria Scheler, the editor of the *Gesammelte Werke* at that time, places the essay I am quoting from as being written in 1913–14 (see GW10 517).

> have been fixed by logic, and, second, of a procedure of *seeing*. (PUE 380/PTC 137)

The problem with this characterization is that, as far as it goes, it sounds very much like physical empiricism. In fact, Scheler himself calls phenomenology the most radical empiricism and positivism (PUE 381/PTC 138). How then can an "empiricism" give Scheler a realm of autonomous values that will stand up against Kant's attacks on the "empirical"? The answer lies in the fact that what Scheler means by the term "empiricism" differs radically from what is usually meant by that label. The usual meaning of this term is the idea that one should get back to the experience of real physical things as a basis of knowledge. Furthermore, this knowledge of real physical things is usually understood in terms of those doctrines that have become known as sense empiricism. When Scheler calls phenomenology an empiricism, he means simply that phenomenology points us back to the given, the fully given, as the source of knowledge. This distinguishes his position from sense empiricism because, as he points out, the sense empiricist does not examine purely and simply what is given in experience, but rather,

> after having taken as their basis an altogether narrow concept of experience (*Erfahrung*), namely, the concept "experience through the senses," they explain that everything which would count as given must be traced back to "experience." . . . That empiricism simply suppresses every given which cannot be made to coincide with an impression or with something derived from an impression, or it explains the given *away*. Thus Hume explains away causality, thing, ego, etc. For Kant the given must be composed of sensations and thought. (PUE 382–83/PTC 140–41)

As Scheler puts it in his criticism of Kant in the *Formalism*, the core error is asking the question "what *can be* given instead of simply asking what *is* given" (GW2 74/F 55). Once this fundamental error is committed, the rest follows easily: "One assumes in this fashion that nothing 'can' be *given* at all when sensory functions (even sense organs and sensory stimuli) for it are lacking" (GW2 74/F 55).

The core claim of sense empiricism is that what we know immediately is based upon "sensations," the "impressions" of things our senses give us. This poses at least two important problems. First is the issue of how we know there is anything beyond ourselves, since all we immediately know are the internal data generated by our sense organs. Second, and what is even worse, such data seem to be subjective not only in their being private, but also because what data you get depends upon your personal makeup as a particular physical entity. Even if we can somehow posit or prove there is something beyond the sense organs that somehow causes the "sensations," what we know is dependent upon the particular arbitrary construction of these organs and ourselves. We are trapped into subjective arbitrariness.

Kant, in accepting the position that what we are given can be nothing but sensations, and thus arbitrary and dependent upon our contingent being as real beings, sought the source of our certain knowledge elsewhere than in the given. Indeed, his answer to this problem actually diminishes the given further. As I noted in chapter 2, in Kant's position the given is an unordered chaos, and it is the forming activity of mind that imposes objective, determinate form upon this raw, unordered "matter" (*Stoff*). Kant identifies the nonformal with this "sensible content" both in his theory of cognition and in his ethics. Thus nonformal values cannot possibly be the grounds for "objective" ethics. If we wish to find stable grounds for ethics, or for that matter for any "objective" knowledge, we must look to the form-giving activities of the mind, not to the given. Whatever finds its validity resting in whole or even in part on the given, the sensory, is, for Kant, resting only on a contingent foundation. This is what Scheler's classic phenomenology challenges by attempting to get back to the fullness of the given.

The *A Priori*

In attacking Kant, Scheler had to adopt, at least initially, the terms by which Kant articulated his position. A basic distinction Kant used to articulate his position is the difference between *a priori* (absolute, universal) knowledge and *a posteriori* (empirical, contingent) knowledge. Now since all knowledge gained through experience was, for Kant, only of "phenomena" (the product of the interaction between the form-giving activities and the sensorially given), all such knowledge is of only *a posteriori* status. For Kant, the distinction between the *a priori* and the *a posteriori* coincides with the distinction between knowledge gained "prior to" experience (in the sense that it was a presupposition of any experience or object of experience) and that gained within experience. *A priori* knowledge is, for Kant, knowledge of the forms which reason imposes upon the unordered chaos of the given. It must be achieved by some technique discovering the formal laws of the operation of the mind in this activity. One must, as it were, purge experience of the given and get back to the pure forms if one is to have *a priori* knowledge.

What Scheler attacks in Kant is not the insistence that we need *a priori,* objective grounds for ethics (where by "objective" is meant grounds that are not caught in the web of empirical contingency) but rather the narrowing of the given (by the sense empiricists and then by Kant) to the point that it is no longer a possible source of noncontingent (*a priori*) knowledge. Kant's identification of the formal and the *a priori,* with the nonformal being relegated to sensation and accessible only in experience and thus only of *a posteriori* status, must be successfully challenged if a nonformal ethics of value is to be possible.

Whereas Kant believed that this meant we must abandon all experience and seek the *a priori* in knowledge of pure form, Scheler does not. He attacks Kant's identification of the *a priori* with the formal directly, redefining the *a priori* when he says: "We designate as '*a priori*' all those ideal units of meaning and those propositions that are self-given by way of an *immediate intuitive* content" (GW2 67/F 48). Furthermore, and most significantly, Scheler does not abandon experience in the search for the *a priori* as Kant had done. Instead, he affirms that "it therefore is not experience and non-experience, or so-called presuppositions of *all* possible experience . . . with which we are concerned in the contrast between the a priori and a posteriori; rather, we are concerned with two *kinds* of experience" (GW2 71/F 52).

The *a priori* is thus not something added by the mind to what is given, but rather is to be found in the given itself. This is why Scheler calls phenomenology the most radical of empiricisms. By showing how sense empiricism has blinded us to whole realms of the given, phenomenology gives us access to the experience of a new realm of "facts," gives us access *within* experience to the noncontingent (*a priori*). Yet if the distinction between the *a priori* and the *a posteriori* is to be found within experience, what is the difference in experience that marks it? For Scheler, phenomenological experience gives us noncontingent (*a priori*) knowledge. But what, precisely, is phenomenological experience, and how can it give us such knowledge?

THE *A PRIORI* AND THE PHENOMENOLOGICAL GIVEN

This is perhaps the most difficult, if the most necessary, question a phenomenologist must speak to. It is difficult because the phenomenologist must appeal, in meeting this question, to experience itself rather than to anything he or she can say or argue about it. Again, if one believes that there is no way to get beyond language, this very attempt is doomed from the start. Nor need one follow the complex contemporary debates over this issue to end up trapped within language. If, in the following, the reader concentrates merely on the verbal assertions I and Scheler present, he or she will remain totally unconvinced and even uncomprehending. The reader must use what is said to go to his or her own *lived* experience to see what is being talked about. If, on the other hand, with the best will in the world you do try to see what we are talking about and cannot do so, then we have truly failed, either because we are wrong or because we did not direct you well enough. So, with this warning sounded, I will now try to help you to an understanding of Scheler's phenomenological experience, to the *given* that is for Scheler the key to the *a priori.*

Scheler spoke of the difference between the *a priori* and the *a posteriori* as a difference between two types of "facts." Verbally, Scheler puts the distinction between phenomenological "facts" (the *a priori*) and nonphenomenological "facts" (the *a posteriori*) very plainly. A phenomenological fact is a fact given in phenomenological intuition (*Anschauung*),[7] and " '*what*' this intuition gives

[7] The fact that the German word *Anschauung* is translated as "intuition" is most unfortunate. The English word "intuition" has the sense of some sort of unreliable and mysterious process by which one can learn things that others cannot. In German the word does not have these overtones. Quite the contrary, it carries with it the sense of clear, plain, obvious, evident "seeing."

cannot be given to a lesser or greater degree, comparable to a more or less exact 'observation' of an object and its traits. Either this 'what' is intuited and, hence, 'self'-given (totally and without subtraction, neither by way of a 'picture' nor by way of a 'symbol') or this 'what' is *not* intuited and, hence, not given" (GW2 68/F 48).

Either we are given phenomenological facts directly, fully, and immediately or we are not, and if not, what we have is not a phenomenological fact. But to put matters this simply tells us precious little of how, in practice, we are to distinguish what is given to us directly, fully, and immediately (what *is* the "intuited" phenomenological fact) from what is not so given. Thus this verbal distinction is of little help until we can see *what* is being distinguished.

Fortunately, Scheler does develop a number of contrasts between phenomenological and nonphenomenological experience that will be of help in clarifying the distinction he is drawing here. In order to point to the phenomenological fact or the phenomenological given (the immediately given), we will first contrast the immediately given with the nongiven; then we will contrast the immediately given with the mediately, or indirectly, given. It is through such contrasts that the phenomenological given will become clearer.

The Immediately Given versus the Nongiven

We can begin to approach the grounds for the first contrast, between the immediately given and the nongiven, via an illustration Scheler used in one of his more detailed discussions of the sense empiricist's "sensation." He begins as follows:

> In seeing a materially extended cube, for example, I can ask what is given. It would be basically erroneous to answer that the perspectival side of the cube is given, or even that "sensations" of it are given. The "given" is the cube as a *whole*—as a material thing of a certain spatioformal unity that is not split up into "sides" or "perspectival aspects." That as a matter of fact the cube is only *visually* given, and that visual elements in the content of perception (*Gehalt der Wahrnehmung*) correspond only to such points of the seen

> thing—of all this, nothing is "given," just as the chemical composition of the cube is not "given." Rather, a very rich and complicated series of *ever new* acts (of the same kind, i.e. of natural perception [*naturlicher Wahrnehmung*]), and a combination of them, is necessary for the "perspectivally visible side of the cube" to enter into the experience of it. (GW2 75/F 55–56)

Scheler then gives a "rough sketch of the stratification of such acts" needed before the "perspectival side of the cube" emerges in experience. First is the recognition that the act of perception of the cube as a whole is an act of a particular ego with its own particular world. A second act reveals that "the act of perception (*Wahrnehmung*) happens through an *act of seeing* (*Sehakt*) in which not everything appears that was first given, e.g., the 'materiality' or the cube's 'having an inside.' In this act of seeing, there remains only a certain formed, colored, and shaded *shell* of the whole 'given' " (GW2 75/F 56). Scheler goes on in detail showing the series of ever new acts that are needed to get to a point where we can see the "perspectival side of the cube." This occurs only after we have brought to givenness the relatedness of the seen thing to ourselves as a living organism. Indeed, only after the given seen thing is seen to be givable in variable size qualities can we begin to experientially see the "perspectival side of the cube."

Even here we are, Scheler says, a long way from the "contents of sensation" of the sense empiricist. Indeed, the closest he can come in experience to such entities are those things "which in their coming and going imply some variation of our experienced *lived-body* (*leiblichen*) states" (GW2 77/F 58). Even here such "contents of sensation" are not sounds, colors, or qualities of smelling or taste, but rather "hunger, thirst, pain, lust, and tiredness, as well as all '*organic sensations*' faintly localized in specific organs" (GW2 77/F 58). The kind of sense "impressions" that are, for sense empiricists, the primordial given are not found to be given in any intuition that Scheler can attain. For him unless the thing can be brought to immediate presence in some act of intuition, it is not an immediate, phenomenological given.

The Order of Givenness

Another important feature of the phenomenological given can be brought out through this example. Scheler points out that the cube is, in the initial act, "given as a whole," yet at the same time we learn in a later investigatory act that this act of perception (in which the cube is given as a whole) "happens through an *act of seeing* in which not everything appears that was first given" (GW2 75/F 56).

Yet, as important as this genetic issue is, the given in one act must be accepted in its fullness even if it can be seen to "happen through" an act whose content is less. If the cube as a whole is given in an act of intuition, then it is to be fully accepted as it is so given; reduction to simpler elements is not permitted. Though investigatory acts may be performed, one has no right to then turn back and deny the fullness of what was given in the initial act. The cube as a whole *is* given, no matter what the "series of ever new acts" reveals about its genesis. For Scheler, one does not ignore what is given in one intentional act by trying to reduce it to some "simpler elements" given in another act or by claiming that the original given is nothing but a "complex" synthesized from these simpler elements.

As Scheler points out in "Phenomenology and the Theory of Cognition," this in no way rules out the fact that we can see in natural perception an "order of givenness" such that "a phenomenon B cannot be given if a phenomenon A is not given 'beforehand,' in the order of time" (PUE 416/PTC 182). Such necessary pregivenness lies in the nature of our natural experience and does not bespeak creative synthesis on our part. As Scheler states:

> Thus, spatiality, thinghood, efficacy, motion, change, etc., are not added onto, any more than they are abstracted from, a given by the so-called understanding as forms of its synthesizing and relational activity. Instead, all these are *non-formal phenomena* of a special sort; each one is the object of a careful and painstaking phenomenological investigation. No thinking and intuiting can "make" or "structure" them; all are *encountered* as data of intuition. (PUE 416/PTC 182)

Indeed, the investigation of the "order of givenness" of natural phenomena depends upon the fact that what is necessarily pregiven in natural experience can itself be brought to immediate givenness. The immediately given can appear at all levels of intentional acts, both the initial naive and the investigatory. The immediately given cannot be found by any attempt to reduce the "complex" to some set of "simpler elements," for the "complex" is itself as much immediately given in its intentional acts as the "simpler elements" are in theirs. Nor are all such reductions successful. If Scheler is correct that the "sense impressions" of the empiricists cannot be brought to immediate givenness, some proposed "simpler elements" may turn out to be purely theoretical and nongiven.

Similarly, the nonreducibility of the phenomenological given does not rule out the fact that we may find that there are certain foundational relationships between phenomenological givens. In another essay concerning the nature of phenomenology, entitled "The Theory of the Three Facts" ("Lehre von den drei Tatsachen"),[8] Scheler says that such foundational relationships would not be temporal or causal relationships but rather "the order in which certain intentional acts and the contents they embrace are built upon one another in accordance with their essence" (LDT 449/TTF 222). But once again such "founding" of givenness is not to be traced back to some theoretical synthesizing activity of mind, but rather "must be accessible to an intuition and experience" (LDT 450/TTF 223) in which the essential foundational relationship is given.

Thus for Scheler the phenomenological given, in contrast to what is not given, must appear within some immediate act of intuition as the correlate of that act. The contrast between the phenomenological given and the nongiven is, however, only one way to illuminate the nature of the phenomenological given. We will now turn to another useful contrast, this time between the phenomenological given and the mediately, or indirectly, given.

The Immediately Given versus the Mediately Given

According to Scheler, the phenomenological given is that which is *immediately* given. This means that some givens are *not* given

[8] "Lehre von den drei Tatsachen" is dated by the editor of the *Gesammelte Werke* at 1911–12. It first appeared in Scheler's *Schriften aus dem Nachlass, Band I: Zur Ethik und Erkenntnislehre* in 1933 and is reprinted in volume 10 of the *Gesammelte Werke,* 431–502. The English translation is "The Theory of the Three Facts," in Scheler, *Selected Philosophical Essays,* 202–75. This work will be referred to using the abbreviation LDT/TTF.

immediately but rather only mediately or indirectly. Although in some passages Scheler uses the term "given" alone to refer to the phenomenological, immediately given, in other places he does indicate the distinction between the immediately given and the mediately given which we will now explore.

In one sense it may seem odd to talk of something being given indirectly—one might think that either something is given immediately and is fully present or it is simply not given at all. Yet there are situations in which something is "given," is the correlate of the intentional act, and yet is not immediately present. One common example of this is that which is given via inference. If I see smoke rising, for example, I may well infer that there is fire. Now in this act of intuition via inference, the correlate is the fire, but what is directly before me is the smoke. One might be tempted to say that the correlate here is not the fire but the smoke, but to do so would be to completely misunderstand the inference. The object of the inference is the fire, not the smoke. The fire is truly given, but it is given only indirectly, via the smoke and the inference.

It would be wrong, however, to take inference to be the only—or even the paradigmatic—case of the indirectly given. What is given by inference is only one small part of the realm of the indirectly given. Anything given symbolically or via signs is also given indirectly. It is the symbol or the sign that is directly present, not the thing itself. The function of a symbol or sign is not to be the ultimate object of the intentional act. It is only a vehicle, a mediator, a "way" pointing toward that which is symbolized or signified. Indeed, a symbol or sign works only when we ignore the symbol or sign immediately present before us and focus on that which is pointed to by the symbol or sign and indirectly given by it. As Scheler indicates in "The Theory of the Three Facts," where the symbol or sign is not related to the thing it stands for except through convention, definition, or custom, the indirectness is, as it were, at its ideal limit, with the symbol taking fully the place of the thing it stands for (LDT 457–58/TTF 232).[9]

---

[9] The reader may be wondering here if Scheler has not in this case reduced the indirectly given to the nongiven. After all, the symbol has here taken fully the place of the thing it stands for, and so the thing it stands for is not present at

The Immediately Given's Independence from the Senses

Scheler's concern with distinguishing clearly between the immediately given and the indirect, symbolically given has good grounds because there is an intimate connection between one type of symbolically given and the immediately given which makes the need to distinguish clearly between them central to the independence of the immediately given. Although, as noted above, Scheler rejects the "contents of sensation" of the sense empiricists (since he cannot find any such thing in any act of intuition), he does not reject the senses or "sensory perception." For him the senses, the sense organs, function as narrowly focusing organs which pick out of the world that which is most important to our bodily survival. What these senses focus on is contingent upon our particular biological makeup. The senses pick out whatever can serve conveniently and usefully as a symbol of the whole object—useful, that is, to our physical survival. Thus what sense perception gives us is not an immediately given but rather only an indirectly given. As Scheler says: "Certainly in an act of common sensory perception the physical object as a whole, together with its back side, its inside, etc., is intended. However, this whole is not given directly but only by means of the *appearance* of this physical object. In natural perception the content of this appearance is at the same time a symbol for this *intended* whole" (LDT 457/TTF 232). The fact that the contents of sensory perception function as symbols pointing toward an indirectly given is important because Scheler also asserts that "even if there is a pure intuition of facts, a pure non-sensory intuition of them . . . such an intuition, insofar as a living being performs it or is its bearer, can never be realized other than through and by means of a sensory organization" (LDT 444/TTF 217).

Now, since Scheler admits that the pure intuition of the immediately given occurs only through and by means of sensory orga-

---

all. This does not mean, however, that this indirectly given is nongiven. The distinction between the indirectly given and the nongiven lies in the fact that in the case of the indirectly given, what is directly present functions as a mediator pointing toward what is not present. In the case of the nongiven, what is present does not so point beyond itself to anything else, and so nothing is indirectly given.

nization, and sensory perception only gives us indirectly the "intended whole," has he not in effect said that what is immediately given is given only mediately? Has he not destroyed the independence of the immediately given? In order to see that the requisite independence of the immediately given is still intact, despite its relationship with the indirectly given, we must remind ourselves of what we have already seen through the cube illustration in the *Formalism*. There Scheler affirmed both that the cube as a whole was given immediately and fully *and* that the act of perception of the cube as a whole "happens through an *act of seeing* in which not everything appears that was first given" (GW2 75/F 56)—in other words, through an act of indirect giving.

With such a statement, Scheler is not admitting that the contents of the immediate intuition, the cube as a whole, are dependent upon the sensory perception of the physical cube. All he is admitting is that because I am a flesh-and-blood living being, the immediate intuition of the cube as a whole can be achieved only in accordance with and through my sensory constitution. He writes:

> The real dependence of intuition on a sensory constitution never provides the least proof that such a pure intuition of facts *does not* exist. Nor does the fact of this dependence prove that intuition is exhausted in the combined activity of the sensory functions or that its objects are exhausted in the complexes or partial contents of these functions, or, finally, that the sensory function is not *only* the condition of the *realization* of intuition for a living creature, but belongs to the *essence* of intuition. For this reason establishing these real or causal connections completely misses the point of the question occupying us here. (LDT 445/TTF 217)

Let us once again return to the cube example to see this in operation. If I focus into an examination of a physical cube by my physical organs of sight, there is immediately given to me a theoretically infinite series of ever new views of the "seen thing of the cube," of the "appearance of this physical object." Furthermore, the cube as a whole *is* only indirectly present in such a series of appearances. But this in no way means that at any time there cannot arise and be given to me the cube as a whole, with it being given immediately and totally. Even if I have never experienced a cube in any way, there may come a point in my "looking over" the physical cube where I *grasp* what a cube essentially and fully is because I grasp the cube as a whole immediately and totally.

The contents of such an intuition are independent of any physical act of perception or any series of such acts. Scheler, in distinguishing between the symbolically given of the natural and scientific worldviews and the immediately given of phenomenology (in the "Three Facts" essay), calls the immediately given "pure facts" because they are purified of all possible elements of sensation. He adduces a series of "essential characteristics of pure facts," the first of which is that "the pure fact must maintain itself as a positive something (*Etwas*) and as an intuitive identity when the sense-function through which this fact actually reaches us is varied, provided that the sense-function itself is brought into our intuition and is then varied within the sphere of the phenomenological reduction."[10]

Once we have grasped the essence "cube as a whole," the essential "facts" of its makeup are seen to hold independent of the various sense functions through which this essence was, perhaps, first made accessible to us. The cube as a whole is a cube with the essential characteristics of a cube as a whole, despite the actual characteristics of any physical cube that is, has been, or ever will be. Indeed, once we have grasped the essential cube as a whole, we may then "go back" to the very physical cube that gave us access to this essence in the first place and make a series of "observations" to see whether this particular physical cube does or does not fulfill the cube as a whole that we now hold in a single, gestalt-type grasp of intuition. Scheler points out in the *Formalism* that the idea of deliberate observation presupposes a grasp of the essence (*Wesen*) (GW2 69/F 50)[11] of whatever we are

---

[10] He continues: "What accounts for the differences between these facts must not be explainable in terms of the differences between the sense-functions through which they in fact become accessible to us. The connection between these facts must be absolutely inexplicable in terms of the concrete physiologically and psychologically real connection between our sensory functions" (LDT 446–47/TTF 219).

[11] The content of an immediate intuition, the immediately given, is also called by Scheler a phenomenon, an essence (*Wesen*), or sometimes simply a "what" (*Was*), with phenomenological intuition also called the "seeing of essences"

trying to observe, for without it the observation would lack the desired direction. In the "Three Facts" essay he identifies the second essential characteristic of "pure facts": "The pure fact must have the character of an ultimate *foundation* of the merely sensory components of natural facts. In other words, when other pure facts are added the specific sensory content of the phenomena is altered, while the addition of an altered sensory content does not alter the pure fact."[12]

Once we have achieved an immediate intuition, changes in the physical sensory perception no longer have any effect on the now grasped phenomenological facts. In the case of our example of the cube, changes in the perceived physical cube would in no way affect the essential cube as a whole. On the other hand, changes in the phenomenological, immediately given would mean I no longer have a cube as a whole but rather some new, immediately given phenomenon, some new essence (a rectangular polyhedron, for example).

The phenomenological given is thus in a sense given absolutely.[13] It is absolute not in the sense that everyone "must" see the same thing, but rather that once a particular phenomenological given *is* seen by anyone, it is seen to be what it is and nothing else. Phenomenological facts do not change. If there is a change in what is phenomenologically given, you have a *new* phenomenological given. Once I grasp the essence "cube as a whole" I have it absolutely, and if I later grasp a "solid rectangular polyhedron" I grasp it as a new essence, not merely as an "elongated

(often translated "essential intuition") (*Wesensschau*). Such essences are ideal rather than real.

[12] He continues: "Or, more briefly: if pure facts exist, then they must be the *independent variable,* while the sense-content is the dependent variable. The possible, indeed, even the actual, sensory appearances of the intuited object must be determined only by its purely objective nature, even though these appearances are univocally determined only when we include the actual performance of the sense-functions belonging to the percipient creature. However, it can never be the case that the nature of the intuited state of affairs changes when the manifold sensory contents which enter into it change—contrary to what sensationalism teaches" (LDT 447/TTF 219–20).

[13] As noted above, the term "absolute" has fallen into disrepute, primarily, I believe, because of its use as a reductive, metaphysical claim of victory. Again, my use of it in this book implies no such claim but is meant rather to point to the independence, the noncontingency, the "*ab-solus*" status of what is so labeled and nothing more.

cube" (though I may well through another act of intuition see similarities between the two essences).

Such independence and absoluteness of the immediately given is what allows Scheler to counter Kant's contention that the *a priori* grounds of ethics could only be found in the formal. At the same time, however, there is a serious possibility of misunderstanding in calling Scheler's given *a priori* or absolute. Unlike Kant's *a priori,* Scheler's is not a universal "forming activity" of the mind. Scheler's *a priori* is a *given,* and we have access to it in phenomenological *experience.*

Thus, in Scheler's case one can mis-take the given, or even not see it at all. As Scheler says:

> If what is *seen* by *A* is a *genuine essence,* then it must be capable of being seen (*erscheinbar*) by everyone,[14] since its inclusion in the content of all possible experience is essentially necessary. The question can only be: "What happens when *B,* after *A* has made an attempt to show him this, asserts that he does not see it?" This can have the most diverse causes. For example, *A* claims that he has seen something which, in fact, he has only observed in himself; he deceives himself in the phenomenological sense of the word, that is, he claims to have insight where he has none. Furthermore, the way he goes about exhibiting the phenomenon can be poor and inadequate. *B* can fail to have understood *A*. *B* can "deceive" himself phenomenologically. There is no so-called universal criterion here. Each case must be decided on its own. (PUE 393–94/PTC 155)

Furthermore, the fact that a *genuine essence* must be part of "the content of all possible experience" does not mean that it will be, in actuality, accessible to all persons. Scheler says: "The essence of an object and of being . . . does not exclude the possibility that only *one man* in *one* act brings something to self-givenness for himself. Indeed, it does not even exclude the possibility that a particular object can be given in this way to *one person* alone" (PUE 393/PTC 154). Thus, as absolute and *a priori* as Scheler's phenomenologically given essences are, access to them cannot be *guaranteed* by either a transcendental deduction or even by a phe-

[14] I disagree with Lachterman's translation of the *erscheinbar* clause in this passage. He translates it as "then everyone must be able to see it." This could be taken to mean that everyone must, in fact, be able to see it, and this is clearly not Scheler's meaning here.

nomenological "method." Controversy is possible, and since such disputes are rooted in what is given through immediate experience, they are particularly hard to resolve. Indeed, such controversy is settled, if it is, only when B can bring to givenness what A has seen. Nothing else will do.

With the requisite independence of the immediately given from the sensorially given thus adduced, Scheler goes on, in the third "essential characteristic of the pure facts," to adduce the independence of the immediately given from all symbols. As he puts it, "The identity and difference of pure facts must be completely independent of all the *symbols* with which it is possible for us to designate them and of the symbols which are used in presenting the facts of which they are parts" (LDT 447/TTF 220). Symbolic knowledge is, of course, very valuable, but for Scheler:

> Phenomenology has reached its goal when every symbol and half-symbol is completely fulfilled through the "self-given," including everything which functions in the natural world-view and in science as a *form* of understanding (everything "categorical"); when everything transcendent and only "meant" has become *immanent* to a lived-experience and intuition . . . what constitutes the unity of phenomenology is not a particular region of facts, such as, for example, mental or ideal objects, nature, etc., but only *self-givenness* in *all* possible regions. (PUE 386/PTC 145)

With this eloquent statement of a key goal of phenomenology we complete our development of Scheler's understanding of the immediate, phenomenological given.

The Obscurity of the Phenomenological Given

A serious question must still be raised. If Scheler is correct about the nature of the phenomenological given, why have people not recognized their experience of such givens, such essences, beyond their experiences in geometry and mathematics, before now? Why, to take the example most relevant to our concerns, have people not immediately recognized that there are nonformal, material essences that can be given *a priori*? Why did Kant, for example, miss them, and turn to acts of transcendental synthesis to explain the orderliness of phenomena, thereby condemning the given as unordered chaos with the *a priori* found only in the formal? Why, simply, are the *a priori,* phenomenological givens not as immediately obvious as they are immediately given?

One difficulty of meeting this question arises out of a fact already mentioned. A phenomenologist cannot simply present verbal arguments to back up his or her assertions. Only if the reader can go to his or her own experiences and there check to see if what Scheler is claiming tallies with those experiences will there be evidence for his claims. The "proof" Scheler provides is not an argument but rather is found only in experience. To ask for anything else is to ask for what cannot be given. To see, for example, that the essence "cube" is no more dependent upon the particular physical cube than it is upon a picture of a cube, or a fantasized cube, or any other particular real or imaginary bearer of that cube is to see what Scheler is talking about—namely, the essence "cube." But why do people not easily and quickly see the essence "cube"?

Perhaps because they are not looking in the right place, or in the right way. It is, as our discussion of sense experience and Kant has suggested, quite easy to not be able to see things because one is not looking at them. Let us return, for a moment, to Scheler's cube. To arrest your view of the cube on a particular level of givenness is to blind yourself to what else can also be given; for example, to insist that all that can be given of the physical cube is the "perspectival side view" is to ignore the fact that the physical cube can be given (albeit indirectly) as a whole. Similarly, to fix on this physical cube can blind us to the equally evident fact that the essence "cube" can also be given to us in experience. Or, to use an example more immediately relevant to our study, if you believe that the only way that you can experience values is as part of empirical "goods," you may very well never be able to experience the essence of nonformal values, and never see that nonformal values can be given *a priori,* can be autonomous.

Autonomous Values

At the very beginning of the *Formalism,* Scheler works to show that such a narrowly fixated view is not a necessary one, that nonformal values can be experienced independently from their bearers. It is worth now reading Scheler's own words as he begins to work to bring the reader to the experience of the autonomy of nonformal values, in a subsection entitled "1. Goods and Values":

> No more than the names of colors refer to mere properties of corporeal things—notwithstanding the fact that appearances of colors in the natural standpoint come to our attention only insofar as they function as a means for distinguishing various corporeal, thinglike unities—do the names of values refer to mere properties of the thinglike given unities that we call *goods*. Just as I can bring to givenness a red color as a mere extensive quale, e.g., as a pure color of the spectrum, without regarding it as covering a corporeal surface or as something spatial, so also are such *values* as agreeable, charming, lovely, friendly, distinguished, and noble in principle accessible to me without my having to represent them as properties belonging to things or men.
>
> Let us first attempt to demonstrate this by considering the simplest of values taken from the sphere of sensory agreeableness, where the relation of the value-quality to its concrete bearer is no doubt the most intimate that *can* be conceived. Every savory fruit always has its particular *kind* of pleasant taste. It is therefore not the case that one and the same savor of a fruit, e.g., a cherry, an apricot, or a peach, is only an amalgamation of various sensations given in tasting, seeing, or touching. Each of these fruits has a savor that is *qualitatively* distinct from that of the others; and what determines the qualitative difference of the savor consists neither in the complexes of sensations of taste, touch, and sight, which are in such cases allied with the savor, nor in the diverse properties of these fruits, which are manifested in the perception of them. The value-qualities, which in these cases "sensory agreeableness" possesses, are *authentic* qualities of a value *itself.* (GW2 35/F 12–13)

After pointing out that the independence of values from their bearers can be seen even more clearly in other value spheres beyond that of sensory agreeableness (which is a realm where values are experienced in a very tight bond with our sensory states), Scheler illustrates his point using aesthetic values, and then moves to a sphere where the bearers of values are not physical objects but rather the person:

> The above also applies to values belonging to the ethical sphere. That a man or a deed is "noble" or "base," "courageous" or "cow-

> ardly," "innocent" or "guilty," "good" or "evil," is not made certain for us by constant characteristics which can be discerned in such things or events; nor do such values *consist* in such characteristics. In certain circumstances a *single* deed or a *single* person is all that we need to grasp the *essence* of the value in question. On the other hand, if the sphere of values is excluded in attempting to establish a common characteristic of, for example, good or evil men, we are theoretically led not only into an epistemological error but also into a moral illusion of the gravest kind. Anyone who has presumed to bind good and evil to self-sufficient *criteria* from outside the domain of values—whether such criteria are demonstrable bodily or psychic predispositions and properties of men or whether they are those of membership in a class or party—and has accordingly spoken of the "good and just" or the "evil and unjust" as if they were an objectively determinable and definable class, has necessarily succumbed to a kind of "pharisaism," confounding possible bearers of the "good" and *their* common characteristics (as simple bearers) with the corresponding *values themselves* and with the essence of these values for which they function only as bearers. (GW2 36–37/F 14)

He summarizes his position with the following statement:

> The ultimate independence of the being of values with regard to things, goods, and states of affairs appears clearly in a number of facts. We know of a stage in the grasping of values wherein the *value* of an object is already very clearly and evidentially given *apart from* the givenness of the *bearer* of the value. Thus, for example, a man can be distressing and repugnant, agreeable, or sympathetic to us without our being able to indicate *how* this comes about; in like manner we can for the longest time consider a poem or another work of art "beautiful" or "ugly," "distinguished" or "common," without knowing in the least which properties of the contents of the work prompt this. Again, a landscape or a room in a house can appear "friendly" or "distressing," and the same holds for a sojourn in a room, without our knowing the *bearers* of such values. This applies equally to physical and psychical realities. Clearly, neither the experience of values nor the degree of the adequation and the evidence (adequation in a full sense plus evidence constitutes the "self-givenness" of a value) depends in any way on the experience of the bearer of the values. Further, the *meaning* of an object in regard to "what" it is (whether, for example, a man is more "poet"

> or "philosopher") may *fluctuate* to any degree *without* its *value* ever fluctuating. In such cases the extent to which values are, in their *being, independent* of their bearer clearly reveals itself. This applies equally to things and to states of affairs. Distinguishing the values of wines in *no* sense presupposes a knowledge of their composition, the origin of this or that grape, or the method of pressing. Nor are "*value-complexes*" (*Wertverhalte*) mere values *of* states of affairs. The grasping of states of affairs is not the condition under which they are given to us. It can be given to me that a certain day in August last year "was beautiful" without its being given to me that at that time I visited a friend who is especially dear to me. Indeed, it is as if the *axiological nuance* of an object (whether it be remembered, anticipated, represented, or perceived) were the *first* factor that came upon us, and it is as if the value of the totality of which this object is a member or part constituted a "medium," as it were, in which the value comes to develop its content or (conceptual) meaning. A value precedes its object; it is the first "messenger" of its particular nature. An object may be vague and unclear while its value is already distinct and clear. In any comprehension of our milieu, for example, we immediately grasp the unanalyzed totality and its value; but, again, in the value of the totality we grasp partial values in which individual represented objects [*Bildgegenstände*] are "situated." (GW 40/F 17–18)

These passages are only the beginning of Scheler's attempt to bring the reader to the experience of the complex world of autonomous, nonformal values. We will return again to his development of understanding of the world of values, but for now we must stay focused on his understanding of the phenomenological approach, for seeing values as autonomous phenomena is not easy.

Phenomenology as a "Procedure of Seeing"

This brings us to the next stage of what phenomenology was to Scheler and why he believed it provided a knowledge of *a priori*, autonomous, nonformal values that would be the basis for an ethics. In the passage characterizing the nature of phenomenology with which we started, he said phenomenology was, first, a seeing of new realms of facts, and second, "a procedure of seeing." For Scheler, this second aspect of phenomenology, the "procedure of seeing," *is* of secondary importance, for one must first see that there *are* new realms of facts that can be brought to givenness before it is worthwhile to lead others to see what you have seen or to worry about developing procedures that will help both you and them to see more clearly this new realm. It is only after the explorer has discovered the new land that he or she starts preliminary mapping and tries to interest others in setting up expeditions. It is only after you have seen autonomous values that you worry about why you can see them and others cannot.

Yet despite the secondary importance of Scheler's procedures of seeing, it is now worthwhile for us to explore them. We are not pioneering explorers here, but followers, and as such we need all the help we can get in seeing what Scheler saw. Scheler himself follows the priorities he claims. Both the phenomenological procedures of seeing and the way he marks off phenomenological intuition and facts from other types of seeing and other types of facts clearly follow from his original experience of these facts and his "naive" use of the procedures. This is often forgotten today when we find ourselves being introduced to elaborations of phenomenological techniques, and even theories about them (not to mention refutations), before being led to any phenomenological experiences. In such a case it is difficult to see how the techniques shown are developed out of the phenomenological experiences.

Fortunately for us, as Scheler worked to uncover hitherto unrecognized (at least by Kant) *a priori* essences such as values, he also made contributions toward articulating his procedures of seeing. In approaching Scheler's comments on procedure, it is, first of all, important to understand that his procedures of seeing must not be confused with external criteria, where by "criteria" are meant external tests or procedures that can be stated apart from the experiencing of the realm of essences themselves. Scheler believed that such criteria could not be given and specifically distinguishes the phenomenological approach from the "critical" approach on precisely this point: "The criterion question is posed by the eternally 'other,' the man who does not want to find the true and the false, or the values of good and evil, etc., by experiencing, by investigating the facts, but sets himself as a judge over all of these. It has not become clear to such a man that all criteria are first derived from contact with the things-themselves, that even *the* criteria are to be so derived" (PUE 382/ PTC 139–40).

Now this does not mean that there are no "criteria," if by this term you mean describable differences in experiencing or in the content of experiences. In that sense of "criteria" all that Scheler says about the nature of essences and the immediately (versus indirectly) given constitute "criteria" for phenomenological intuition and essences. Furthermore, some of Scheler's descriptions at least imply a kind of test. For example, when he defines phenomenological facts as facts that do not vary when the sense function that gives them varies, he is simultaneously suggesting a possible test procedure. Even here, however, we do not yet have neat, hard-edged procedures or simple either-or tests. In fact, Scheler's main concern is not with setting up tests at all but rather with emphasizing that in order to find tests and criteria you must first be able to *see* the phenomenon in question. In this regard there is one very important procedure of seeing we must explore. It is intended to help us see those things we are blind to.

We have already seen that one way you can blind yourself to whole realms of the given (the given essences, particularly) is to fix upon one level of givenness. For example, to fix upon the "perspectival side of a cube" is not to see the "cube as a whole" which can just as validly be given, and to fixate on the bearers of nonformal values is not to see the autonomous essence of nonformal values.

To grasp the blinding force of such a prejudice, let us look at such a "level" fixation more carefully. In the first place, one who is so fixated would probably object to our characterization of his or her position. This person might well complain that in fact he or she does recognize that the cube can be experienced as a whole. It is not the "naive" experience of the cube as a whole he or she objects to, but the fact that the person having this experience does not realize that the experience is not of a *reality* but rather of a construct. To such persons, anyone who thinks he or she is experiencing a cube as a whole is mistaken and is only experiencing a constructed entity. They may well claim that what we *really* experience is the "perspectival side-views of the cube." Similarly, a person who wishes to argue that the world is really nothing but atomic physical objects in causal interaction may well wish also to argue that anyone who thinks he or she has experienced an essence "cube" is experiencing only an intellectual abstraction of the physical *real* world. These two types of people may well, incidentally, themselves debate over whether reality is physical objects or individual "perspectival views" (perhaps sensations, even), and the history of philosophy is replete with such arguments, attempting to define, once and for all, "reality."

The problem with all of these debates is that they begin with perhaps the most difficult of all questions, the question of what is real, already settled. Indeed, they begin with the assumption that there is only one level or type of reality and perception of reality. Now since phenomenology began, in Scheler's case at least, with the suspicion that some philosophers' epistemological or metaphysical positions had arbitrarily impoverished the given, it is not surprising that approaches which start out with the issue of what is real and what is not real settled ahead of time are suspect.

Nor is it only the theories of philosophers that can blind us to whole realms of phenomena. Not all reality-unreality distinctions are philosophers' theories. Quite the contrary, we find ourselves in a world within which such distinctions force themselves upon us both "naturally" and "socially" long before we begin to reflectively develop philosophical theories. To give one simple example: to stay alive I must find out very early in life what is, relative to my physical constitution, really food and really poison. If not, I will quickly die of poisoning (unless I am incredibly lucky). Such "interests" and others tend to focus and fixate me all the time. The theories of philosophers, which blind them to everything except what will fit their theories, are weak and puny things compared to the naturally adopted worldviews needed for biological survival.

Indeed, it is the power not only of theories of reality but of reality itself that creates one of the most basic differences between Scheler's phenomenological approach and that of others, notably Husserl. From Scheler's point of view, the simple intellectual suspension of a "judgment" of reality is not enough. As Frings puts it in *The Mind of Max Scheler:*

> While the concept of reality bears heavily on Scheler's later *Philosophical Anthropology,* it should be mentioned that the concept of

> reality is, in part, a result of Scheler's sharp critique of Husserl's phenomenological reduction. This reduction must not center in a method, Scheler charges, but in a "technique" of nullifying (*aufheben*) the factor of the reality in the life-world itself so that pure phenomena can appear in consciousness. Husserl's reductive method simply takes real being as having a place in time to be bracketed by a judgment (*Daseinsurteil*).[15]

It should be noted that in this passage Frings draws upon Scheler's last-period thought, which I will develop below. Yet even before Scheler began to develop his understanding of reality, he criticized Husserl's *epoche* as not being fully adequate to "suspend" reality.

Thus, if we are ever to see a new realm of facts ("new" meaning here precisely a realm that is not permitted within the range of some "old" viewpoint) we must learn to free ourselves from such fixation. Scheler was very much aware of the power of natural reality itself to blind us, but the intellectual biases, theories, and worldviews that enthrone judgments of what is real are dangerous enough. If we are to see the essences given within and through experience (even sensory experience), we must not *begin* either blinded by reality itself or intellectually blinded by theories about reality that divide what we experience neatly according to what is judged to be real and what is judged to be nonreal, with the nonreal being relegated to an inferior and dependent status. For example, if I am to see the autonomous, nonformal values carried by physical bearers of these values, I must not fixate on a world-

[15] Frings continues: "In a judgmental method, therefore, phenomena remain tied, no matter how slightly, to the *reality* of the life-world that is to be nullified in the first place. Because of the sensory linkage the method has, which stems from the 'thought-procedure' of the phenomenological reduction itself, phenomena do not yet appear as they should, that is, as *pure* facts alone. Hence the reduction is not radical enough. For this reason Scheler proposes to eliminate the very root that posits reality. This root, however, lies in the capacity that posits reality: impulsion. While consciousness or 'mind' in general can only posit the whatness of something, it is 'impotent' (*ohnmächtig*) to posit the reality of something. A temporary nullification of impulsion is necessary, therefore, and it can be achieved only by a psychic technique to accomplish the 'phenomenological attitude' necessary to reach a pure fact. This technique alone promises a momentary access to what is in 'pure intuition' as facts, severed from the realities of the natural world view or life-world and that of the world of science" (1997, 191–92).

view within which all there "really" can be are physical objects. If I do so, I will never see that values can be given to me as an autonomous realm of facts. I will never see the values themselves but will focus on "physical reality," on the physical bearers of the values. Similarly, if I begin with sense empiricism or Kant's epistemological-metaphysical views, the very possibility that *a priori,* nonformal values can be directly and immediately given is forever precluded.

Thus, in order to open us to new "facts," phenomenology must first concern itself with the fundamental act that suspends the blinders of insistent reality if we are ever to see beyond what is given to us through our interests. Yet beyond this most basic and necessary suspension, phenomenology must also work to counter the intellectual biases, prejudices, and worldviews that can intellectually blind us as well.

Scheler worked to identify blinding interests and realities, as well as the intellectual theses that flow from them. This is shown as he defines the *a priori* in the *Formalism:*

> We designate as "*a priori*" all those ideal units of meaning and those propositions which are self-given by way of an *immediate intuitive* content in the absence of any kind of positing (*Setzung*) of subjects that think them and of the real nature of those subjects, and in the absence of any kind of positing of objects to which such units of meaning are applicable. The point, therefore, is to leave aside all kinds of *positing,* including the positing of "real" or "non-real," "illusion" or "real," etc. (GW2 67–68/F 48)

It is important to note here that Scheler is not only warning the reader to suspend positing concerning the reality versus non-reality of the *objects* we perceive. In fact, the first positing to be suspended, he notes above, is "positing of subjects that think them and of the real nature of those subjects." What, however, does Scheler mean by "positing on the subject-side"? Again we must go to reflective experience to see what is meant by this phrase. Let us begin with a simple example. As a human being I see via physical eyes. Yet if I fixate on this level I may well prejudge what I can "see" on the basis of my knowledge of the limitations of these physical eyes. The act of seeing is not identical with that which the physical eyes can provide, unless I make it so by ignoring all other givens of "seeing."

There are more subtle but no less dangerous prejudgments possible. I have, so far in this book, used the word "see" to refer not only to the literal act of seeing (pure or physical) but also to grasping a given in general. This type of metaphor is dangerous, for it might well set up a hidden limitation to the type of grasping "seeing" can be if we take physical seeing as the paradigm, even if we do not limit ourselves in the simple fashion just noted.

Yet when it comes to what we can be phenomenologically given, and how it can be given to us, one of the subject-side prejudices that is most destructive of our ability to see *a priori* values is, according to Scheler, again rooted in the rational-sensible dichotomy adopted by Kant.

The Phenomenological Given and Kant's Rationalism

We have already seen one feature of Kant's dichotomy on the object side, with his belief that the given of sensation is nothing but an unordered chaos. But Kant's understanding of the subject side of the dichotomy is just as limiting. For him the mental or spiritual (*geistigen*) is nothing but the rational. Kant reduces any and all spiritual (*geistigen*) acts to logical-intellectual-rational acts. To do so, according to Scheler, is to ignore acts that are as spiritual (mental) as rational acts but not reducible to them, and among these nonrational spiritual acts are precisely those acts within which values are phenomenologically given.

Just as the fullness of the given was lost in the physical empiricists' sensation theory, the fullness of mental or spiritual life is lost in Kant's rational-sensible dichotomy. This dichotomy either ignores the mental or spiritual nonrational, attempts to reduce it to the rational, or banishes it to the sensible—thereby expelling it from the mind or spirit. As Scheler says:

> Whether there are original as well as essential differentiations in rank among the essences of acts and functions at the base of the alogical of our spiritual life, that is, whether these acts and functions have an "originality" comparable to that of the acts in which we comprehend objects in pure logic—in other words, whether there is also a *pure intuiting and feeling, a pure loving and hating, a pure striving and willing,* which are *as* independent of the psychophysical

> organization of man as pure thought, and which at the same time possess their own original laws that cannot be reduced to laws of empirical psychic life—this question is not even asked by those who share this prejudice. (GW2 259/F 254)

Once one has suspended the idea that all is to be divided between rational "thought" and the sensible "chaos," this question can be asked and can be answered in experience; and for Scheler, the answer is in the affirmative. Indeed, for him it will be acts of pure intuiting and feeling, and pure love and hate, that give us access to autonomous, nonformal values.

Summary, and Transition to a New Problem

In this chapter we have seen Scheler go beyond experience of the physical (physical cubes and empirical "goods") to the experience of a new realm of phenomenologically given "pure facts" (essential cube, pure values) as he worked to show that Kant was wrong and that we can have immediate intuition of the essences of nonformal (material) values. It is because Scheler believed we did have immediate experience of autonomous, nonformal (material) values that he believed Kant was wrong to retreat to the formal as a way of finding a stable, autonomous basis for moral direction. Indeed, the very first "presupposition" of Kant that he indicated he would be challenging in the *Formalism* was the belief that "every non-formal ethics must of necessity be an ethics of goods and purposes" (GW2 30/F 6). With his adoption of the phenomenological approach, Scheler believed he had within his grasp the way needed to meet the first of the three challenges that Kant's work presented to any nonformal ethics of values, the need to show there are noncontingent nonformal (material) values.

With the passage just quoted above, however, we see Scheler making a claim that raises Kant's second challenge. Scheler speaks of pure feeling, pure loving and hating, pure striving and willing. This is to take his quest for a new ethical personalism into new areas, areas fraught with dangers. For as we saw in the previous chapter, Kant ultimately rejected feeling as a way of access to autonomous, nonformal values just as surely as he rejected such values. Yet this is precisely the area that Scheler must enter if he is to make good on his claim that it is through feeling that we have noncontingent access to absolute values.

Scheler must not only show that there are autonomous, noncontingent, nonformal values; he must also show how we have access to them. Furthermore, if he is correct that such access is nonrational, he must show that Kant's presupposition that all nonformal ethics are hedonisms rooted in sensible states of pleasure is wrong. Thus Scheler must not only rescue values from Kant's indictment, he must rescue feeling as well. We will turn to Scheler's attempt to meet this second Kantian challenge, the need to show that there are noncontingent feelings that can be a stable and effective way to moral judgments, in the next chapter.

4

Feelings

Introduction

The battle between "Head and Heart," as Andrew Tallon (1997) entitles his new attempt to reconcile and integrate these often warring elements of the human person, is old. Just as old is the idea that one way or another the head ("dispassionate," "calculating," "cold" reason) ought to win out over the heart ("passionate," "intuitive," "warm" feeling). For despite their "warmth," feelings seem to lead us to destruction more often than to redemption. Indeed, the idea that feelings can give us reliable access to "objective" values—or, for that matter, anything stable and reliable—seems ludicrous. If there is anything more capricious, arbitrary, or out of our control in our lives than our feelings, it seems hard to imagine what it is. We have all uttered words and committed deeds while angry, or envious, or resentful, or just plain scared, that we would give almost anything to take back. Even when we are not uttering such words or committing such deeds, the moods of sadness, or depression, or anxiety we all suffer now and then (and some, sadly, suffer continually) are experiences we all wish to avoid or overcome.

Now most people will admit that feelings *can* have a positive role in the moral realm. An "open heart," a fine affective sensibility, can open our eyes to subtle elements that a cold and calculating reason might well ignore. We are all, I hope, fortunate enough to have intimate contact with such souls. They can awaken and quicken us to whole realms of value we had never dreamed existed (whether in the world or in ourselves).

Unfortunately, not all that our "moral feelings" give us is of positive moral value. The champions of reason are quick to point out that the world of moral feelings is not simply the world of finer sensibilities. All too often, instead of giving us new positive moral insight, feelings blind us to higher values as we are overwhelmed by passions, hatreds, angers, fears, envies, and resentments that take over both our hearts and our minds and work their havoc in and through us. Furthermore, such negative feelings often seem to confirm us in our wrath. There has never been a moment in human history when there were not human beings feeling deeply that what they were doing was right, or good, or noble, while they laid waste to all about them. "Feelings run high" in any massacre, be it of bodies, or ideas, or beauty. Many there are of the moral monsters who feel deeply their rectitude. Thus the idea that it is through "feelings" that we are to find the promised land of a reliable standard for morals, that "feelings" will give us access to the wisdom needed to settle moral disputes, seems to many people to be dangerous folly. Even if "feelings" are the initial way by which we judge the worth of a thing, as soon as we can we ought to move from this chaotic and anarchic realm and purify what the feelings give us by reasoned analysis and thought. Even if feelings do occasionally give us insights, we must refine what is given us through the cold fire of reason. We must always control feelings by use of this "higher function" of reason, lest they beguile and overpower us.

This is, indeed, one of the most disturbing and worrisome things about "feelings," the idea that all feelings are, at their root, passions that are out of our control. If we are to be moral beings, we must, in some meaningful sense of the term, be *free* beings. It makes no sense to talk of being held, or of holding ourselves, morally responsible for what we could not in any way *help* doing. In this Kant was correct. And the passions that can and do overcome us and sweep us away are not something we choose. They negate choice: they destroy the very *possibility* of choice. As I write this text today, "tribal" hatred continues to dismember both nations and bodies with a heart-wrenching brutality presented to us nightly through the wonders of technology (mixed, of course, with more local and individual acts of hatred). I will not identify the particular European and non-European "tribes" that are hating, killing, and maiming both bodies and spirits at this moment because of the sad knowledge that by the time this book is published the particulars may well change, as they have over the years I have been writing this book, but the carnage will most likely not. Unfortunately, as the "hatred," murder, and mayhem continue to show, the appeals of reason are rarely effective in the face of passion. Thus, even if we admit that feelings can sometimes play a positive role in our seeing of values, there seem to be very good grounds for believing that feelings can, at best, only provide the raw materials for moral judgment—that reason must purify the chaotic hodgepodge given to us in feeling.

Scheler's Manifesto

As old and as reasonable as the idea that feelings must be subordinate to reason may seem, it is an idea that Scheler challenges directly. He is aware that such a challenge is not easy to mount. As he states in the *Formalism* concerning the prejudice that upholds the division between "reason" and "sensibility" (with the alogical relegated to the side of the sensible): "The consequence of this prejudice is that ethics has in the course of its history been constituted either as absolute and a priori, and therefore rational, or as relative, empirical, and emotional. That ethics can and must be both absolute *and* emotional has rarely even been considered" (GW2 260/F 254).

Although Scheler acknowledges that Augustine and Pascal did try to undermine this "prejudice," he claims that no one has been able to *elaborate* an opposing viewpoint. That he intends to do so is plain from his comments endorsing Pascal's famous statement that *le coeur a ses raisons* (the heart has its reasons) and complaining that Pascal has often been misread:

> It is strange to see how these remarks of Pascal have been misunderstood by so many of his interpreters! . . . [T]he word reasons (*raisons*) is taken somewhat ironically. Supposedly Pascal does not mean to say that the heart *has* reasons or that there is anything which is *truly equivalent* to "reasons" in its rank and meaning, i.e., "*ses*" *raisons,* or its *own* reasons not borrowed from understanding; rather he means that one must not always seek "reasons" or their "equivalents," but must occasionally let the "heart" speak—blind feeling! But this is the exact *opposite* of what Pascal means. The stress of his proposition is on *ses raisons* and *ses raisons.* That there is a complaisance of the conscientiousness of thinking with regard to so-called needs of the heart, or that the so-called world view is "comple-

> mented" by assumptions which feelings and "postulates" suggest—even "postulates of reason"—when reason cannot provide an answer: surely Pascal's proposition does not imply any of this! On the contrary, there is a type of experiencing whose "objects" are completely inaccessible to reason; reason is as blind to them as ears and hearing are blind to colors. It is a kind of experience that leads us to *genuinely* objective objects and the eternal order among them, i.e., to *values* and the order of ranks among them. And the order and laws contained in this experience are as exact and evident as those of logic and mathematics; that is, there are evident interconnections and oppositions among values and value-attitudes and among the acts of preferring, etc., which are built on them, and on the basis of these a genuine grounding of moral decisions and laws for such decisions is both possible and necessary. (GW2 260–61/F 255)

From this manifesto it is clear that Scheler believes both that we have access to "objective" values and their hierarchy only through feeling *and* that such access is not simply a vague, nascent forerunner which must be subsequently clarified by reason. But how can he hold such beliefs? In the face of Kant's "colossus of steel and bronze," how can Scheler meet what we have called (in chapter 2) the second requirement that Kant's work makes clear any nonformal ethics of value must meet: how can Scheler show that feelings are not rooted in the empirically contingent? And how can he show that Kant's fourth "presupposition," the claim that all nonformal ethics are hedonisms (GW2 31/F 6–7), is not well founded? Furthermore, how can he account for the variableness of judgments rooted in feelings?

The Complexity of "Feelings"

In order to see how Scheler lays the foundations for answering these challenges, we must first realize that for him the word "feeling" does not refer to a single, simple phenomenon. Language does not always accurately capture the full complexity of a phenomenon, and the word "feeling" is particularly vague and ambiguous. Unless we can get beyond the general term "feeling" and begin to sort out the very different phenomena covered by this single word, we will never be able to see why it is only in "feeling" that "objective" values are accessible. Let us now follow Scheler as he begins to make the necessary distinctions.

"Feeling of Something" (*Fühlen von etwas*) versus "Feeling States" (*Gefühlszuständen*)

The first distinction is between the intentional "feeling of something" (*Fühlen von etwas*) and mere "feeling states" (*Gefühlszuständen*) (GW2 261/F 255). The clearest evidence that one can make such a distinction is the experience of *feeling* a "feeling state." Take, for example, a sensible feeling state such as a pain. We can intentionally feel such a state in a number of ways: we can "suffer" the pain, "tolerate" it, "observe" it, and so forth. Further, all such variance is in the act of *grasping* the pain, not in the *state of pain* itself. As Scheler says:

> There are changing facts involved when I "suffer," "endure," "tolerate," or even "enjoy" "pain." What varies here in the functional quality of *feeling* it (which can also vary by degrees) is certainly not the *state of pain*. Nor is this variation to be found in general attention, with its levels of "noticing," "heeding," "noting," "observing," and "viewing." Pain observed is almost the opposite of pain suffered.[1]

But this is only one example of the difference between feeling states and feeling. Scheler goes on to a more general description of the difference. He points out that feeling states are only mediately related to objects and that we often have to investigate to find the connection or cause. What is important to our concerns, however, is the fact that in the case of an intentional "feeling of" there is

[1] Scheler continues: "In addition, all these kinds and levels of attention and interpretive viewings may freely vary to any extent within such qualities of feeling without any dissolution of the feeling itself. The limits of the feelable variations of the givenness of pain are quite different from those of a feeling-state in its relation to excitation and different also from the degrees of such a state. For this reason the ability to suffer or to enjoy has nothing to do with sensitivity to sensible pleasure and pain. An individual can suffer the same degree of pain more or less than another individual" (GW2 261/F 256).

> an original relatedness, a directedness of feeling toward something objective, namely, *values*. This kind of feeling is not a dead state or a factual state of affairs that can enter into associative connections or be related to them; nor is such feeling a "token." This feeling is a goal-determined movement, although it is by no means an *activity* issuing forth from a center (nor is it a temporally extended movement). . . . This feeling therefore has the same relation to its value-correlate as "representing" has to its "object," namely, an intentional relation. It is not *externally brought together* with an object, whether immediately or through a representation (which can be related to a feeling either mechanically and fortuitously or by mere thinking). On the contrary, feeling *originally* intends its *own* kind of objects, namely, "values." (GW2 261–63/F 257–58)

Yet, despite the importance of distinguishing between intentional feelings and feeling states, there are any number of "feelings" that are not merely feeling states but which seem incapable of serving as a means of access to "objective" values. We seem to have a certain intentionality when, for example, we are angry, for are we not angry "at" or "over" something? Scheler must distinguish the intentional feeling of value from such acts, and he does so immediately. To go back to the text where we broke off:

> Feeling is therefore a meaningful occurrence that is capable of "fulfillment" and "non-fulfillment." Consider an affect in contrast to this. An affect of anger "wells up within me" and then "takes its course in me." The connection of anger with the "about" of my anger is not intentional or original. A representation or a thought or, better, the objects in these that I first "perceived," "represented," or "thought" are what "cause my anger." And it is later—even though in normal cases very quickly—that I relate this anger to these objects, and then always through a representation. Surely I do not "comprehend" anything in this anger. Certain *evils* must be "comprehended" beforehand in *feeling* if anger is to be aroused. (GW2 263–64/F 258)

It is intentional feelings that give us values, not the affects such as anger. Without this distinction between the intentional feeling of values on the one hand and feeling states and affects on the other, Scheler's claim that it is in feeling that we have access to "objective" values would be impossible to sustain. The acts of feeling that give us access to values must be independent of our contingent makeup, from the feeling states and passions ("affects") that happen within us. Yet this distinction between feeling states and affects and the intentional acts of the "feeling of" values is only a beginning. To simply see a realm of values, even a realm of absolute values given objectively, is not yet to have the basis for moral choice and decision. Why should we choose one value over another? What is it about these values that allows for a differentiation between them?

"Preferring" (*Vorziehen*) and "Placing After" (*Nachsetzen*)

The answer to this question is that the values have a hierarchical relationship, an order of ranks, among themselves. Some ranks of values are "higher" than others. Here, too, Scheler works to show that our access to this hierarchical character of values is not tied to our contingent makeup as he makes his next distinction:

> It is necessary to distinguish emotional functions from the experiences that are based on "*preferring*" and "*placing after*" ("*Vorziehen und Nachsetzen*"). The latter constitute a *higher* stage in our emotional and intentional life, and *in* them we comprehend the ranks of values, their being higher and lower. "Preferring" and "placing after" are not conative activities like, say, "choosing," which is based on acts of preferring. Nor is preferring (or placing after) a purely feeling comportment. It constitutes a special class of emotional act-experiences. The proof is that we can "choose," strictly speaking, only between actions, whereas we can "prefer" one good to another, good weather to bad, one food to another, etc.[2]

[2] Scheler continues: "Moreover, this 'preferring' occurs immediately on the basis of the felt value-material and independent of its thing-bearers. It does not presuppose pictorial goal-contents or contents of purposes, whereas choosing does. On the contrary, the contents of goals in conation—contents that are not contents of purposes, which, as we saw, presuppose a reflection on preceding contents of goals and belong only to willing within conation—are *formed* with the cocondition of preferring. Therefore, preferring belongs to the sphere of *value-cognition, not* to the sphere of striving. This class of experiences, experiences of preferring, is in the strict sense intentional; these experiences are 'directed' and sense-giving, but we classify them with loving and hating as '*emotional acts,*' in contrast to intentional functions of feeling" (GW2 265/F 260).

In the *Formalism,* Scheler explains what he means by saying that the acts of preferring and placing after constitute a higher stage in our emotional and intentional life: "Since all values stand essentially in an order of ranks—i.e., since all values are, in relation to each other, higher or lower—and since these relations are comprehensible only 'in' preferring or rejecting them, the 'feeling' of values has its foundation, by essential necessity, in 'preferring' and 'placing after' " (GW2 107–8/F 89).

Scheler's distinction between higher and lower "stages" in our emotional and intentional life is of the greatest significance for his entire project. This is because, as noted above, what "feeling" gives us seems to be so variable that Scheler must show not only that we have access to "objective" values and their hierarchical ranking via "feelings," but also why such access is not uniform and universal. Why do people differ in what they feel of values? To see why we must now explore one of Scheler's most profound insights—his view of the nature of love and hate.

Love and Hate

We now turn to the final "level" Scheler distinguishes, indeed the "highest level of our intentional emotive life," the level of love and hate. For Scheler, our vision of the hierarchical ranking of values is determined by the functioning of these most fundamental of "emotional acts." He puts this almost poetically as he starts a discussion of "The normative and descriptive meaning of *'Ordo Amoris'*" (in the essay "*Ordo Amoris*"):[3]

> I find myself in an immeasurably vast world of sensible and spiritual objects which set my heart and passions in constant motion. I know that the objects I can recognize through perception and thought, as well as all that I will, choose, do, perform, and accomplish, de-

[3] Max Scheler, "*Ordo Amoris,*" appears in volume 10 of the *Gesammelte Werke,* 347–76. The original German manuscripts date from 1914–15 and 1916. The English translation, also entitled "*Ordo Amoris,*" is in Scheler, *Selected Philosophical Essays,* 98–135. This Latin phrase can be translated as "the order or ordering of love," but since it marks such a basic element in Scheler's thought the tradition is to leave it untranslated. This work will be referred to using the abbreviation GOA/EOA.

> pend on the play of this movement of my heart. It follows that any sort of rightness or falseness and perversity in my life and activity are determined by whether there is an objectively correct order of these stirrings of my love and hate, my inclination and disinclination, my many-sided interest in the things of this world. It depends further on whether I can impress this *ordo amoris* on my inner moral tenor (*Gemüt*). (GOA 347/EOA 98–99)

Love and hate are not only at a different level, they are different in nature as well. As Scheler says:

> In love and hate our spirit does much more than "respond" to already felt and perhaps preferred values. Love and hate are acts in which the value-realm accessible to the feeling of a being (the value-realm with which preferring is also connected) is either *extended* or *narrowed* (and this, of course, independent of the present world of *goods,* i.e., real valuable things, which are not presupposed in the plurality, fullness, and differentiation of felt values). In speaking of this "extension" or "narrowing" of the value-realm given to a being, I do not mean to imply in the least that values are created, made, or destroyed by love and hate. Values cannot be created or destroyed. They exist independent of the organization of all beings endowed with spirit. I do not mean to say that the nature of the act of love is such that it is directed in a "responding" fashion to a value *after* that value is felt or preferred; I mean, rather, that, strictly speaking, this act plays the *disclosing* role in our value-comprehensions, and that it is only this act which does so. This act is, as it were, a movement in whose execution ever *new* and *higher* values flash out, i.e., values that were wholly unknown to the being concerned. Thus this act does not *follow* value-feeling and preferring, but is ahead of them as a *pioneer* and a guide. And we must therefore attribute a "*creative*" role to this act to the extent that the range and nature of feelable and preferable values of a being, but not the existing values themselves, are concerned. Hence *all* of ethics would reach its completion in the discovery of the laws of love and hate, which, in regard to the degree of their absoluteness, apriority, and originality, go beyond the laws of preferring and those obtaining among their corresponding value-qualities. (GW2 266–67/F 261)

For Scheler, love is an act that opens our hearts to a wider and truer vision of the full hierarchy of values. This is a dramatic insight. Love does not simply "see" values or their proper ranking in the hierarchy of values, but is an act that *enables* us to see new values. Hatred is the opposite, for it destroys our ability to see positive, higher values.

With this we complete Scheler's description of the complex world of the feeling of values, and we can see why he believes the intentional acts of "feelings," the acts of preference, and the act of love are not passions that overcome us, but rather the complex way we "feel" noncontingent, "objective," nonformal values. If Scheler is correct, Kant may well be as wrong to condemn all feelings as contingently empirical as he was to condemn nonformal values.

Furthermore, as noted above, the complex levels of "feeling" and Scheler's understanding of love and hate also allow him to throw light on why people's view of values seems so variable, why what intentional "feelings" give us is not always insight into higher values but all too often precisely the kind of error we all wish to avoid, for hatred can produce profound value blindness and errors of "vision." I will develop this insight next.

The Refutation of Relativity

One of the great challenges to any "objective" ethics, whether formal or nonformal, is the apparent relativity of moral judgment. There seems to be little or no moral agreement between people—all moral judgment can seem relative and contingent. Although Scheler points out that much of the supposed variableness in moral judgments does not show any fundamental disagreement over the existence or rankings of values, he believes that such disagreement does indeed occur. In his book-length study of resentment, entitled *Ressentiment* ("Der Ressentiment im Aufbau der Moralen" [GR/ER]), Scheler states:

> The recognition that there have been *several* "moralities" in the world, not just one, is one of the most important results of modern ethics. . . . When we say that there have been several moralities, we mean that *the rules of preference between the values themselves* have varied, quite apart from all changes in the external conditions of life. A "morality" is a system of preference between the values themselves, a "moral constitution" which must be discovered *be-*

> *hind* the concrete valuations of a nation and an era. This system itself can undergo an evolution which has nothing at all to do with the growing adaptation of actions and judgments to changing conditions. In the latter case, the evaluations of certain actions, convictions, or types of men may have changed, but the ultimate criterion (such as general welfare) has remained the same. But there have been primary transformations of the moral systems themselves, independently of mere adaptations. Actually, the so-called ethical "relativists" have always been the absolutists of their own particular periods. They interpret the variations in moral judgments as stages in the "development" toward present-day morality, by which they wrongly measure the past. They do not even see the primary variations in the ways of judging, the rules of preference themselves. It is ethical absolutism, the doctrine which teaches that there are eternal evident laws of preference and a corresponding eternal hierarchy of values, which has recognized and could afford to acknowledge this much more far-reaching relativity of value judgments. (GR 68–69/ER 59–60)

This last statement seems to be a bold and risky assertion, for it would seem that such a far-reaching relativity provides the best of grounds for denying "evident laws of preference and a corresponding hierarchy of values." Why does Scheler make such a statement? He does so because, for him, the grasp of values and their hierarchy is not simply an "all or nothing" proposition. It is not simply a matter of seeing everything clearly or being totally blind. He goes on to say: "The relation between the various moralities and that eternally valid ethics is approximately the same as that between the different astronomical systems (for example, the Ptolemaic and the Copernican system) and the ideal system sought by astronomy. That intrinsically valid system is represented more or less adequately in the different moralities" (GR 69/ER 60).

Scheler's position is that there is an "objective" ranking of values and that love can give us reliable access to it, despite the fact that such access is not, *in practice,* universal. The problem he faces is that he must be able to show that we all have enough access to make good on the claim that there is such a realm and that we all do have reliable access to it, yet at the same time he must account for the limits and distortions in our access in a way that does not undercut this claim. Scheler's approach to this task is rooted in an understanding of the damage that hatred can do to our vision of values. Scheler actually indicates two different ways hatred might lead us to misread the rankings of values. The first is rooted in the fact that finite human persons, both individually and collectively, have imperfect visions of the totality of the world of values. We are all blind to *some* values, and thus to some parts of the "objective" hierarchy of values. The second is that we can and do distort what we "see"—we can and do, to use Nietzsche's term, "transvalue" values. But how does hatred create such problems?

Value Blindness

We will begin to explore Scheler's insights into the working of hatred by showing how our view of the hierarchy of value ranks can be *limited* (later we will show how it can be *distorted*). Why, exactly, do some people "see" values and their hierarchical rankings, while others do not? To answer this question I must develop Scheler's understanding of both love and hate. I will begin with love.

The Role of Love

Again we must turn to another of Scheler's essays (another early work which he revised and expanded in later years) for illumination. It is entitled *The Nature of Sympathy* (*Wesen und Formen der Sympathie*),[4] and within it Scheler undertakes, among other things, to describe love. In a key passage, he begins:

> Love, we said, is a movement pointing from a lower value to a higher one, though it is *not* necessary for *both* values to be *given* in

---

[4] *Wesen und Formen der Sympathie* is a revised and expanded version of *Zur Phänomenologie und Theorie Sympathiegefühle und von Liebe und Hass,* published in 1913. It is reprinted as volume 7 of the *Gesammelte Werke* (1923; rpt. Bonn: Franke Verlag, 1973 [now Bonn: Bouvier Verlag]). The English translation is Max Scheler, *The Nature of Sympathy,* translated by Peter Heath, with an introduction by W. Stark (London: Routledge and Kegan Paul, 1954). This work will be referred to using the abbreviation GW7/NS.

> the process. Usually it is the lower value that is given, either in the intimation of value which produces the love, as in love at first sight, or as a sequel to the occurrence of an act of preference between several given objects. But whichever it may be, "love" for the object or bearer of value concerned only begins with the commencement of that movement towards a potentially higher value in the beloved object; a movement which is as yet completely unconcerned as to whether this higher value is already in existence (having been merely unperceived or undiscovered hitherto, for instance), or whether it does not yet exist and merely "ought" to do so (in an ideal, individual sense, not as a general obligation). This *indifference* with regard to either possibility is a characteristic feature of love. It would therefore be wrong to depict love as an attitude of constantly prospecting, as it were, for new and higher values in the object, for this *could* only be due to *un*satisfied love. Yet it would be equally wrong to describe it as endeavoring actually to "raise" the value of its object, either by merely wishing its betterment, or by actively willing and trying to secure this, as when we seek to "better" a person or help them in any way to acquire a higher value. Though this too can certainly result from love. I said earlier in the case of personal love, that the movement of love itself "sets up an ideal paradigm" of the person's value which is not "drawn" from the empirical values he is felt to have, though it is erected upon that basis; but I do not take this to mean the same as an attempt to heighten the value of the beloved object, or a desire for its improvement. (GW7 159–60/NS 156–57)

In this passage, Scheler is trying to indicate the nature of love by distinguishing love, as the most basic of "movements" of the heart, from what results from love. After contrasting this sense of love as movement toward higher values with conceptions that obscure this core sense of love, he notes:

> We said that love is directed towards the "enhancement of value"; but this is not the same as being directed towards "a higher value." If I seek a value in an object higher than the given one, such a seeking demands some grasp of this higher value in respect of its ideal *quality*. But the higher value with which love is concerned is in no way previously "given," for it is only disclosed in the *movement of love*—at the end of this, as it were. All that it necessarily includes is the orientation towards an enhancement of value (which may be qualitatively determined in various ways). (GW7 161/NS 158)

Again we see love as the movement opening us to new, higher values, a movement and an opening that is quite distinct from and precedes all other acts. After next rejecting the idea of love as a pedagogical promotion of higher values, Scheler writes:

> The statement that "Love is directed upon things as they are" is undoubtedly correct. If one is entitled to expect *love* and encounters only the pedagogic gesture "Thou shalt," the result is *obduracy* and injured pride. And that is quite to be expected. But this "as they are" should not be misunderstood. It should not be equated with "we love things, possessing the values we discern them to possess," or "through the medium of these values." For this is to deprive love of that character as a *movement* which assuredly belongs to it. The "being" we are concerned with here is that "*ideal* being" postulated in love which is neither an empirical and existential one, nor one which it "ought" to have, but a *third* thing, which is as yet indifferent with regard to *this* distinction; the same being that is implied, e.g. in the phrase "Become what thou art," which means something quite different from "Thou shouldst be thus and thus," while it is also quite different from the being of empirical existence, for what one "is" in this latter sense, one does not need to *become*. (GW7 162/NS 159)

Finally, after rejecting the idea that love creates higher value, or that love blinds us to the "true" qualities of the beloved, Scheler closes:

> If we now consider this phenomenon, stripped of all its empirical and other trappings, it can also be said that *love is that movement wherein every concrete individual object that possesses value achieves the highest value compatible with its nature and ideal vocation; or wherein it attains the ideal state of value intrinsic to its nature.* (Hatred, on the other hand, is a movement in the opposite direction.) We are not concerned here with whether the love in question refers to oneself or to others, or with any other distinctions which might be drawn in this connection. (GW7 164/NS 161)

Yet despite the fact that Scheler has come to this final delineation, it seems oddly unsatisfying, for how does the beloved object "achieve" its "highest value" when Scheler has, earlier in this very passage, denied that the act of love in any way tries to bring about the highest value?

Scheler's phenomenological description, and final "delineation," of the phenomenon of love makes sense if one realizes that what he is calling love is one of the most fundamental of all acts possible to a person. Love is, I believe, the fundamental *enabling* act. It is that act which helps enable us to "become what we are." It does so because it is an act that does not demand, does not strive, does not anticipate, but rather, in its movement, opens up for both the lover and the loved what was always there as true potentiality. It is in making these higher potentials accessible that love lays the foundation for all other acts that follow. This is why any attempt to *capture* in positive description or definition the essence of love tends to go beyond love and include acts that are founded in love, grow out of love, and are made possible by love, but are not themselves the fundamental act of love. Love is, simply, that fundamental act, that fundamental movement, which makes all other acts of growth and development possible.

The Limited Vision of Values

With this view of love before us, we can now see one of the basic ways that Scheler accounts for the variableness of the perception of values and their hierarchy. As he himself puts it in the "*Ordo Amoris*" essay:

> Man, before he is an *ens cogitans* or an *ens volens,* is an *ens amans.* The fullness, the gradations, the differentiations, and the power of his love circumscribe the fullness, the functional specificity, and the power of his possible spirit and of the possible *range* of contact with the universe. Of all that is actually worthy of love—the essences of which circumscribe a priori the concrete goods which are accessible to his power of comprehension—he has access to only a part. (GOA 355/EOA 110–11)

What we see of the ranks of values varies because what we have access to of the hierarchy of values depends upon what love has opened to us—it depends upon our specific *ordo amoris.*

Although Scheler's specific idea is novel, the general approach is not. Any approach that has some sort of "seeing" at its core must appeal to some sort of "blindness" to account for differences in what is "seen." What is novel about Scheler's approach is his belief that the "blindness" is not simply a matter of either seeing a single thing (the simple value "good" of G. E. Moore, for example) or not seeing it. It is rather a matter of seeing clearly, but only seeing *part* of a vast, complex whole. Since we are speaking of a hierarchical ranking of values, to see only part of it leads naturally to judgments that absolutize what is, truly, only relative—that is, we take the highest value we see to be the objectively highest value there is, whether it is, in fact, the highest or not.

Scheler's doctrine accounts for relativity of insight within the framework of an absolute hierarchy of values, but it raises an important question. Since love opens us to more and more of the hierarchy of values and allows us to become more and more fulfilled as persons, why do we not always engage in this enabling act of love? Why are some people less loving than others, and thus more limited in the range of values they can see?

The Role of Hate

To answer these questions we must turn to the antithesis of love. For Scheler, hatred is a positive act. As he states in *The Nature of Sympathy:*

> In the first place love and hatred cannot be radically distinguished on the grounds that hatred is simply love for the non-existence of a thing. For hatred is really a *positive act,* involving a presentation of *disvalue* no less immediate than the presentation of *positive* value in the act of love. But love is a movement, passing from a lower value to a higher one, in which the higher value of the object or person suddenly flashes upon us; whereas hatred moves in the opposite direction. It can be seen from this that hatred looks to the possible existence of a lower value (itself of negative value, on that account), and to the removal of the very possibility of a higher value (which again has a negative value). Love, on the other hand, looks to the establishment of higher possibilities of value (which itself has a positive value), and to the maintenance of these, besides seeking to remove the possibility of lower value (which itself has a positive moral value). Hate, therefore, is by no means an utter repudiation of the whole realm of values generally; it involves, rather, a *positive* preoccupation with lower possibilities of value. (GW7 155–56/NS 152–53)

Yet even if hatred is a "positive" act in the sense that it "looks to the positive existence" of lower values, it does differ from love in one key respect. Love opens up for us new values, new "territory," while "hatred, on the other hand, is in the strictest sense *destructive,* since it does in fact destroy the higher values (within these spheres), and has the *additional effect* of blunting and blinding our feeling for such values and power of discriminating them. It is only because of their destruction (within these spheres) by hatred, that they *become* indiscernible" (GW7 157/NS 154).

When we hate, what we can feel of the "objective" hierarchy of values is diminished. In hating we become blind to what love could make visible. With this we now see how it is that some people see more and some less of the hierarchy of values. But such incomplete seeing is only one of the ways we can come to misread the hierarchy. The second way is to feel values and their hierarchy, but in a distorted fashion.

Value Distortion

We must now turn to Scheler's work on uncovering the roots not simply of *blindness* to values, but of the *distortion* of what is seen. Here too hatred is the key. This is because although love and hate are antithetical modes of emotional life—we cannot in one act love and hate the same thing with respect to a given value—they are not "equi-primordial modes of behavior." As Scheler states: "*Our heart is primarily destined to love,* not to hate. Hate is only a reaction against a love which is in some way false" (GOA 369/EOA 126). "Hate is always and everywhere a *rebellion of our heart* and spirit *against a violation of ordo amoris*" (GOA 370/EOA 127). "The act of *hate,* the antithesis of love, or the emotional negation of value and existence, is the result of some *incorrect* or *confused* love. However rich and various may be the motive of hatred or the state of valuelessness which exacts hatred, *one* form of lawfulness runs through all cases of hatred—every act of hate is founded on an act of love, without which it would lack sense" (GOA 368/EOA 125).

To see how hatred is the root of a distorted vision of the hierarchy of values, we must explore what could cause this "confusion of love" that hatred is. If, as we have seen, love is one of the most basic of acts, what can disrupt it, what can confuse it? This is an area that is, in my judgment, perhaps the most difficult of all to penetrate, despite our great desire to do so. Yet even here Scheler does develop at least one way in which such a disorder can arise, namely resentment, which we must now consider in some detail.

Ressentiment

The recognition that resentment, or more precisely *ressentiment,*[5] can play a key role in determining basic perception of values and their hierarchy, and thus of the judgments based upon such perception, is not original with Scheler. Although Scheler disagrees with Nietzsche's belief that Christian love is rooted in *ressentiment,* he saluted Nietzsche's recognition of the role that *ressentiment* could play in value judgment. Scheler devotes an entire study to developing insight into the essence of *ressentiment.* For Scheler:

> *Ressentiment* is a self-poisoning of the mind which has quite definite causes and consequences. It is a lasting mental attitude, caused by the systematic repression of certain emotions and affects which, as such, are normal components of human nature. Their repression leads to the constant tendency to indulge in certain kinds of value delusions and corresponding value judgments. The emotions and affects primarily concerned are revenge, hatred, malice, envy, the impulse to detract, and spite. (GR 38/ER 29)

As Scheler then develops, these emotions and affects are not themselves *ressentiment,* but rather the ground within which *ressentiment* grows. When an affront cannot be answered because we fear defeat or failure and feel our impotence as we postpone reaction, we are on the way to *ressentiment.* Scheler describes the stages of repressed reactions, a "progression of feeling which starts with revenge and runs via rancor, envy, and impulse to detract all the way to spite, coming close to *ressentiment*" (GR 39/ER 30), with

[5] Scheler used the French term *ressentiment* because, as we shall see below, it is much deeper than what is signaled by the English word "resentment." For this reason I will use the term *ressentiment* in my discussions.

each step becoming increasingly detached from a specific object, becoming increasingly generalized.

Scheler then develops a variety of situations in which *ressentiment* can occur, as well as examples of it in action. Our concern is, however, not with specific examples of *ressentiment*-laden deeds but with precisely what *ressentiment* is and how it can lead to a confusion of the *ordo amoris*. After pointing to the "psychological law" that we tend to overcome the tension between desire and impotence by downgrading the value of the desired object (the "sour grapes" phenomenon), and pointing out that this does not yet distort our vision of the proper ranking of values themselves, but only of the value of the object desired (GR 63–64/ER 53–54), Scheler finally begins to get to true *ressentiment*. If the sense of impotence is not overcome by action or true forgiveness, our view of values themselves becomes poisoned. Scheler describes the poisoning when the repressed soul, now suffused with generalized negative feeling, continues to strive to relieve the tension between desire and impotence, and yet again and again is confronted with realized positive values he or she cannot achieve. It is then that we move from the falsification of the "worldview" to the perversion of the "sense of values" itself, and

> in this new phase, the man of *ressentiment* no longer turns away from the positive values, nor does he wish to destroy the men and things endowed with them. Now the values themselves are inverted: those values which are positive to any normal feeling become negative. The man of *ressentiment* cannot justify or even understand his own existence and sense of life in terms of positive values such as power, health, beauty, freedom, and independence. Weakness, fear, anxiety, and a slavish disposition prevent him from obtaining them. Therefore he comes to feel that "all this is vain anyway" and that salvation lies in the opposite phenomena: poverty, suffering, illness, and death. This "sublime revenge" of *ressentiment* (in Nietzsche's words) has indeed played a creative role in the history of value systems. It is "sublime," for the impulses of revenge against those who are strong, healthy, rich, or handsome now disappear entirely. *Ressentiment* has brought deliverance from the inner torment of these affects. Once the sense of values has shifted and the new judgments have spread, such people cease to be enviable, hateful, and worthy of revenge. They are unfortunate and to be pitied, for they are beset with "evils." Their sight now awakens

> feelings of gentleness, pity, and commiseration. . . . *Ressentiment* man, on the other hand, now feels "good," "pure," and "human"—at least in the conscious layers of his mind. He is delivered from hatred, from the tormenting desire of an impossible revenge, though deep down his poisoned sense of life and the true values may still shine through the illusory ones. There is no more calumny, no more defamation of particular persons or things. The systematic perversion and reinterpretation of the values *themselves* is much more effective than the "slandering" of persons or the falsification of the world view could ever be. (GR 66–67/ER 56–57)

Ressentiment thus produces a transvaluation of values, a distortion of the hierarchy of values, on the level of their givenness. It is not simply a matter of not seeing values, and thereby mistakenly assigning to values a height they do not have since we simply do not see the higher values. In this case we "see" the higher values, but can no longer "see" their proper height. As Scheler completes the passages just quoted:

> What is called "falsification of the value tablets," "reinterpretation," or "transvaluation" should not be mistaken for conscious lying. Indeed, it goes beyond the sphere of judging. It is not that the positive value is felt as such and that it is merely declared to be "bad." Beyond all conscious lying and falsifying, there is a deeper "organic mendacity." Here the falsification is not formed in consciousness, but at the same stage of the mental process as the impressions and value feelings themselves: *on the road* of experience into consciousness. There is "organic mendacity" whenever a man's mind admits only those impressions which serve his "interest" or his instinctive attitude. Already in the process of mental reproduction and recollection, the contents of his experience are modified in this direction. He who is "mendacious" has no need to lie! In his case, the automatic process of forming recollections, impressions, and feelings is involuntarily slanted, so that conscious falsification becomes unnecessary. Indeed the most honest and upright convictions may prevail in the periphery of consciousness. The apprehension of values follows this pattern, to the point of their complete reversal. The *value judgment* is based on this original "falsification." It is itself entirely "true," "genuine," and "honest," for the value it affirms is really felt to be positive. (GR 67–68/ER 57)

It is because hatred (in this case *ressentiment*), like love, works at such a depth within our being that it can both limit and distort what we see of the true ranking of values. With his development of the working of hatred and *ressentiment,* Scheler shows the roots of the limitations and distortions in our access to the true hierarchy of values, and he begins to account for the relativity of moral judgments in a way that denies neither the noncontingency of the nonformal values we see nor the nonrational way we see them. Thus he has both shown the noncontingency of intentional feelings and accounted for the variability of what we see of the realm of nonformal values, the second challenge set by Kant.

Yet as important as this task is to countering the blinding rationalism of Kant, it is only part of the task Scheler faced in refuting Kant. We have now shown Scheler repudiating three of the eight presuppositions he set himself to challenge in the *Formalism,* as noted in chapter 2. In order to challenge the other five, Scheler must develop a new vision of the person. How he did so will be shown in the next chapter.

5

Persons

Introduction

In the last two chapters I showed why Scheler believed that Kant was wrong to forswear nonformal values and feelings in his search for moral wisdom. But defending nonformal values and feelings was only the beginning of Scheler's task in the *Formalism in Ethics and Non-Formal Ethics of Values*. Scheler was acutely aware of the fact that Kant's attacks on nonformal, "material" values and our access to them was only one of the stumbling blocks Kant placed in the way of nonformal ethics. Scheler not only had to rescue values and our access to them by "feelings" from the uncertainty of the "empirical," but he had to rescue the person as well. Kant's formalism claims not only that all material values are caught in the web of empirical contingency, but also that only formalism can rescue the person from the same fate. Thus Scheler must work to show that the *whole* person—the person of feeling and not just the "person" seen by the rationalist and the formalist—is autonomous.

Scheler's awareness of the centrality of this task is shown in several ways. First of all, five of the eight presuppositions of Kant that Scheler lists concern the person (GW2 30–31/F 6–7). Second, the development of the *Formalism* shows that he was aware of the central importance of the person to his project from the beginning. This is signaled by the fact that the subtitle of the book is *A New Attempt toward the Foundations of an Ethical Personalism,* and the section of this book dealing with the person ("Section 6: Formalism and Person" [GW2 370–580/F 370–595]) is the longest section of the book, constituting over 39 percent of the volume.

Sections of this chapter appeared in my essay "Person, Acts, and Meaning: Max Scheler's Insight," *New Scholasticism* 59, no. 2 (1985): 200–12, and are reproduced here with permission.

Scheler's Critique of Kant's Person

Scheler believes that one need not turn to a formalism to show the autonomy and dignity of the person. Indeed, he believes that formalism itself presents a degraded view of the person. Scheler begins by criticizing Kant's identification of the person with the rational (GW2 370–71/F 371). The problem with the rationalist's view of the person is that it is too narrow, because the person is more than a "logical subject of rational acts" (GW2 370/F 371). Worse, in reducing the person to nothing but what his or her rational formalism would allow, Kant destroys individuality as persons become "in the end an indifferent thoroughfare for an impersonal rational activity" (GW2 372/F 372–73). Although Scheler points out that it is Fichte and Hegel who show this "consequence" of Kant's work, and Kant himself avoids this extreme, even Kant's more moderate position fails to show adequately the fullness of the human person's dignity. As Scheler puts it:

> It is true that in Kant's case the idea of the person acquires the appearance of an existence and full-bloodedness that transcends the X of a rational will through his identification of this X with the *homo noumenon,* i.e., with man as "thing in itself," which he opposes to the *homo phenomenon*. But, logically, the *homo noumenon* is nothing but the concept of the unknowable constant "thing in itself" applied to man. The same unknowable constant also pertains, without *any* inner possibility of differentiation, to every plant and every rock. How could *this* constant render man a dignity different from that of a rock? (GW2 373/F 373)

In chapter 2 we saw how Kant's retreat to rational formalism ignored all but the formal value of universality, ignoring the fullness of the nonformal values relevant to our moral life. Analogously, Kant reduces the person to only one element, the rational, and in doing so fails to do justice to the dignity of the full person, the person of heart as well as head.

Scheler's Person

Scheler's rejection of rational formalism's narrow view of the person does, however, raise the question of how, exactly, Scheler is going to be able to defend the whole person as autonomous and noncontingent. In order to understand how he does so, we must first see the quite unique definition of the person that Scheler accepts. It is at the end of his criticism of Kant's personalism that Scheler begins to develop his vision of the person:

> Once we have separated the *kinds, forms, and directions of acts,* having bracketed their real bearers and the natural *organization* of such bearers, and once we have demonstrated what their essences and foundational laws consist in, we are confronted with a final question: What, in fact, is it that forms the *unity* of these acts quite independent of the natural *organization* of those bearers (e.g., men) with whose reduction the essences of acts came to the fore—in other words, what forms the unity of these *different* act-essences themselves, not of the factually performed acts of a certain real individual or a species? (GW2 380/F 380)

For Scheler, a phenomenological examination of acts shows that they are no more to be identified with their sometimes physical bearers than values are. Yet once you have separated acts from their bearers you do have a problem of unity. What holds acts together? Scheler solves the problem of the unity of acts with a bold stroke:

> Neither the being nor the problem of the "*person*" would exist if there were beings (whose natural organization we set aside in the reduction) endowed *only with knowing* (as thought and intuition) and those acts belonging to this (specifically theoretical) sphere. (Let us call such beings purely rational beings.) Of course these beings would still be (logical) subjects that execute rational acts: but they would not be "persons." Nor would they be persons if they had both inner and outer perception and often dealt with knowledge of the soul and nature, that is, even if they found an object "ego" in themselves and others and could perfectly observe, describe, and explicate experiences of "the ego" as well as all individual egos. The same would hold for beings whose entire contents were given only as projects of willing. They would be (logical) subjects of a willing, but not persons. For the person is precisely that unity which exists for acts of all possible *essential differences* insofar as these acts are thought to be executed. Hence, by saying that it belongs to the nature of the differences of acts to be in a *person* and *only* in a person, we imply that the *different logical subjects* of

> essentially different acts (which are different only as otherwise identical subjects of such act-differences) can only *be in a form of unity* insofar as we reflect on the possible "being" of these subjects and not merely on their nature.
>
> We can now enunciate the essential definition in the above sense: *the person is the concrete and essential unity of being of acts of different essences* which in itself . . . precedes all essential act-differences (especially the difference between inner and outer perception, inner and outer willing, inner and outer feeling, loving and hating, etc.). *The being of the person is therefore the "foundation" of all essentially different acts.* (GW2 382–83/F 382–83)

After reading this passage, one might well wonder why I say that Scheler has solved the problem of the unity of acts, or why he claims to be defining the person. It seems that instead of solving the problem, Scheler has merely defined the person *as that* which unifies the essentially different acts executed by the person. To read him thus leads immediately to the following question: What is this "person" that unifies acts? But Scheler does not identify the person as *that which* unifies the acts. He identifies the person *as* the unity of acts. And, as we shall see, that makes all the difference.

Person as Act

In Scheler's view, the person is not something separate from the acts—the person is *in* the acts. There is no need to posit something above or behind or separate from the acts. The person *is* the acts, but not acts abstracted. The person is the acts unified, acts of essentially different natures unified in a particular concrete way: acts *are* the person.

This lays the foundation for the noncontingency of the person because, as already noted, for Scheler neither acts nor persons are empirical entities, indeed they are not even "objects." In a section entitled "The Being of the Person Is Never an Object," Scheler contrasts act with the ego, which is an object:

> An act is never an object. No matter how much knowledge we have of an act, our reflecting on its naive execution (in the moment of such execution or in reflective, immediate memory) contains

> nothing like the objectification which marks, e.g., all inner perception, especially all inner observation.
>
> If an act can therefore never be an object, then the *person* who lives in the execution of acts can a fortiori never be an object. (GW2 386/F 387)

Since this belief is at the core of Scheler's view of the person, we must now turn to a development of what he means by his assertion that neither acts nor persons can be objects, because this claim seems to raise as serious a difficulty as any it allows Scheler to meet. If acts and persons are not objects, how can we ever know them? What access do we have to them? As Nicolai Hartmann put it: "If there were no possibility of a presentation of acts and persons as objects, ethics would itself be an impossibility. For man as a person is the object of ethics."[1]

The difficulty of understanding Scheler's position is not eased by the fact that despite his denial that acts and persons can ever be objects, he asserts again and again that we do have reflective access to acts and to persons. Indeed, the quote I just presented from the *Formalism* goes on to say, immediately after the assertion that persons cannot be objects:

> The only and exclusive kind of givenness of the person is his *execution of acts* (including the execution of acts reflecting on acts). It is through this execution of acts that the person experiences himself at the same time. Or, if we are concerned with other persons, the person is experienced in terms of post-execution, coexecution, or pre-execution of acts. In these cases of the execution of acts of other persons, there is no objectification. (GW2 386/F 387)

Thus, Scheler clearly believes that we do have phenomenological access to acts and to persons, even if such access occurs only in the "execution of acts." Why, then, is he so adamant in his refusal to accept the idea that acts are, in some special way, "objects" of knowledge?

The simple, direct answer is that acts do not need to be objects for us to have phenomenological access to them. Indeed, to confuse acts and objects is one way to mis-take the being of acts and persons and the nature of our access to them. Scheler attempts

---

[1] Hartmann is quoted in Thomas J. Owens, *Phenomenology and Intersubjectivity* (105), in a passage where Owens develops this question himself.

to forestall such confusion because as a phenomenologist he was unusually sensitive to the correlation between *what* is given and the *way* in which it is given, as well as the need to suspend all theories about both sides of this correlation. The question of why Scheler does not accept the idea that acts can be objects of knowledge rests upon the twin assumptions that the only phenomena we can be given are *objects,* and the only *way* we can reliably know anything is as an object.

Scheler does not make these assumptions. In another essay, first presented in 1911 and later expanded in 1915 under the title "Die Idole der Selbsterkenntnis" ("The Idols of Self-Knowledge"),[2] Scheler, in a passage where he is distinguishing between acts and functions, says:

> An act can *never* become the object of any sort of perception; it can never turn into an object at all, never become an "entity" ("*Dasein*"). The being of a genuine act consists rather in its performance (*Vollzug*) and therefore is *absolutely,* not relatively, distinct from the concept of an object. This performance can come about straightforwardly or with "reflection." Still, this "reflection" is no "objectification." (DIS 233–34/ISK 26)

It is clear that Scheler believes both that acts are not objects and that we can have access to acts themselves through a reflection that does not objectify these acts. But my documentation of Scheler's beliefs does not show if he is correct. Evidence for this can be gained only by bringing acts to phenomenological givenness, since for a phenomenologist only the phenomenon itself can be evidence for a belief.

A Phenomenological Description of Acts and Persons

Unfortunately, Scheler rarely devotes time to the kind of phenomenological description of acts that will show forth their fun-

---

[2] This essay first appeared in 1911 under the title "Über Selbsttäuschungen" ("On Self-Deceptions") in the first issue of the journal *Zeitschrift für Psychopathologie.* The later, expanded version we are quoting from is Max Scheler, "Die Idole der Selbsterkenntnis," which first appeared in 1915 and is reprinted in volume 3 of the *Gesammelte Werke.* Scheler, *Vom Umsturtz der Werte,* 215–92. The translation is "The Idols of Self-Knowledge," in Scheler, *Selected Philosophical Essays,* 3–97. This essay will be referred to using the abbreviation DIS/ISK.

damental nature. His main concern in his description of acts is usually to point to the differences between various acts. However, his writings do affirm that fundamental characteristic of all acts which, when brought to givenness, will show why he is so adamant in his insistence that acts are not objects and cannot be given as objects. This characteristic is affirmed in two coordinate claims made by Scheler. On the side of *what* is given, he claims of each act: "There is no phenomenal time-duration (*Zeitdauer*) in it; an act in this sense is something that cuts through all phenomenal time-duration and never spreads itself over a duration of time" (DIS 234/ISK 27). As he metaphorically puts it in the *Formalism:* "Acts spring from the person into time" (GW2 387/F 388). Shifting to the *way* acts are given, Scheler makes the coordinate claim, as we have already seen in the passages above, that acts and persons can be given only in the execution of acts.

Since only acts themselves can provide evidence for Scheler's beliefs and claims, I must now bring you to a reflective experiencing of acts. My description of acts will initially focus on the claim that acts are nondurational, and it will begin with the description of a mundane act. As a particular act of friendship I take someone to the store. Such an act involves all sorts of physical events: getting into my car and driving to my friend's house to pick him up, driving to the store, shopping, carrying groceries, and so forth. The list of physical events is quite long, and all of them take time. Thus we face the immediate question of why Scheler, or anyone, would want to say that this particular act of friendship, like any act, is nondurational.

The Nondurational Act

To see the nondurational nature of this act, we must not look at the diversity of physical events involved but rather to the essence of this particular act of friendship.[3] What makes *this* particular set of physical events *this* particular act of friendship? Why do we

[3] Notice that we are not looking for the essence of friendship as such. Rather, we are trying to get at the fundamental nature of *this* act of friendship (taking someone to the store) as a way of getting at the nature of an *act*.

recognize this series of physical events as this particular act of friendship, and yet another series of perhaps the same physical events as not so?

We do so because this series of physical events in time has the *meaning* "act of friendship of taking someone to the store." We grasp, we are given, this series of physical events as this *particular* act of friendship. This sequence of events has unity, has completion, *as* this act of friendship. That is what gives *meaning* to this sequence of physical events. Any and all of the events could and can occur without this unity, without this meaning, and then they are not this act of friendship. But this set of events participates in a meaningful unity (this act of friendship of taking someone to the store), and that makes all the difference.

I must now issue a warning. If one does not take what I am saying as a phenomenological description, one may well think, at this point, that I am begging the question. After all, we are trying to *find out* why these events "mean" this act of friendship, and I am not explaining why they do so, but simply asserting that they do. Such an assertion of the "obvious," one might add, is no help whatsoever.

To so read my statement as an unsupported assertion would reflect a mis-taking of what a phenomenological description does. My report of the "obvious" fact that these physical events are *given* as unified, as meaning this act of friendship, is not intended as an explanation, but rather to help you see that there is nothing *obvious* about this given meaning, this unity, at all. Indeed, what is *unique* about these physical events as this act of friendship is precisely their particular unity, their particular meaning as this act of friendship. It is quite possible to have these physical events given in experience *without* this unity, or, as we will see below, as part of a *different* unity. In such a case the physical events are not this act of friendship. Indeed, if they are given without *some* unity they are not even acts. Thus my "assertion" is not an assertion at all, but rather a phenomenological description, an attempt to direct your reflective gaze in such a way that you will focus upon the level of unification, of meaning, for that is where acts are.

But what, one may ask, does seeing acts in the unification of events, in their meaning, have to do with seeing the essentially nondurational nature of all acts? Just this: the meaning of a set of physical events is nondurational. Meanings do not occur within time as physical events do. If the meaning "act of friendship of taking someone to the store" did occur within time, it would not provide unity to the "*diversity* in time" of the various events that are the physical bearers of what, when they are so unified, *is* this act of friendship. All of the physical events that are the physical bearers of this act of friendship of taking someone to the store do occur in time, but their unity, their meaning, in Scheler's words, "cuts across phenomenal duration."

In order to more easily see the nondurational nature of acts, let us now turn to another act, an act that is, in some regards, different from this act of friendship. Such contrasts often help one see what is the common element in both. Since the act of friendship described above realizes itself in the physical world (we physically went and got groceries), let us turn to an act not realized in the physical world but rather in the "world of ideas." Let us turn to the act of understanding of what I am now "writing down."

As I write this chapter I give unity to the various "marks" of the English language so that they mean something. The marks I leave on the page are the "physical bearers" of that meaning. And when you read what I write it is possible for you to "see" what I mean, but you will do so only if *you* can and do execute an act of understanding that is, to use Scheler's terms, a post-execution or co-execution of the act of understanding *I* now am executing as I "compose" this chapter, as I "act into time" in "writing it down." But both of our acts of understanding, purely as acts, are nondurational. The meaning is not in the objects (in this case "the marks on the paper") that are the "physical bearers" of the meaning we can, when we perform the act of understanding that gives unity to these marks, both *see.*

Again, the fact that it takes time for me to physically "put it down on paper," and that it takes time for you to physically "read" and mentally grasp what I put down, does not invalidate the essentially nondurational nature of both of our acts of understanding. The meaning of these marks on this page "cuts across phenomenal duration." If it did not, the "marks" would not have the *unity,* the *meaning,* that they do have when we "understand" them.

The Experiencing of Acts

As important as seeing the nondurational nature of acts is, it grounds only half of Scheler's claims. We must now shift our focus in order to explore Scheler's correlative claim that we have access to acts *only* in their performance, their execution. Let us focus then on the *way* acts are given, again using the same two acts, starting with the act of friendship of taking someone to the store.

In order to be able to see whether Scheler is correct in his claim that we have access to this act of friendship only in its performance, I propose a simple experiment. Take this act of friendship and look at the individual events that "make it up" as if they were *not* "part of" this act of friendship, as if, for example, you were puzzled about what was "going on here." In such a case you see me get into a car and drive to a house, someone comes out of the house and gets into the car, we drive to a store and buy groceries, I drive back to the house and we carry the groceries inside, and so forth. Notice that in this case, as you observe all of these physical events, you experience them in a disconnected fashion and have questions about their overall meaning: Am I an employee doing a chore? Is this a "cover" for an espionage meeting? Am I doing this out of a sense of obligation? Is it an act of friendship?[4] Individual events are given with meaning (my getting into a car and driving to a house, for example), but the overall meaning unifying all of these individual events is not given.

What I want you to reflectively grasp here is that you do not see such unity, such meaning, simply by blankly staring at the events. You see it by *acting,* by co-performing or post-performing an act unifying all of these events in this one way. (Indeed, your search for the overall meaning is also a co- or post-execution of different acts to see which, if any, do "fit," that is to say, do unify the given physical events.) This is the whole point of my experiment. The experience you have in seeing the overall meaning, in contrast to when you do not see it, when reflected upon, shows

[4] The number of possible fundamentally different "overall meanings" is quite large and includes not only the ones I suggest here but some that are complex combinations of the ones I suggest.

that you have access to the act of friendship of taking someone to the store *only* in the *execution* of this act. (There is, of course, one essential difference between your "execution" of this act of friendship and mine: my act of friendship of taking someone to the store is a realization in the physical world, while your act of understanding is not. But your act of understanding unifies these events in the same way as my act; you have access to this unification, this meaning, this act of friendship of taking someone to the store, only as you *act* to unify these events in this one way, only when you *execute* this act.)

Turn now to our second example, the one of understanding what I am now writing down on this page. Again repeat the same experiment you have just undertaken with the act of friendship. This time, however, be a little more destructive. In our experiment with the act of friendship, each "individual event" (getting into a car and driving to a house, etc.) had a separate "meaning," and what was not initially given was the "overall" meaning. Now as you experience the "marks on the page" do not suspend simply the "overall" meaning; instead, suspend *totally* all acts of understanding of the "marks on the page." As you do this *all* unity begins to disappear; when complete, the "marks on the page" become absolutely meaningless. (Indeed, if the suspension is complete enough, they would not even retain the meaning "marks on the page.")

The point of this new experiment is the same as that of our experiment with the act of friendship. Any meaning the "marks on the page" have (even the meaning "marks on the page"), they have because there is some act of understanding being performed. If you look for any kind of meaning of the marks on the page (as lines, marks, words, sentences, paragraphs, intellectual, affective, etc.) in the absence of an act of understanding that gives them unity, you will fail because the meaning these "marks on the page" have does not reside in them, it does not *endure* in them. You can see the act that gives unity, gives meaning, to these "marks" *only* as it "cuts across phenomenal time" and unifies the objective bearers of the meaning you are grasping. Again, it is only in the execution of an act of understanding that you can reflectively grasp that act of understanding.

With this I have completed my very limited description of acts (focused on their nondurationality) and our phenomenological access to them (only in their execution). There is much more that can be pointed to, but the ultimate concern of our study is not phenomenological access to the nature of acts alone. We are interested in acts as an avenue of approach to persons, and we are now ready, again with Scheler's help, to turn to persons and our phenomenological access to them.

The Experiencing of Persons

Scheler's phenomenological description of persons is more complete than his description of the nature of acts. Furthermore, as we shall see, it builds upon what the above description of acts has revealed. This is because, for Scheler, just as the act is that which gives unity to events, the person is that which gives unity to acts. In this regard, Scheler insists that persons are always "concrete beings" because a person is a combination of multiple acts of different essences (each of which can be given as an individual "abstract essence") into a "concrete essence." Furthermore, as Scheler points out, this combining does not result in simply an interconnected complex:

> The person can never be reduced to the X of a mere "point of departure" of acts or to some kind of mere "interconnective complex" or network of acts, as a form of the so-called actualistic theories which conceives of the being of the person in terms of his doings . . . would have it. The person is not an empty "point of departure" of acts; he is, rather, a concrete being. Unless we keep this in mind, all of our talk about acts can never catch the fully adequate essence of any act, but only an abstract essence. Abstract act-essences concretize into concrete act-essences only by belonging to the essence of this or that individual person. Therefore a concrete act can never be fully and adequately comprehended without the antecedent intending of the essence of the person. (GW2 383–84/F 384)

Yet since "*the being of the person is . . . the 'foundation' of all essentially different acts*" (GW2 382/F 383), we face the same temptation we did with acts, namely, considering the person to be a separate "thing," but as Scheler points out: "Surely the person *is* and experiences himself only as a being that *executes acts,* and he is in no sense 'behind' or 'above' acts, or something standing 'above' the execution and processes of acts, like a point at rest. For all of this is a picture taken from a spatiotemporal sphere; and it stands to reason that this does not hold for the relation between *person* and *acts*" (GW2 384/F 385). Furthermore, since a person *is* the unity of acts of different essences, which, in that person, are unified into a concrete act, "the *whole person* is contained in *every* fully concrete act, and the whole person '*varies*' in and through every act—without being exhausted in his being in any of these acts, and without 'changing' like a thing in time" (GW2 384/F 385).

It is worthwhile to elaborate on this last short passage. First, the "whole person" is contained in every fully concrete act because the "whole person" *is* the unity of acts of different essences in a concrete act. Second, the person "varies" in and through every concrete act, because the individual "abstract" acts of different essences that are so unified in this person are different in different concrete acts. Each different concrete act is a unique concretion of them. Third, the person is not "exhausted" in any of these concrete acts because the person is the *unity* of these acts, not their *content.* Fourth, the person does not "change" like a thing in time, because acts themselves are, as developed above, essentially nondurational phenomena. Furthermore, one does not need a substance to safeguard the integrity of the person because the variations the person undergoes, the pure "becoming different," is itself not a durational process, and so no durationally enduring "substance" is needed. As Scheler puts it: "Identity lies solely in the qualitative direction of this pure becoming different" (GW2 385/F 385).[5]

[5] The idea of a "pure becoming different" raises the question of how, if acts are nondurational, there can be a nondurational "becoming different." Although Scheler does not develop his insight at this point, he does allow acts and persons to occur in a time which he calls "absolute time." As Manfred Frings notes in *The Mind of Max Scheler,* Scheler did develop this idea later. Frings summarizes the nature of absolute time: "Absolute time, Scheler held, has three inherently interwoven aspects: 1) inseparable coincidence between meanings and their phases; 2) phases are simultaneously becoming and unbecoming; 3) the run-off of absolute time during transitions between an A and a B; for instance, during the actualization of a potency A" (1997, 263). As this passage indicates, "absolute" becoming does not occur in clock time with its reference to the past and the future, but rather in the "inward self-becoming of a process (*das Werde-*

Since the person *is* the unity of acts, there are parallels not only between the nature of acts and persons but also in the kinds of phenomenological access to them. Just as we saw that acts can be given only in their performance, so too with persons. As Scheler says:

> Because the person lives his existence precisely in the *experiencing* of his possible *experiences,* it makes no sense to try to grasp the person in past lived experiences. As long as we look only at the so-called experiences and not at their *being* experienced, the person remains completely transcendent. But every experiencing, or, as we can also say, every *concrete act,* contains all act-essences that can be distinguished in phenomenological investigations. It contains them according to a priori orders of foundation, which are established by the results concerning act-founding. Therefore every concrete act always contains inner and outer perception, lived-body consciousness, loving and hating, feeling and preferring, willing and not willing, judging, remembering, representing, etc. All these divisions, necessary as they are, yield only abstract traits of the concrete act of the person—if we are looking at the person. The concrete act of the person can be understood as a mere sum or a mere construct of such abstract act-essences no more than the person can be understood as a mere interconnective complex of acts. Rather, it is the person himself, living in each of his acts, who permeates every act with his peculiar character. No knowledge of the nature of love, for instance, or of the nature of judgment, can bring us one step nearer to the knowledge of how person *A* loves or judges person *B;* nor can a reference to the contents (values, states of affairs) given in each of these acts furnish this knowledge. But, on the other hand, a glance at the person himself and his essence immediately yields a peculiarity for every act that we know him to execute, and the knowledge of his "world" yields a peculiarity for the contents of his acts. (GW2 385–86/F 386)

Each individual person, each unifier of these essentially different acts, unifies these acts in a unique way. From the standpoint of an understanding of a particular abstract act, say "love," we *can* grasp the abstract essential nature of "love." But when an individ-

---

sein)" (263). Although Scheler does not develop the idea of absolute time until later, it is clear that his phenomenology of the person points to it quite early in his thought.

ual person loves, when that "abstract act of love" becomes part of a concrete act of that person, then *in* that concrete act we can also see *that* person. Just as we could only see the abstract act of love in its being performed, we can see the person only as that abstract act of love becomes part of a concrete act of love of that person. Persons are unique in their concreteness as the abstract acts become theirs in the unity of the concrete acts they are, and it is only in the *performance* of these concretizing acts that persons are accessible.

Scheler's person is not an object, yet we have direct, immediate phenomenological access to the person. Neither acts nor persons are part of the contingencies of the empirical. This is the core insight that allows Scheler to meet the last of the three requirements Kant's work set for any nonformal ethics. With this insight Scheler clearly believes he has rescued the person from the contingency of the empirical just as surely as he rescued values from the contingency of the world of "goods and purposes." The person, the unifier of acts, is nontemporal, nondurational, and therefore noncontingent and autonomous. With this Scheler shows forth the dignity of the whole person, who, as the unifier of all acts, includes the acts of the heart just as surely as the acts of reason. Thus the dignity of the whole person, not simply the reduced "person" of reason, is safeguarded and shown forth.

Solving the First Enigma: Why Does Scheler Not Provide Phenomenological Evidence for His Claims about Values and the Person?

With the work of these last three chapters now completed, I am finally in a position to begin to address the first of the three enigmas presented to even the most sympathetic reader of Scheler's work. This enigma, as indicated in chapter 1, is the fact that Scheler fails to provide phenomenological grounding for his insights. Before I address the puzzle, however, I would like to develop it in some detail.

The criticism that Scheler does not provide the kind of phenomenological evidence he should seems to be a fair one. Although he does provide descriptions of "feelings" in works we drew upon in the last chapter, Scheler rarely provides detailed descriptions of the person. Perhaps more surprising is the fact that he does not provide the kind of detailed descriptions of the realm of nonformal values that one would expect from someone claiming to be developing a nonformal ethics of values. Indeed, Scheler himself recognized the importance and need to provide just such descriptions when, for example, he says: "We expect an ethics first of all to furnish us with an explicit determination of 'higher' and 'lower' in the order of values, a determination that is itself based on the contents of the essences of values—insofar as this order is understood to be independent of all possible positive systems of goods and purposes" (GW2 117/F 100). Furthermore, he is aware of how important accomplishing this task is, later stating that "the most important and most fundamental a priori relations obtain as an *order of ranks* among the systems of qualities of nonformal values which we call *value-modalities*. They constitute the *non-formal a priori* proper in the intuition of values and the intuition of preferences. The facts of these modalities present the *strongest* refutation of Kant's formalism" (GW2 122/F 104–5).

What is so perplexing is the fact that Scheler does not even attempt to undertake this task. Indeed, immediately after the above statement that we expect from an ethics an explicit determination of the order of values, he states: "It is not our aim at this point in the discussion to furnish such a determination. It will be sufficient here to characterize more fully the *kinds* of a priori orders among values" (GW2 117/F 100). And, after stating how important the order of ranks would be as a refutation of Kant, he says: "Rather than giving a full development and establishment of these systems of qualities and their implicit laws of preferring, the following presents an explanation through examples of the kinds of a priori orders of ranks among values" (GW2 122/F 105). These twin disclaimers are appropriate, for what Scheler then gives us is less than ten pages of what is little more than a series of brusque assertions (we will consider these passages in the next chapter as we develop Scheler's personalistic ethics).

Now Scheler is a phenomenologist, and his work on "feelings" shows that he is capable of providing at least initial descriptions. And yet when he comes to his "presentation" of the "objective" ranking of values he gives a terse, formal, almost dogmatic recitation. He does not even give a hint of a phenomenological description needed to ground his claims. Furthermore, despite the centrality of his new view of the person to everything he was trying to accomplish, again he fails to provide the kind of detailed description he provided for love and hate. Why these serious lapses?

I believe the answer lies in the *breadth* of the task Scheler set himself in the book. Scheler never intended the *Formalism* to be a book in which he developed a complete ethics, or even the full foundations of one. The book was intended to show the *possibility* of such an ethics in the light of Kant's attack upon all nonformal ethics. As I have demonstrated in the last three chapters, if you take seriously Scheler's claim that the goal of this work is both to show that Kant was wrong to condemn nonformal values, feelings, and the person to the empirical realm and to thereby lay the foundations for a nonformal ethics of values, what he does and what he does not do in this work is eminently logical. Scheler did not need to provide detailed evidence for all of his claims; all he needs to do is provide a philosophically plausible case. To look for what he did not need to provide, and did not intend to provide, is not logical.

The Need for an Ethics

Scheler has, as we have shown, freed values, the person, and our access to them from empirical contingency. This does begin to provide a foundation for the possibility of a nonformal ethics of values. But despite the fact that he need not provide phenomenological evidence for all of his claims about values, the heart, and the person, there is one more thing he did need to do in the *Formalism in Ethics and Non-Formal Ethics of Values*. He needed to show how it was possible to develop an ethics using these values and this person.

Simply showing there is a noncontingent person who can grasp a realm of noncontingent values is not yet an ethics. An ethics must give us a basis for resolving conflicts of morality, the kind of moral dilemmas we began with, the kind we face every day. Ultimately, the upshot of all ethical inquiry is intensely practical.

An ethics, in the end, must tell us (or allow us to decide) what to be, what to do. It must tell us *how* to act. Scheler freed material, nonformal values, feelings, and the person. We must now look at what kind of ethics he devised in the *Formalism in Ethics and Non-Formal Ethics of Values* with these newly won elements. I turn to this task in the next chapter.

3

THE CHALLENGE OF SCHELER'S NEW ETHICS

6

Scheler's New Ethics

Introduction

I entitle this third part of my study the *challenge* of Scheler's ethics for two reasons. First, although Scheler does not develop an ethics in the *Formalism in Ethics and Non-Formal Ethics of Values: A New Attempt toward the Foundation of an Ethical Personalism* (GW2/F), he does sketch out the basic nature of a new ethics appropriate to the *foundations* for an "ethical personalism," an ethics true to the nonformal values and the full person he had defended against Kant's attacks. Thus, Scheler's approach to ethics is a challenge both to Kant's formal ethics and to other approaches. Second, and perhaps more importantly for my task of showing the logic of the development of Scheler's thought, the new approach to ethics Scheler sketches sets new challenges for him, for it raises as many new problems as it solves. Before we get to these problems, however, we must begin with Scheler's sketch of his personalistic ethics.

The Hierarchical Ranks of Values

Scheler was well aware that simply showing that a nonempirical person had access to noncontingent material values was not enough to constitute an ethics. An ethics must show how we make moral choices and must give us a way of resolving moral dilemmas. Thus an ethics based upon a complex realm of compet-

---

Sections of this chapter appeared in my essays "Max Scheler's Practical Ethics and the Model Person," *American Catholic Philosophical Quarterly* 69, no. 1 (1995): 63–81, and "Scheler's Ethics vs. the Ethics of Success," in *Person und Wert: Scheler's "Formalismus" Perspektiven und Wirkungen,* ed. Christian Bermes, Wolfhart Henckmann, and Heinz Leonardy (Freiburg/München: Verlag Karl Alber, 2000), 192–203, and are reproduced here with permission.

ing values must answer, in some detail, how we go about using such values to decide what to do and be.

In order to use Scheler's nonformal values to found an ethics, we must be able to make morally relevant distinctions between those values. The first distinction to be made between values is relatively simple. Values are positive or negative, and as Scheler says: "This fact lies in the *essence* (*Wesen*) of values; it is independent of our being able to feel specific opposites of values (i.e., positive and negative values), such as beautiful-ugly, good-evil, agreeable-disagreeable, etc." (GW2 100/F 81–82). This fact is not new with Scheler, as he himself acknowledges when he goes on to sketch the "axioms" of the relationships between positive and negative values (the existence of a positive value is itself a positive value, etc.) (GW2 100/F 82).

What *is* novel is Scheler's development of the hierarchical ranking of values already noted in previous chapters. For Scheler we do not simply have individual values ranked higher than others (again a far from novel insight)—we have entire sets of values ranked higher than other sets of values. Scheler distinguishes four ranks of values: the first rank are the values ranging from the agreeable to the disagreeable; the second are the vital values, such as the noble-vulgar series; the third are the mental or "spiritual" values, such as aesthetic values; and, finally, we have the holy-unholy series. Since the nature of this hierarchical ranking is so central to Scheler's ethics, I will now present in some detail Scheler's own articulation of the four ranks of the nonformal values, for despite the fact that what appears seems more a curt and dogmatic recitation than a full phenomenological description, it does effectively hint at what Scheler wishes us to see. Scheler delineates the four ranks as follows:

> 1. The values ranging from *the agreeable to the disagreeable* represent a sharply delineated value-modality. . . . The function of *sensible feeling* (with its modes of enjoying and suffering) is correlative to this modality. The respective feeling-states, the so-called feelings of sensation, are pleasure and pain. As in all value-modalities, there are values of *things* (Sach*werte*), values of *feeling-functions,* and values of *feeling-states.*
>
> This modality is "*relative*" to beings endowed with sensibility in general. But it is relative *neither* to a specific species, e.g., man, *nor*

to specific things or events of the real world that are "agreeable" or "disagreeable" to a being of a particular species. Although one type of event may be agreeable to one man and disagreeable to another (or agreeable and disagreeable to different animals), the difference between the values of agreeable and disagreeable as such is an *absolute* difference, clearly given prior to any cognition of things. . . .

2. The essence of values correlated to *vital feeling* differs sharply from the above modality. Its thing-values, insofar as they are self-values, are such qualities as those encompassed by the "*noble*" and the "*vulgar*" (and by the "good" in the pregnant sense of "excellent" [*tüchtig*] as opposed to "bad" rather than "evil"). . . . The feeling-states of this modality include all modes of the feelings of life (e.g., the feelings of "quickening" and "declining" life, the feelings of health and illness, the feeling of aging and oncoming death, the feelings of "weakness," "strength," etc.). Certain emotional reactions also belong to this modality—(a certain kind of) "being glad about" or "being sad about," drive reactions such as "courage," "anxiety," revengeful impulses, ire, etc. Here we cannot even indicate the tremendous richness of these value-qualities and their correlates.

Vital values form an entirely *original* modality. They cannot be "reduced" to the values of the agreeable and the useful, nor can they be reduced to spiritual values. Previous ethical theories made a *basic mistake* in ignoring this fact. Even Kant tacitly presupposes that these values can be reduced to mere hedonistic ones when he tries to divide all values in terms of good-evil on the one hand and agreeable-disagreeable on the other. . . .

The particular character of this modality lies in the fact that "*life*" is a *genuine essence* and not an "empirical generic conception" that contains only "common properties" of all living organisms. . . .

3. The realm of *spiritual values* is distinct from that of vital values as an original modal unity. In the kind of their *givenness,* spiritual values have a peculiar detachment from and independence of the spheres of the lived body and the environment. Their unity reveals itself in the clear evidence that vital values "ought" to be sacrificed for them. The functions and acts in which they are apprehended are functions of *spiritual* feeling and acts of *spiritual* preferring, loving, and hating. They are set off from like-named *vital* functions and acts by pure phenomenological evidence as well as by their *own proper lawfulness* (which *cannot be reduced* to any "*biological*" lawfulness).

The main types of spiritual values are the following: (1) the values of "*beautiful*" and "*ugly*," together with the whole range of purely aesthetic values; (2) the values of "*right*" and "*wrong*" ("*des Rechten und Unrechten*"), objects that are "values" and wholly different from what is "correct" and "incorrect" according to a law. . . . (3) the values of the "*pure cognition of truth,*" whose realization is sought in *philosophy* (in contrast to positive "science," which is guided by the aim of controlling natural appearances). Hence "*values of science*" are consecutive values of the values of the cognition of truth. So-called *cultural values* in general are the consecutive (technical and symbolic) values of *spiritual* values and belong to the value-sphere of *goods* (e.g., art treasures, scientific institutions, positive legislation, etc.). The correlative feeling-states of spiritual values—for instance, the feeling-states of spiritual joy and sorrow (as opposed to the vital "being gay" ("*Froh*") and "not being gay")—possess the phenomenal quality of appearing *without mediation*. That is to say, they do not appear on an "ego" as its states, nor does an antecedent givenness of the lived body of a person serve as a condition of their appearance. Spiritual feeling-states vary *independent* of changes in vital feeling-states (and, of course, sensible feeling-states). Their variations are directly dependent upon the variations of the values of the *objects themselves* and occur according to their own proper laws.

Finally, there are the reactions belonging to this modality, including "pleasing" and "displeasing," "approving" and "disapproving," "respect" and "disrespect," "retributive conation" (as opposed to the vital impulses of revenge) and "spiritual sympathy" (which is the foundation of friendship, for instance).

4. Values of the last modality are those of the *holy* and the *unholy*. This modality differs sharply from the above modalities. It forms a unit of value-qualities not subject to further definition. Nevertheless, these values have *one* very definite condition of their givenness: they appear only in objects that are given in intention as "absolute objects." This expression, however, refers *not* to a specific or definable *class* of objects, but (in principle) to *any* object given in the "absolute sphere." Again, this modality is quite independent of all that has been considered "holy" by different peoples at various times, such as holy things, powers, persons, institutions, and the like (i.e., from ideas of fetishism to the purest conceptions of God). These latter problems do not belong to an *a priori phenomenology of values* (*apriorische Wertlehre*) and the theory of ordered ranks of values. They concern the *positive representations of goods* within this

> value-sphere. With regard to the values of the holy, however, *all* other values are at the same time given as symbols for these values.
>
> The feeling-states belonging to this modality range from "blissfulness" to "despair"; they are independent of "happiness" and "unhappiness," whether it be in occurrence, duration, or change. In a certain sense these feeling-states indicate the "nearness" or the "remoteness" of the divine in experience.
>
> "Faith" and "lack of faith," "awe," "adoration," and analogous attitudes are specific reactions in this modality.
>
> However, the act through which we *originally* apprehend the value of the holy is an act of a specific kind of *love* (whose value-direction *precedes* and *determines* all pictorial representations and concepts of holy objects); that is to say, in essence the act is directed toward persons, or toward something of the *form of a personal being, no matter what* content or what "*conception*" of personhood is implied. The self-value in the sphere of the values of the "holy" is therefore, by essential necessity, a "*value of the person.*" . . .
>
> As we have stated, these modalities have their own a priori order of ranks that precedes their series of qualities. This order of value-ranks is valid for the *goods* of correlative values because it is valid for the *values* of goods. The order is this: the modality of vital values is *higher* than that of the agreeable and the disagreeable; the modality of the holy is *higher* than that of spiritual values. (GW2 122–26/F 105–10)

The significance of these passages does not lie in Scheler's absolute accuracy in sketching out the hierarchical ranks of values. It is possible that Scheler's own vision of values is imperfect, for reasons already developed above in chapter 4. What is significant is the recognition that values are not only positive and negative but also hierarchically ranked, with entire realms of values higher than others. However, even with such a hierarchy of value ranks we do not yet have an ethics. We must still show what it is to be a morally "good" person. To put it simply, what is the relationship between moral good and evil and this hierarchy of value ranks?

The Moral Good

One way to answer this question is to place good and evil among the other values. To be a good person is to realize the value "good." Kant rejects this approach as he separates good and evil from all other values. As Scheler puts it, for Kant "the meaning of the words *good* and *evil* is wholly exhausted in *lawful* or *unlawful form*" (GW2 46/F 24–25). Thus for Kant there can be no relationship between good and evil and values other than the formal value of lawfulness. Scheler does agree with Kant that good and evil differ from all other values, but he disagrees with Kant's judgment that there is no relationship between good and evil and the values other than lawfulness.

Scheler's understanding of the relation between good and evil and the other values is that "the value 'good'—in an absolute sense—is the value that appears, by way of essential necessity, on the *act* of *realizing* the value which (with respect to the measure of cognition of that being which realizes it) is the highest. The value 'evil'—in an absolute sense—is the value that appears on the act of realizing the lowest value" (GW2 47/F 25). This definition allows Scheler to have a relationship between moral values and all other values while still agreeing with Kant that a moral value cannot be a content of will, since for Scheler "this value appears *on* the act of willing. It is for this reason that it can *never* be the content of an act of willing. It is located, so to speak, on the back of this act, and this by way of essential necessity; it can therefore *never* be intended in this act" (GW2 48–49/F 27).

Scheler may seem to be splitting very fine hairs here, but the relationships he is trying to make clear *are* complex, and we sense that complexity in our everyday moral judgments. For example, even our everyday language crudely points to the fact that one cannot directly will the "good." A direct attempt to "do good" *is* off track (and the "do-gooder" is looked upon with suspicion), even if we do try to act in ways that "are good," and we say that what a person is doing "is good." We sense that "good" is separate from, but related to, what we do and create. Scheler's distinction between, on the one hand, the moral values, and on the other hand, the nonmoral values that, when realized, also realize goodness, gives us a way of beginning to grasp the roots of the complexity we sense; a complexity that is, confusedly, reflected in common language.

With this definition of good and evil, Scheler supplies the connection between the moral values and the other values in a way that reflects the fullness and complexity of our moral experience, for it ties moral values to all other values. As he sums up: "There *exists,* therefore, despite Kant's denial, an interconnection between good and evil on the one hand and the remaining values on the other. And with this there exists the possibility of a *nonformal* ethics that can determine, on the basis of the ordered ranks of the other values, which kind of value-realizations are 'good' and which are 'evil' " (GW2 48/F 26). Yet, despite the promise such a nonformal, personalistic ethics of values holds, the distinctions and relationships just sketched raise a serious difficulty that must be addressed.

The Noncontingent Realization of Moral Values

The problem is rooted in the fact that nonformal values and the person must be free from the contingency of the empirical. Yet, in defining the moral good (and evil) Scheler makes the moral values dependent upon the *realization* of nonmoral values. Has he not, in doing so, undercut all he has gained through his insights into the independence of values, the person, and intentional "feeling" from the contingency of the empirical? Has he not made the morality of the person dependent upon that person's success in the empirical world? How does Scheler, in introducing the realization of values at the very core of his ethics, avoid this seemingly fatal error of again embedding morality in the contingency of the empirical?

The Person as Bearer of Moral Values

One reason why Scheler's linking of the realization of moral good to the realization of nonmoral values does not tie morality to empirical contingency is rooted in the fact that persons are the bearers of moral values. As we developed in chapters 3 and 4, neither values nor persons are empirical things. Thus, neither are contingently empirical even if, in the act of realization, a thing is created. Yet what of the nonmoral values realized when moral values are co-realized? Is this realization not contingent upon the success in the empirical world, and does this not make morality also dependent on such success?

Not necessarily. In the first place, not all acts of realization are physical. Indeed, when Scheler began to sketch the *a priori* relationships between values, he did not start with the relationships between the value modalities we already quoted above. Instead, he began with the "*A Priori* Relations between the Heights of Values and 'Pure' Bearers of Value," and the distinction he began with was between the "Values of Persons and the Values of Things" (*Sachwerte*):

> The values of the person pertain to the *person* himself, *without any mediation. Values of things* pertain to *things* of value as represented in "goods" ("*Güter*"). Again, goods may be material (goods of enjoyment, of usefulness), vital (all economic goods), or spiritual (science and art, which are also called cultural goods). In contrast to these values there are two kinds of values that belong to the human person: (1) the value of the *person* "*himself,*" and (2) the values of virtue. In this sense the values of the person are *higher* than those of things. This lies in their *essence.* (GW2 117/F 100)

Besides again emphasizing the centrality of the person in Scheler's ethics, this passage shows that not all acts of realization have physical bearers. "Spiritual" goods realized in the person, for example, do not have a physical bearer. This is not to say that no act of realization of spiritual values has a physical object as its bearer (for example, aesthetic values are realized in physical objects). Yet what of those cases where the bearer of the nonmoral value realized is physical? In these cases, how can Scheler *not* make good and evil dependent upon our success in the real physical world?

Scheler's Ethics versus an Ethics of Success

Scheler devotes an entire section of the *Formalism,* entitled "Non-Formal Ethics and Ethics of Success," to just this task. He recognized its importance by making the third Kantian presupposition, which the *Formalism* was to counter, the claim that "every nonformal ethics is of necessity an ethics of success" (GW2 30/F 7). As Scheler put it, an ethics of success is "an ethics which makes the value of persons and of acts of willing—indeed, of all acting—dependent upon the experience of the practical *consequences* of their efficacy in the real world" (GW2 127/F 111).

Scheler begins his defense against this Kantian "presupposition" by agreeing with Kant that "it is, in principle, nonsense to make the moral relevance of practical acting dependent upon a calculation of probable consequences based on real states of affairs and their causal relationships" (GW2 127/F 111). Scheler then explores Kant's attempt to locate the values of good and evil within the "basic moral tenor" of a person. Although Scheler approves of Kant's attempts to free this basic moral tenor from the empirical, he believes Kant's attempt is ultimately flawed because of Kant's retreat to the formal. For Scheler the "basic moral tenor" is not simply an unexperiencable form of positing an intention but rather "the directedness of willing toward a higher (or lower) value and its content," and it "contains a *non-formal value-quality* (*Wertmaterie*) that is independent of success, even of all further levels of an act of willing" (GW2 130/F 115).

What Scheler here (following Kant) calls the "basic moral tenor" parallels what we have already seen him exploring when he developed his idea of the *ordo amoris*. This is confirmed as he goes on in this section to say:

> Therefore the basic moral tenor does not unilaterally determine intentions, something done on purpose, or deeds. But whatever *can* become their content is nevertheless dependent on the value-content of the basic tenor in that the peculiarity of its content determines what *can* become in a special case of intention, something done on purpose, or a deed. Hence the importance of the basic moral tenor consists in the delineation of *a non-formal a priori field* for the formation of possible intentions, acts done on purpose, and deeds, *including* the kinematic intention that directly guides a deed. The basic moral tenor permeates all levels of a deed up to its success with its own value-content. (GW2 130–31/F 115)

What is significant here is that Scheler is showing that the ground of morality, the bearer of the moral values good and evil, the core of the person, is not dependent upon the empirical world or success in it, but it is not disconnected from it either. The basic moral tenor is the ground of the moral, and in it are grounded intentions, willing, and deeds.

Basic Moral Tenor and Deeds

The exact relationship Scheler works out between these elements is complex and will not be reproduced here in detail. However, there are several points important to our present concerns. First of all, even when we get to the level of deeds (*Handlung*) (a deed is the experience of the realization of a state of affairs in acting [GW2 142/F 127]), the empirical does not control what happens, even where the realization is physical. Even here the moral value, dependent upon the realization of the nonmoral value, is not dependent upon the *success* of this realization in the physical world. Scheler makes this especially clear in a passage in which he distinguishes between seven elements that are united in any deed. The sixth element is "the experienced realization of the content (the 'performance')" (GW2 137/F 121). This sounds very much like the experience of success, but Scheler counters this reading of it immediately upon completing the list when he says of this sixth element:

> No doubt the sixth belongs to a *deed.* But the causal effects of a deed, which can be *inferred* on the basis of an *assumption* of the realization of the content (*before* or *after* a deed), do *not* belong to a deed. A *deed* must be sharply distinguished from its *effects;* for the latter, unlike the realization of a deed, are not experienced in a deed itself. If one considers a deed or its ultimate component of realization as a mere "effect" of willing, a *false* ethics of the moral tenor is introduced at once. Whereas a deed with its ultimate element (its experienced realization) is a *bearer of moral values,* its causal effects can *never* be regarded as such. If a deed were a mere "effect of willing," it could not be considered a bearer of moral values. The realization of a deed, however, is a "part" of it, belonging to its *unity.* This difference must not be taken as only a "relative" or "arbitrary" one. For *whatever* is *experienced as belonging* to my deed, and whatever is phenomenally manifested as its simple effect, can never be "relative." Objective causal relations that are *taken into consideration* in a deed have *nothing* to do with this fact. It may be that a *content of willing,* i.e., what I will to be *real,* represents a remote effect of what I am realizing in acting—e.g., an effect that I previously "calculated." But this effect does not belong to my *deed,*

nor is it the "success of my deed" [*Handlungserfolg*]; it is, rather, the "success of my speculation and calculation."[1]

Thus we see that the remote success is not part of the deed, of the realization of the value that co-realizes moral good or evil. Yet, despite this, it may be suggested that although Scheler does separate values and the persons from dependence on the remote success (consequences), there is still the need to succeed in the physical world in that immediate experience (the deed). Does this not make success (however immediate) necessary, and does this not tie values and the person to this contingency of the empirical (at least in those cases where the realization is in the physical world), however limited that tie may be?

The answer is no, and this is shown when Scheler considers whether a physically disabled person can have moral worth equal to that of an able-bodied person. While defending the idea that the deed represents only a "symbolic value of the moral tenor," Scheler states:

> But this is not to deny that a deed *as* a deed possesses its *own* value. An example may clarify this point. The ethics and the notion of the basic moral tenor that we are criticizing here would maintain the following in regard to this situation: If a paralyzed person happens to see someone drowning, he is *no less* moral than someone else not paralyzed who actually rescues the man—provided, of course, that the paralyzed person has the *will* to come to the rescue. In both cases the *same* type of moral tenor can be present, and hence the two men would be of equal moral value. But it would be too much to assert that the same act of willing with its moral

[1] Scheler continues: "At the beginning of a deed, then, *this* very content is 'given,' not as *content* of the will-to-do, but as the 'consequence of this doing,' which is not contained at all in the *phenomenal content* of acting. The fulfillment (or non-fulfillment, i.e., conflict) consists in the execution with respect to the *will-to-do* (when I *experience myself as doing what* I will to do), not in the execution with respect to *what* I will to be *real*. This distinction is clearly manifest in the differences between a *misdeed* [*Fehlhandlung*] and the mistakes and errors that we make in our calculations concerning causal relations in which we are about to be engaged, or concerning the means and tools that we use in such an engagement. The nature of a *misdeed* consists in my not actually experiencing my doing what I will to do, not in my not accomplishing what I will. One may think of 'mis-taking' something, as opposed to an object's being something other than what I took it for" (GW2 137–38/F 121–22).

> value is present in the "paralyzed" person. For this *cannot* be the case, simply because in his situation there is *no* possibility of a "willing-to-do." Much as the paralyzed man may "*wish*" to perform the rescuing act, he cannot "will" it. Concerning his relation to this willing-to-do and its value, he is in the same situation as someone absent from the scene who has the "same moral tenor" and recognizes the fact that drowning people ought to be rescued. Hence we are *not* faced with the *same moral state of affairs* in these two cases. The paralyzed person is, of course, not at all subject to moral reproach. But neither is he subject to any part of the moral praise that belongs to the rescuer. Any opinion that would refute the above view and regard the moral tenor as the *only* bearer of moral value must be reduced to the *ressentiment* of "disabled" people. (GW2 134–35/F 119)

Now this may sound as if Scheler is allowing that the moral worth is dependent upon the contingent realization of the rescue, but he is not. The difference lies not in whether the paralyzed person actually realizes the rescue in the deed, but whether or not he can actually perform the deed. Willing is an integral part of the unity of the deed,[2] and as Scheler notes later:

> I maintained that he is not in a *position* to will the rescue of the drowning man because he is not in a position to *will* the rescue. He may be "prepared" to will, but not in reality. But in another case a different interpretation is possible, namely, when he *experiences* his paralyzed state on the occasion of such an event. For then he would have the experience of resistance, setting in against his kinematic intention and the subsequent graduated series of kinematic impulses, as an experience of the practically "impossible." In that case there is an attempt to act on his part which is equal to a factual deed of rescue (at least insofar as a moral evaluation is concerned). (GW2 136/F 120)

Notice that in this latter case the actual realization does not occur, yet because the willing does, it has some moral worth.

For Scheler, the deed, with its immediate realization of the value as part of its unity, does not control the moral worth of that unity of acts (that person). He goes on to note that "a deed is immediately directed toward the realization of a specific value . . .

[2] It is the third of the seven elements Scheler distinguishes (see GW2 137/F 121).

a deed *emanates* from a moral tenor and is at the same time guided by it" (GW2 137/F 120). Thus the realization of a value, even the immediate realization as contrasted with the remote consequences (success), does not threaten the autonomy of values or the person because the realization of the nonmoral values, even when it is a realization in the physical world, is the subordinate part of the unity that *is* the person. Although the deed is part of the co-realization of both the nonmoral value in a physical bearer and the moral value in the person, the deed controls neither the act of realization nor the person. Up from the acts of love and hate that determine the nonmoral values accessible to the person, the acts of preference and "placing after" that place those values in their rank, on up through intention, willing, and the deed—all of these acts are part of the unity that is the person. As a person, the realization experienced in a deed is only a part of what is experienced in the unity when a moral value is being realized. Thus, that small part which is empirical and contingent is in no way controlling of either the values realized or the person, even though physical realization is an integral part of the total unity of acts that is the person when moral value is realized in the person (and as we saw in the example of the paralyzed person, an important part).

Scheler, Kant, and Utilitarianism

What Scheler is developing here is of the greatest significance, and not only for his countering Kant's formal ethics or for his protecting the autonomy of nonformal values and the person. There has always been a complementary incompleteness to deontological ethics (such as Kant's) on the one side and teleological ethics (such as utilitarianism) on the other. As it is sometimes simplistically put, deontological ethics ignores "consequences," while utilitarian ethics ignores "intentions." For the deontologist, what really happens in the physical world has little or no moral worth because it is what we will that is morally significant. For the utilitarian, the consequences are all, and the moral worth of what we do is thus determined, ultimately, by often remote physical consequences of our actions, physical consequences over which we have, at best, only partial control or foreknowledge. Both approaches lead to absurdity, and worse, because both must leave out half the story of our moral life.

Scheler is pointing out here that our moral *experience* is not that of either of these extremes. What I intend (as what I will, not simply what I "wish") is relevant, but so is what I do, my actions, my deeds in which I realize something. Yet that realization is not some remote "causal consequence" of my deed, but what I experience as realized *in* the deed, *in* the act. What I *do* may well, ultimately, *fail* in the world in the light of its ultimate consequences, but if, in the *act*ual doing of "the deed," a positive, higher value is realized, as a person I become the bearer of the moral value "good."

This does not mean, of course, that I can simply ignore the consequences—even the remote consequences—entirely, for they too have value. Indeed, another set of distinctions Scheler draws between the "Heights of Values and Their 'Pure' Bearers" is that between "Values of the Basic Moral Tenor, Values of Deeds, and Values of Success" (GW2 118/F 101). Even success has its own value. We must not, however, conflate these different values, especially not the value realized in the deed, with the quite separate and sometimes remote "success" of the causal sequences initiated by that deed.

Thus we can now see that moral values are not dependent upon the achievement of success in the physical world. The independence of the person and of moral values from the empirical has not been compromised simply by Scheler's introduction of the idea of the realization of nonmoral values as a core element of his ethics.

Despite the fact that the introduction of the realization of values does not compromise the autonomy of either values or the person, there is still another core problem related to the realization of values that must be solved. If realization does not mean "success" in the physical world, exactly what *does* it mean to realize a value? Again, this is an especially acute problem for Scheler, since we have access to the realm of material, nonformal values worthy of being the basis for a morality through a phenomenological approach that suspends the reality of the bearers of values in seeking the values themselves. Thus Scheler must have a distinction between nonreal values and real values. Although he does not deal with this problem in the *Formalism,* he does (as we will begin to develop in the next chapter) eventually face it, and in doing so he will create for himself such basic difficulties that he will be forced to abandon theism. To see how this comes about, we must first see how Scheler's attempt to sketch a practical ethics leads to God.

Core Elements of Scheler's Foundations for Ethics, with Practical Problems

To enable us to see how Scheler's search for a practical ethics leads to God, let me begin by presenting the rough outlines of a few of the core elements of Scheler's foundations for an ethics. There is a realm of absolute nonmoral values arranged in hierarchical ranks, each rank consisting of a range of values stretching from the positive to the negative (holy-unholy, for example). The seat of morality is the nonempirical person, who has, through the special acts of "feeling," limited access to these values and their hierarchy. By realizing these values, the person becomes morally good or evil.

With these core elements, Scheler does have, I believe, the foundations for an ethics, but he is also faced with a basic practical question that must be answered if a fully functional ethics is ever to be built on these foundations. The question is this: exactly which of the wide range of positive, higher values to which I have access am I to realize? The general direction that we are to realize positive, higher values affords little practical direction. This problem is especially acute for Scheler because his ethics opens before us the entire range of nonmoral values as a field relevant to morality, and so some sort of specific direction is sorely needed. Thus Scheler must not only sketch the foundations of a nonformal ethics of values but must also provide at least a sketch of a "practical ethics." He must show how we can make practical moral judgments of what to do and what to be.

Scheler's Practical Ethics

Scheler recognized the need for a practical ethics in the preface to the *Formalism,* where he comments: "Ultimately ethics is a 'damned bloody affair,' and if it can give me no directives concerning how 'I' 'should' live now in this social and historical context, then what is it?" He adds in the margin: "The path 'from eternity,' or '*amor intellectualis sub specie quadam aeternitatis,*' where one can catch a glimpse of it, to Here and Now must cross an enormous gap. It is precisely philosophy that attempts to bridge it—however indirectly" (GW2 591/F xxxi n. 14).

Now, as both Scheler and I have emphasized, the goal of the *Formalism* is not the full development of an ethics, either theoretical or practical, but rather the showing of the possibility of a nonformal ethics of values, and so one cannot expect a detailed practical ethics in the *Formalism*. At the same time, however, Scheler must indicate what type of practical direction we can expect his ethics to provide, and he does so in the final section of the book, entitled "The Person in Ethical Contexts" (GW2 469–580/F 476–595).

Although much of this final section of the *Formalism* continues to develop the nature of the person, exploring exactly when a human being becomes a fully actual person, differentiating between the individual and the collective person, and distinguishing Scheler's position from other "personalistic" ethics, in it Scheler begins to wrestle with the kind of direction his ethics affords.

The Uniqueness of Individual Persons

Given Scheler's belief in an absolute hierarchy of value ranks, a hierarchy to which we do have access, we might expect him to set up a legalistic type of direction. In such a system, when confronted with a question of what to do, one simply reads off the highest positive value appropriate to the situation from the publicly agreed-to list of values and then realizes that value. Scheler, however, rejects this simple "table of values" schema. In the first place, it presupposes that the entire hierarchy is accessible to everyone in such a way that we could develop a full public list of the hierarchical ranks of values, but as we showed in chapter 4, this is not the case. Over and above the human inability to clearly and fully see values and their rankings, Scheler now raises another impediment. The "list of values" schema presupposes that all persons are interchangeable, that *any* person, in a like situation, ought to act the same—ought, in that case, to choose the same value to be realized. Scheler does not accept this universal interchangeability. In a section entitled "Person and Individual" he develops the idea of the "*individual-person value-essence,*" and as he says, "there are essences that are given only in one particular individual. And for this very reason it makes good sense to speak of an individual essence and also the individual value-essence of a person. It is this value-essence of a personal *and* individual nature that I also designate 'personal salvation' " (GW2 481/F 489).

Scheler then sketches doctrines of the "ought" which he rejects (Simmel and Kant) and contrasts them with his own idea, which he states as follows:

> If, however, an ought becomes a moral and genuine ought whenever it is *based* on *insight into objective values*—i.e., in this context, into the *morally good*—there is also the possibility of an evidential insight into a good whose *objective* essence and value-content contain a *reference* to an individual person, and whose ought therefore comes to this person and to him alone as a "call," no matter if this "call" is addressed to others or not. . . .
>
> It is . . . precisely this theory which claims that there is a true good-in-itself which not only allows but also *demands* that there be a *good-in-itself* for *each* person in particular. (GW2 482–83/F 490–91)

Scheler is quite well aware that this emphasis on the individual raises problems, for he quickly asks: "What, then, is the relation of *universally valid* values and their dependent, universally valid norms to the *personal* essence and the ought founded on it? In the past ethicists have for the most part given the answer which Kant has set forth in its most extreme form: the person acquires a *positive moral value* only by realizing universally valid values or by *obeying a universally valid moral law*" (GW2 483/F 491).

Scheler's answer to this question is:

> The following obtains: all universally valid values (universally valid for persons) represent, in relation to the highest value, i.e., the sainthood of the person, and in relation to the highest good, i.e., "the salvation of an individual person," only a minimum of values; if these values are not recognized and realized, the person cannot

> attain his salvation. But these values do *not in themselves* incorporate all possible moral values *through* whose realization the person attains salvation. Any deception concerning universally valid values, and any action contrary to norms derived from them, is therefore evil or conditioned by evil. But true cognition and recognition of them, as well as obedience to their norms, are *not* at all the positive good as such. The latter is fully and evidentially given only insofar as it implies individual-personal salvation. (GW2 484/F 492)

What Scheler is objecting to is any ethic that would reduce the totality of the value realm to that "minimum" which is universally shareable at any given moment in the development of the human race or of the individual. As he emphasizes at one point:

> *Every moment of life in the development of an individual* represents at the same time a possibility for the individual to know *unique* values and their interconnections, and, in accordance with these, the necessitation of moral tasks and actions that can never be repeated; such tasks and actions are predetermined, as it were, in the objective nexus of the factual-moral value-order for this moment (and for this individual, for example) and, if not utilized, are lost forever. (GW2 485/F 493)

We have all sensed such a call from time to time and, if we did not heed it, regretted not doing so as sharply as we regret *doing* that which realizes evil. Often it is hard to get consolation for our regret, since it is hard to get another to understand why we believe we ought to have done just *that* just *then*.[3]

Public and Private Insight

There is another serious question that Scheler's position raises. Do the unique values that only a particular individual at a particular time sees *stay* private? Scheler's emphasis on our uniquely individual access seems to leave open this possibility. This could make moral development a radically private matter.

Fortunately, Scheler does not rule out the possibility that what

[3] For a creative development of Scheler's understanding of the individuality of the person, see the work of John F. Crosby, for example, his 1999 essay "The Individuality of Human Persons: A Study in the Ethical Personalism of Max Scheler."

was initially known to only one person can subsequently become shared. This becomes clear in a passage close to the end of this section when he says:

> There are qualities and relations of preferring that can be known by all at any time. These are simply the *universally valid values* and *laws of preferring*. There are, however, qualities and relations of preferring that suit only *individuals*. They are originally syntonized only with individuals and are therefore experienceable and realizable only by these individuals. At the same time these qualities and relations can be seized only at a *unique* moment in historical development, so that ever new values and relations of preferring become visible with every new stage of development. If this does not happen, there is a stagnation of "moral culture." Still, every rule of preferring, once known, remains in existence. (GW2 485–86/F 494)

The ability to see values never seen before is essential if we are to grow, even if the initial "sighting" is done by individuals. Scheler speaks elsewhere of the "moral-religious genius" who has the ability to open a whole culture to new realms of values he or she alone first saw (GW2 309/F 305). Yet since we can all respond to values accessible to no one else, even if we lack the extraordinary skills of the great moral pioneers to introduce new values to entire cultures, if we realize the new values we alone first saw, they are then available to others.

It is the *uniqueness* of the person's insight and response that Scheler is here defending, not the impossibility of sharing what is initially a unique insight. Yet since the role of each person's seeing of unique values is so great, it is clear that for Scheler what is universally accessible at any given time cannot tell the entire story. He finishes this section as follows:

> It stands to reason that *ethics* as a philosophical discipline can never exhaust moral values. Ethics deals only with the universally valid values and their nexus of preferring. And it is the point of ethics to show expressly and to make understood this indubitable fact, i.e., it is its task to *explain*, that there is an ethical cognition through *wisdom* which lies wholly above ethics and without which all immediate ethical knowledge of universally valid values (a fortiori the scientific description of what is thus known) is essentially *imperfect*.

> Ethics can never replace individual conscience, nor should it. (GW2 486/E 494)

Scheler's rejection of a legalistic practical ethics makes even more pressing the question of where I can turn for practical direction. What type of practical moral direction is possible for Scheler?

The Model Person

The answer to this question lies in the fact that Scheler's ethics is not founded on nonformal values alone, but is rather founded ultimately on the person. Indeed, the person is the *center* of Scheler's ethics. Thus his practical ethics turns to the person, not laws, for moral direction.

For Scheler the person is a *qualitative* being. The person is a being of nonformal value, not just of formal, rational logic. It is because Scheler sees persons as dynamic, qualitative beings of value that he has a basis for looking to persons for moral direction. We see this toward the end of the *Formalism* when he finally develops where we can find practical moral direction, in a section entitled "The Law of the Origin of the Prevailing Ethos: Model Persons":

> An ethics which, like the one developed here, locates the highest and ultimate moral meaning of the world in the possible being of (individual and collective) persons of the highest positive value must finally come to a question of great significance: Are there specific *qualitative types* of persons within the idea of the person of highest positive value which can be differentiated in an a priori fashion, i.e., without recourse to positive historical experience; and if there are such types, to what extent do they exist? This question becomes all the more important in our ethics because of the insight that we gained earlier, namely, that all norms have their foundation in values, and that the (formally) highest value is not a thing-value (*Sachwert*), a value of a feeling-state, or a value of law, but *a value of the person*. It would follow syllogistically from this that the idea of the person of highest nonformal value is also the norm for moral being and comportment. But the ideal ought which originates as a requirement in the intuited personal value of a person is not called

> a norm, a name pertaining only to universally valid and universally ideal *propositions* of oughtness which have as content a valuable *action*. This ideal ought is called *a model,* or *an ideal.* A model is, like a norm, anchored in an evidential value of the person. But a model does not pertain to mere action, as is the case with a norm. It pertains first of all to a To-Be. One who has a model tends to *become* similar or equal to it, in that he experiences the requirement of the ought-to-be on the basis of the value seen in the content of the model person. In addition, the *individual* value-essence of the person who serves as a model is not extinguished in the idea of the model, as is the case with a *norm,* which is universal by virtue of its content and validity. (GW2 558–89/F 572)

Thus we see that for Scheler the best practical direction we can obtain is from the qualitative types of persons themselves, from model persons (exemplars). As Scheler goes on to say of the relationship between a person and his or her model:

> The experienced relation that a person has with regard to the content of the personality of his model is *fidelity* (*Gefolgschaft*), based on love for this content, in the becoming of his morally personal *being.* This relation cannot be reduced to executing the same acts as the model has executed or merely imitating the model's actions and ways of expression. This relation is of a unique nature and requires an investigation of its own. For it is, above all, the *only* relation in which the morally positive personal values of a person *A* can *immediately* determine the origin of the same personal values for *B,* i.e., the relation to the *pure and good example.* Nothing on earth allows a person to become good so originally and immediately and necessarily as the evidential and adequate intuition (*Anschauung*) of a good person *in* his goodness. (GW2 560/F 574)

The relationship between a person and his or her model is central to Scheler's practical ethics but difficult to convey. This is because it functions so deep within persons. As I developed above, for Scheler, at the core of persons, in the depths of our soul, our loves and our hatreds define us, defining all that we know, are, and can be. Our love and our hatred create an *ordo amoris,* an "ordering of love and hatred," which determines what we experience. Love and hate are the most fundamental of enabling (and disabling) acts that open and close true access to whole realms of values, and it is at this level that the exemplar functions.

As Scheler puts it in a separate essay contrasting the exemplar with the leader, entitled "Exemplars of Persons and Leaders":[4]

> "To lead" means acting, pointing ways, initiate good or bad directions of life ("the seducer"). But "exemplar" taken as a (objective) bad or good exemplar, means much more and something quite different from this. For an exemplar amounts to the *cast of a value formed by personhood* and it is envisioned by an individual's or a group's soul. Depending on whether or not the soul finds itself in harmony with its exemplar, the soul grows into this exemplary cast, it forms itself into it. It measures its own being, life, and actions by this exemplar, either in a secret or deliberate fashion; it affirms, praises, negates or disapproves of itself after this cast of value. (VF 267/EPL 139)

Each exemplar is a "model," a "prototype" of a particular *ordo amoris,* and this is why exemplars are the best route to moral wisdom. They function at the core of the morality of the person, at the level where the person as a moral being is defined.

Unfortunately, given our focus in this book, we cannot further explore Scheler's insights into the nature of exemplarity, but must return to the question of whether or not there are pure "types of models." There are, and just as ethics can discover universally accessible ranks of values, corresponding to them we can also uncover pure types of value-persons. Scheler lists the saint (corresponding to the holy-unholy series), the genius (the cultural values series), the hero, the leading spirit, and the *bon vivant.*[5]

If one does not grasp the full significance of what Scheler is pointing to, it might seem that we still have a relatively simple schema of practical moral direction. One does not look to laws to learn how to be a good person, but rather to the highest model person. Yet in addition to the profound subtlety of the relationship to a personal model already hinted at above and the depth at

[4] Max Scheler, "Vorbilder und Führer," which dates from 1912–14 and first appeared in *Schriften aus dem Nachlass, Band I: Zur Ethik und Erkenntnislehre* (1933). It is reprinted in volume 10 of the *Gesammelte Werke,* 255–344. The English translation is Max Scheler, "Exemplars of Persons and Leaders," in *Person and Self-Value: Three Essays,* translated by Manfred S. Frings (Dordrecht: Martinus Nijhoff, 1987), 125–98. This work will be referred to using the abbreviation VF/EPL.

[5] GW2 568–71/F 583–85. Note, however that the correspondence is not exact; we have here five types of model persons, but only four levels of values.

which exemplarity functions, there are other complications as well. In the first place, just as there are individual values beyond the universally accessible values, there are also individually valid types of value-persons (GW2 570/F 584–85). Thus, although the universal types are of use as models, one cannot look only to the universally valid model-types for moral direction.

The Tragic Limits of Finite Persons

There is another difficulty with universal types. Scheler puts it best in the "Exemplars and Leaders" essay when he says of the universal types: "However, these schemata expressing the basic directions of all human love, and the basic values in the form of the person, are, by themselves, completely insufficient to nurture our minds and moral lives in a vivid and powerful manner. These tender and shadowy casts must drink the appropriate blood from the wells of the experience of history. It is only when they do this that they become *concrete models*" (VF 269/EPL 142).

This need for concrete models complicates matters further, for as Scheler points out in the *Formalism:*

> It is essentially, not contingently, impossible for one finite (individual or collective) person to represent simultaneously an exemplar of the saint, the genius, and the hero. Therefore no possible opposition of *will,* that is, no possible "strife" between the exemplars of types of the value-person (as models), *can be settled* by a finite person. For this "strife" could be settled in a *just* manner only by a finite person who was the exemplar of all three models in identical ways. (GW2 575/F 590)

Scheler calls this "*the essential tragic of all finite personal being* and its (essential moral) *imperfection*" (GW2 575/F 590). He also says: "Only the hero fully values the hero; only the genius fully values the genius. Who should value both wills when it is impossible to be both perfect hero *and* perfect genius?" (GW2 576/F 591).

The difficulty this tragic imperfection of finite persons presents is a basic one. The model person enables me to *become* a better person. Now the different model persons correspond to different levels of values (in this case, the hero to the level of vital values, the genius to the higher level of cultural values). Yet if we cannot "value" a model at a different, higher level, how then can we ever break free from the level we are at and move to a higher level? Thus this "tragic imperfection" not only leads to a "strife" between persons which no finite person can resolve, but also seems to lock us into whatever level of values and model in which we find ourselves. If it is through concrete models that we gain the best moral direction, the direction seems tragically limiting. Is there no way to overcome this limitation?

The Infinite Person: God

Scheler does introduce one possible source of hope in the *Formalism* as he speaks of God as an "infinite person" and says:

> It should be clear that the idea of God, unlike the ideal types of the person discussed above, does not function as an *exemplary* model (*Vorbildmodelles*). For it is senseless to say that a finite person takes the infinite person as a model or even as the pure type of his model persons. Nevertheless, the essential goodness of God expresses an idea in which the universally valid types of the value-person (although not "as" models) are in their order "co-"contained in infinite perfection as fully exemplary. But the Godhead also contains individually valid essences of the value-person. This "cocontaining" means that the essential goodness of God does *not* exhaust itself in the infinite exemplariness of the universally and individually valid being of the value-person. It means that the essential goodness of God is primally infinite as an *indivisible* essential value-quality. It is *only through* a possible experiential and cognitive relation of a finite person to the infinite person that divine goodness divides into unities of value-essences = value-types and their declining sequence of ranks. (GW2 573/F 588)

This assertion is significant because it shows that the tragic division of all finite persons is overcome in the infinite person of God. Thus there is hope that in our relationship with God we will, ultimately, be able to obtain the kind of moral direction we seek.

Yet just as Scheler raises this hope, he ends the *Formalism* with the following statement:

> With this general theory of the effectiveness of models and their counterparts as the *original form* of moral becoming and alteration,

> and with the explication of the idea of the order of ranks for pure types of value-persons, these investigations into the *foundations* of ethics come to an end. But it is not difficult to see that two additions are needed.
>
> 1. Because the idea of God is originally determining for all models and their counterparts and for types of the value-person governing their formation, the natural continuation of our investigations requires a theory of God and also an investigation into the types of acts in which the essence of God comes to the fore (theory of religion). However, this involves the question of whether, in the basic religious acts of having faith (not belief) in something, the positing of the reality of the being of the Divine is possible or necessary, and, if this positing is possible or necessary, how it takes place. And since such an investigation would especially require a treatment of the original saint and the saint as follower (with the manifold subdivisions of "divine man," "prophet," "seer," "teacher of salvation," "God's delegate," "the called," "savior," "healer") as types of the value-person, we could not present our theory of the types of value-persons, finished some years ago, without expanding the present work to include both the theory of God and the philosophy of religion. I prefer a separate publication of my investigation into the connection between ethics and the theory of God because I believe it is better not to burden the results of this other investigation with a basic theory of ethics that is *independent* (and valid independently) of all philosophical investigations into religion and *religious* ethos. Hence I will present this work soon in a special volume.
>
> 2. The present investigation requires a concrete elaboration of the theory of *all types of the value-person,* their order of ranks, and their subdivisions. (GW2 579–80/F 594–95)

These "two additions" are essential to the foundation of Scheler's ethics. Indeed, until he undertakes investigations showing how our access to God overcomes the problem of the tragic limitation of finite persons, he has not even shown "the effectiveness of models and their counterparts as the *original form* of moral becoming and alteration."

Solving the Second Enigma: Why Does Scheler Turn to God after the *Formalism,* Rather Than Complete His Ethics?

Scheler does not provide a fully developed ethics in the *Formalism.* As we have seen, his sketch of an ethical personalism raises as many new problems as it solves. Yet this very fact allows me to dispel the second enigma that Scheler's work has presented to critics. Why did Scheler undertake, immediately after the *Formalism,* religious and metaphysical investigations that seem to have little connection to his ethics? The answer is that such investigations are absolutely essential to his ethics. Until and unless Scheler can overcome the tragic limitations faced by finite persons and show us how it is possible to use model persons for moral advancement, his ethical personalism is dead in the water. At the end of the *Formalism* it appears that the only way to overcome the limits of finite persons is to turn to the infinite person, God. Thus a study of God is needed to complete Scheler's ethics. Given the centrality of the person to Scheler's ethics, and given the problem that finite persons present in the *Formalism,* there ought to be no surprise that Scheler turns to a study of God (the perfect person) immediately after the *Formalism,* as he attempts to complete his ethics.

What is surprising is the fact that the works he promised, which were to provide the completion of his ethics, do not appear. As a footnote in this last section of the *Formalism* indicates, the title of the proposed study of God is "On the Essence of Godliness and the Forms of His Experience" ("Vom Wesen des Göttlichen und den Formen seiner Erfahrung"), but as the editor adds, this never appeared, and what eventually appears instead is the essay "Probleme der Religion" (GW2 580 n. 1/F 595 n. 323). Nor do we ever see from Scheler the concrete elaboration of the theory of all types of the value-person, or, for that matter, a phenomenological grounding for his claims about the nature of the realm of objective values. As late as 1921, in the preface to *On the Eternal in Man* (*Vom Ewigen im Menschen*) (GW5/E), which contains the essay "Probleme der Religion" (GPR/EPR), and which, Scheler announces, is the first of a projected three-volume study under this title, Scheler says: "Work on the second and third volumes is steadily proceeding, and it is hoped that both will appear before long. The principal section of the second will be devoted to a definite completion of the author's *ethics.* Herein will be considered the importance of the *personal exemplar* of all kinds for the moral and religious being of man as well as for historical variations in forms of ethos" (GW5 9/E 13). Although some work intended for this second volume was published as the "Exemplars and Leaders" essay referred to above, this essay does not constitute a "definitive completion" of Scheler's ethics.

Why did Scheler not follow the plan he indicated he would at the end of the *Formalism,* a plan that is eminently sensible given the results he had achieved up to that point? Given the nature of the objective values and the ethics that Scheler had sketched based upon them, one would have expected at the very least the detailed phenomenological grounding of both the value hierarchy and the types of value-persons, if not this promised exploration of a "theory of God." The very first sentence of the "Introductory Remarks" in the *Formalism* states: "In a major work planned for the near future I will attempt to develop a nonformal ethics of values on the broadest possible basis of phenomenological experience" (GW2 29/F 5). Why did these works never appear? Why, despite his clear intentions, did Scheler never complete his ethics?

A Change of Direction

At the end of the previous chapter we indicated why the *Formalism* itself does not contain the detailed phenomenological groundings for a nonformal ethics of values. We are now faced with a much more serious set of questions. After the *Formalism,* why does Scheler fail to complete the study of God so clearly called for at the end of the *Formalism,* provide the phenomenological evidence for values he promised at the start of the *Formalism,* or complete his ethics?

First, Scheler never provided the phenomenological evidence he promised because the new personalistic ethics of nonformal values he sketched in the *Formalism* presents him with such pressing difficulties that meeting these difficulties overrode his desire to finish his refutation of Kant and his desire to complete the phenomenological evidence for values and the person that would provide the foundations for this ethics. Second, his turn to God in his attempts to complete his ethics led to ever-newer problems that he spent the rest of his life working on. Put simply, Scheler never got back to completing his refutation of Kant because, as he said at the start of the *Formalism,* his main goal was never simply to refute Kant, but rather to lay the foundations for an ethical personalism. He realized that the new problems presented as great a threat to this project as Kant's formal rationalism ever did. As I show below, Scheler began to meet these new problems, but he died before he could complete his ethics or present the kind of phenomenological evidence that would refute Kant.

Thus, if you wish to understand the development of Scheler's thought you must recognize that although Kant's formal ethics set the initial framework of questions for the *Formalism,* after Scheler had sketched the basic defense of the core elements of his new ethics (especially values, the heart, and the person), the problems of the new ethics he began to sketch in the *Formalism* became the framework of his efforts for the rest of his life.

To develop exactly what these new problems are, I will turn in the next chapter to what actually happened when Scheler attempted to complete the task he set himself at the end of the *Formalism*—as he sought God in his attempt to complete his ethics.

7
God and Ethics

Introduction

As we indicated at the end of the last chapter, after the *Formalism* Scheler never produced the definitive completion of his ethics he had promised. Although he continued to produce works that are of great importance to his ethics, including the expanded studies of *ressentiment* and sympathy and the essay "Exemplars and Leaders" (works we have already drawn upon), we never see the definitive works he promised. To understand why he never completed his ethics and why he ultimately abandoned theism, we must now unearth the clues in what did appear in place of the promised completion of his ethics.

We will focus on the well-named "Problems of Religion." This essay appeared in 1921 in the book *On the Eternal in Man* (*Vom Ewigen im Menschen*) (GW5/E), and in it we see Scheler undertake the first of the specific tasks he had set himself at the end of the *Formalism* when he said that "the natural continuation of our investigations requires a theory of God and also an investigation into the types of acts in which the essence of God comes to the fore (theory of religion)" (GW2 595/F 594–95).

As we shall see, however, Scheler's hope that the study of God and our access to this "infinite person" would lead to the completion of his ethics proved vain, as Scheler's study of God leads to difficulties that make the title of this essay sadly appropriate.

The "Problems of Religion"

The "Problems of Religion" essay begins with an acknowledgment of the longing for the divine and an indictment of both positivistic and pantheistic attempts to meet this longing. World War I, the first war in which all of humanity had been involved, had, according to Scheler, shattered the positivistic faith in humanity as a substitute for religion and had provided a blow to pantheism as well. Using Pierre Bayle's question of whether God was at war with himself in a time of war, Scheler undertakes a critique of pantheisms, both those that begin their "equation of god and world" from an existing idea of God and those that begin from an idea of the world. The first approach tends toward an "acosmism" that overlooks the "right and might" proper to the "world," the second toward atheism. Scheler feels it is not surprising that pantheism has tended toward the "lower," the atheistic version. Although the more idealistic version had expressed the "religious formulation of the German temperament so long as the nation's intellectual life was lost in dreams of an ideal world of the spirit" (GPR 109–10/EPR 114), pantheism, in the "face of the immense flood of new reality pouring in from the course of history," also had to account for "an ever lengthening succession of *irrational,* non-divine and, in the event, even *counter*-divine factors . . . within the frame of the pantheistic idea of the world" (GPR 111/EPR 115). Scheler indicates that by the time we get to Schopenhauer we are already at a "pandemonism" rather than a pantheism.[1]

After rejecting positivism and pantheism, Scheler then raises the question of what can meet the present need for the divine. After rejecting the naive belief that need alone automatically provides its relief, and criticizing the idea that Christianity as such is bankrupt, he again returns to the impact the Great War has had on people and indicates that this spiritual dislocation and need for renewal, this spiritual longing and desire, is "nothing *more* than *raw material* for the *true architect* of moral and religious renewal" (GPR 124/EPR 127). But who or what is this "true architect"?

Scheler's answer both echoes the note we heard sounded at the end of the *Formalism* and introduces a new element. The old note newly sounded is the idea that it is persons from whom we will

[1] See GPR 112/EPR 116. It is quite significant that Scheler begins his essay with this attack on pantheism. The core problem he feels pantheism cannot meet—namely, how to account for the reality of evil in the world—is a problem he will himself find most difficult to overcome. This problem was so difficult, in fact, that to meet it he himself eventually abandoned theism and adopted a position that is itself pantheistic.

learn. The new element is a concern for the proper role of and relationship between religion and philosophy in preparing the ground for such learning. Furthermore, despite its somewhat scholarly sound, this new element is not simply of theoretical interest. Just as we saw Scheler argue that feeling gave us a special access to values that reason could never have, here he claims that religious acts have a unique access to God that philosophy does not have. We see this stated powerfully as, immediately after indicating that a "true architect" is needed, Scheler says:

> In the situation I have described, *philosophy,* too, has a new and special task, in so far as religion is its concern. This task is not the highest among those which must be devoted to the renewal of religious awareness. For this highest task will always fall to the lot of the *homo religiosus* himself, the man who has God in his heart and God in his actions, who in his own *spiritual figure* is a transformer of souls and is able in new ways to infuse the word of God into hearts that have softened and yield. (GPR 123/EPR 127)

Scheler goes on to say that such persons cannot be produced, or even sought or anticipated. The best we can do is be ready to hear them if they should appear, and since our understanding of the nature of religion has a profound impact upon our "religious receptivity," Scheler indicates that he will concentrate on offering religion a more rigorous, comprehensive foundation and justification. He points out, however, that the present work is merely intended for a popular audience and lacks the precision of a more systematic treatment to appear later.

The Tasks of Philosophy and Religion

Because Scheler begins to show our access to God through the contrast of philosophy and religion, especially religious persons, developing that contrast a little is worthwhile. We will begin with the role of philosophy. If we gain insight about God from holy people, what exactly *is* the task of reason, of philosophy, in relation to religion? The situation here is different from Scheler's contrast between reason and feeling. There the objects of feeling (values) are totally inaccessible to reason. But, as we shall see, here things are not as absolutely separated. Scheler begins to unravel the complex relationship between what philosophy and religion give us in a new section of the essay entitled "Philosophy and Religion," which opens with the question of "whether and to what extent the objects of religious belief—the existence and nature of God, the immortality of the soul, etc.—together with belief itself and the existential context of these objects, are also objects of philosophical cognition" (GPR 124/EPR 128).

As Scheler recognizes, there are many answers to this question. After sketching a number of possibilities, he begins to develop his own position by pointing out that the origins of religion and philosophy in the human mind are essentially different, as are their methods, goals, and objects. Yet despite these differences (specifically between religion and metaphysics as the "rational knowledge of the ultimate bases of the world's being and essence") there is a point of contact, since "religion's God and the world-basis of metaphysics may be *identical in reality* (*real-identisch*)" (GPR 130/EPR 134). Still, this point of contact must not cloud the deep differences between religion and metaphysics. Scheler completes the sentence we have just quoted with: "but as *intentional* objects they are *different in essence*" (GPR 130/EPR 134).

Both the identity and the difference must be grasped, for both are of equal importance. Emphasize the identity too much and you will confuse and conflate religion and metaphysics. Emphasize the difference and you will forget the real point of contact between them. He clearly states the difference as he says, for example: "The God of religious consciousness 'is' and lives exclusively in the religious act, not in metaphysical thinking about realities extraneous to religion. The goal of religion is not rational knowledge of the basis of the world but the *salvation of man* through vital communion with God—apotheosis" (GPR 130/EPR 134). "The fount of all interest in metaphysics," in contrast, "is *astonishment that anything at all should exist*" (GPR 134/EPR 138). At the same time, however, he emphasizes the point of contact:

> For *a priori* this much is clear: the essential peculiarity of the absolutely real (*absolut Wirklichen*)—the reality underlying all things real—must of necessity be that which decides the salvation or non-

> salvation of all things, including men. It is, so to speak, the last court of appeal for this salvation. And this is also clear *a priori:* the absolutely holy and divine, whose nature is to satisfy the longing of things, can only do this if it is in addition the absolute reality on which all else depends. (GPR 134/EPR 138)

Thus we have the difficult task of both recognizing the gulf that separates religion from metaphysics in experience and remembering their point of contact. Satisfying this need to integrate the results of the essentially different endeavors of religion and metaphysics will not be easy. Yet, as Scheler says:

> We cannot now avoid seeing that the most adequate possession of God, the maximal participation of our being in his, cannot be achieved unless we first attain to a *simultaneous vision,* free from all contradictions and incompatibilities, of the religious God and the metaphysical "world-basis" together. It follows that we cannot achieve this goal by wholly or partly making either the religious God or the metaphysical "God" the yardstick against which we measure the *other* intentional object. (GPR 137/EPR 141)

This task of achieving a "simultaneous vision" is not made any easier by the fact that the differences between religion and metaphysics extend beyond their differences in origin and goal. The way religion and metaphysics have access to their objects, and the status of what they find, differs as well. This is shown dramatically when Scheler indicates the "signs" of a holy man, the second of which is as follows:

> He lives in his own peculiar, real and vital relationship to the divine (*eine besondere, nur ihm eigene lebendige und reale Beziehung zum Göttlichen*) as the eternal source of salvation, and bases his utterances and precepts, deeds and authority on this relation. By virtue of his charismatic quality his disciples believe in his words as subjectively and objectively true. Unlike the sayings of the genius, of the hero, etc., his utterances are never tested for truth and justness against objective norms *external* to himself—norms of morality, logic and ethics—and recognized only because his words, deeds and work are found to be in general agreement with those norms. On the contrary, *he* as a *person* is the norm of his utterances, with the sole authority of his relation to the divine. (GPR 130–31/EPR 134)

Or, as Scheler puts it in another context: "Religion proceeds directly from that basic definition of the absolutely real (of the *ens a se*) which is inaccessible to unaided metaphysics—the personality of God, which attests its existence in revelation" (GPR 146/EPR 149). Metaphysics, on the other hand, is rooted not in the personality of God but rather

> achieves its full value as a branch of learning only when it is grounded, as to its object, in the full depth, range and variety of existence and the world. . . . Knowledge of the "world-basis" is only its final and highest, and truly not its first nor its only object. Properly it represents for metaphysics the intellectual grasp of the point where all those countless threads intersect which lead us from glimpsed essences and essential correlations (these being latent in the empirically known, contingent and objectively real entities of positive science) across the frontiers of the empirically known and in the *direction* of the *absolutely real* (*Absolut Reale*). (GPR 145/EPR 148–49)

Where religion is rooted in direct access to the personality of God, metaphysics

> is able to demonstrate that the *ens a se* must have, as an objective condition, certain definitive attributes if it is to be both real and personal. It must, that is, possess above all *rationality* and *intelligent spirituality*. However, the personality of God is withheld from every kind of *spontaneous* rational cognition in finite beings—not on account of any alleged limitations of the cognitive faculty, but because it belongs to the nature of a *purely* spiritual person in its objective aspect that its existence (*if* it exists) can only be known as a result of self-communication, *i.e.,* revelation. (GPR 146/EPR 149–50)

Having sketched out both essential differences and the important connection between religion and metaphysics, and having rejected other approaches, Scheler proposes that the true counter to error would be a phenomenological investigation of the general "*objects* and *values* of faith," with a study of religious acts secondary (GPR 150–51/EPR 154). He then proceeds to distinguish such a phenomenological investigation from any positivistic "psychology of religion" and from phenomenological investigations of specific religious phenomena as well. What Scheler wishes to study is the essential nature of religion, and he states that such a study has three ends: the nature of the divine, the forms of revelation, and the religious act (GPR 157/EPR 161).

Unfortunately, after sketching out the nature of these three branches of the study, Scheler announces that his present intention is not to undertake such a full study but rather to confine himself "in general to examining the *religious act* in more elaborate detail," since in the religious act we can most plainly see how religious self-evidence comes into being (GPR 159/EPR 162). I say "unfortunately" because immediately after announcing this limitation to his study, Scheler, in order to observe the proper order of treatment of the subject as stated above, says he "must first say a few words about the *essential definitions of the nature* of the divine" (GPR 159/EPR 163). Once again he presents the most important of insights not with full phenomenological grounding but in the form of assertions.

The Nature of God

Scheler begins with a claim about the nature of God. The God that the human person has learned, by "dint of natural religious acts to see, sense or imagine . . . 'is' *in absolute being, and it is holy*" (GPR 159/EPR 163). This insight is gained in awareness of our relative being, but it is a revelation, not an inference based upon a sense of weakness on our part (GPR 160/EPR 163). Scheler points out that the world's dependence on God is not rooted in metaphysical inference either, but rather in the experience of God as "*utterly* active, strong and almighty, and everything else as the utterly passive and enacted" (GPR 161/EPR 165).

Scheler next develops the sense of dependence, of being a creature, a being created by God, as he contrasts the human artist and his or her creation with the world as the creation of God. Just as we sense the presence of the human artist in his or her work, there is an analogous sense of the presence of God in God's creation. Scheler then explores the experienced reactions to the creative power of God, namely, the partial *nothingness* of all *relative* being, and its *creatureliness*.

Scheler asserts that these reactions are not simply causal inferences but are rooted in a *sense of enactment* revealed in a religious act (GPR 163/EPR 167), and he points out that this sense of enactment precedes the sense of creatureliness proper, for the latter postulates an analogy with personal human volition and the idea of the divine as personal and intelligent: "For to *create* is something other than to be the mere cause, and implies the intelligent personality of the cause in question" (GPR 163/EPR 167). And, since theistic religion approaches God as a person, we do have a sense of our creatureliness (GPR 163/EPR 167). Scheler goes on immediately to say:

> Nevertheless, metaphysics can for *its* part demonstrate three things: 1. it is intrinsic in the contingent existence of an object in *any* given sphere of being that the existence must have an effective cause; 2. the phenomenon of reality is originally given only in the empirically known *resistance* of an object to the exercise of volition; 3. the only model on which we apprehend the mode of *possible* realization of a purely qualitative essence is that of the manner in which we apprehend the original realization of a merely imagined thing when, in and through volition, we enact a project of the will—irrespective of the intermediary processes of a psycho-physical organism and mechanism. (GPR 163–64/EPR 167)

Scheler is here again showing the cooperation possible between religion and metaphysics in our search for God. But this passage is of interest to our study for another reason as well. It begins to develop a key element of Scheler's ethics, the idea of *realization,* which we will return to later in this chapter.

God as Mentality (*Geistigkeit*)

At this point in the development of the essay, however, Scheler is most immediately concerned with keeping clear what metaphysics can provide to the quest and what religion must supply. After the above statement concerning what metaphysics can provide, he points out that although metaphysics may well attempt to show by logic the necessary connection between the *ens a se* as active force and the value modality known as holiness, it is not through logic that religion achieves this insight. Scheler then develops a rather interesting connection between phenomenology and negative theology. Both attempt to use language to point us beyond what language can capture. Thus the positive characteristics attributable to God by religious insight are only *analogical* definitions, and the cognitive value, if any, of such analogical definitions depends upon the "self-givenness" of the divine shareable through such phenomenological or negative theological descriptions (GPR 164–69/EPR 168–72). Furthermore, religious acts, and their objective domain of being and value, form a closed and irreducible realm.

Scheler then draws a distinction between the three formal attributes of God he had already identified (infinitude, omnipotence, and holiness) and all others. Beyond these three the "essential structure of facts and values belonging to the finite world . . . now enters as *co-determinant* of all further attributes" (GPR 171–72/EPR 175). Only when we reach these other attributes (spirit, mind, reason, will, love, mercy, omniscience, goodness, creatorship) do we see the world as a possible revelation of God's nature, work, and creation. It is at this point that religion begins to use analogical inferences. This is how we get to these *positive* attributes of God. But despite the legitimacy of this process, Scheler emphasizes that all such positive attributes of God are of "utterly *inadequate, inexplicit and merely analogical validity*" (GPR 173/EPR 176).

After developing these "prices" we pay in gaining positive attributes, Scheler gets to the "most fundamental and the principal positive (analogical) attribute of God": mentality (*Geistigkeit*) (GPR 178/EPR 182). Since this positive attribute is arrived at analogically, Scheler immediately raises the question of how the human person comes to bestow on God this positive attribute, given the fact that mind is found only in the world, and indeed, only in that part of the world that the human person *is*. Scheler's answer is that since we cannot arrive at God's mentality analytically from the concepts of *ens a se* and holiness, the only meaningful basis must lie in the fact that "man feels and considers not only himself but the whole world to be *inspirited,* pervaded by mind" (GPR 179/EPR 182).

Scheler then claims that the noetic principles by which the religious act comes to understand God as mind are simple. The first condition is that we have a vital sense that we are, at the core, at the center of our self, mental acts, and not a body. Without this, we will never be able to execute the cognitive religious act in which we grasp God as mind. This does not mean that we can never know it, for it is a truth open to metaphysics, but such is not religious knowledge. As Scheler points out:

> Herein lies yet another basic difference between metaphysical and religious knowledge. For the truth that the world-basis is by nature mental or spiritual is one that metaphysics can also know *without* this personal moral condition of "living in the spirit," of *having one's substance* in the mind. But the mere possession of this knowledge in the judicative sector of consciousness means absolutely nothing in a *religious* sense. A man may form this judgment and yet be feeling that his centre, his *ego,* resides not in his mental "act-center" but in his belly. In that case he has no kind of *religious* knowledge that God is mind. (GPR 180/EPR 183)

We again see in this passage that religious knowledge has more basic, more direct, and more immediate knowledge of God as mind than does metaphysics.

The Interrelation of the World and Mental Acts

The idea that there is a connection between the world and God is not entirely new for Scheler. In a section of the *Formalism* exploring the relation of the person and the "world," specifically the question of whether there was "*one identical real world,*" Scheler asserts that to posit such a "macrocosm" requires the positing of "the idea of an infinite and perfect person of spirit" and that "this 'person' would have to be concrete simply to fulfill the essential condition of a reality" (GW2 406/F 396). Although Scheler denies in a footnote that he is, in this book, "positing the reality of the 'essence' of God" (GW2 406 n. 1/F 396 n. 34), he does say that "the *idea of God* is *cogiven* with the unity and identity and singularity of the world on the basis of an essential interconnection of complexes. Therefore, if we posit one concrete world as real, it would be absurd (though not 'contradictory') not to posit the idea of a concrete spirit (*Geistes*)" (GW2 406/F 394).

Once again we see an idea, first stated earlier in the *Formalism,* developed and extended in the "Problems of Religion," where Scheler asserts that once we are convinced that God is mind, we "cannot remain unaware of an instantly perceptible *interrelation of the world and mental acts*" (GPR 180/EPR 184). Scheler develops this insight by first admitting that the being and thusness of the world are independent of the existence of any individual act envisioning that being as object, but claiming that despite this independence it is equally evident "that every possible extra-mental entity stands *in (inter-) dependence on a possible mental entity*" (GPR 181/EPR 184).

From this basic insight, Scheler then draws some interesting corollaries. An *absolutely* unknowable being is self-contradictory, and it is senseless to try to envision "some pre-existent *cognitive intention* corresponding to no kind of existent." Furthermore, this truth applies not only to the relationship between contingent being and contingent minds, but to "*any possible world*" (GPR 181/EPR 184–85).

Scheler then says that we are now ready to consider together and as one the two axioms which yield the religious intuition that God is mind and that the holy *ens a se* is mind. These two axioms are the world's radical independence from the concrete human mind and its simultaneous dependence on *mind in general*. Scheler does so in the form of the syllogism:

> 1. The being of the world is independent of the existence of *my* mental act and the existence of *any* act of the same nature; each one of the world's objects is, if immanent at all, only *partly* and inadequately immanent in such mental acts.
> 2. Nevertheless, to the being of any possible world there corresponds a possible mind, and to every object there belongs *full possible immanence* in that mind.
> 3. Thus there corresponds to the world a mind which, *if* I posit the world, I must necessarily posit with it and which (by the first premise) cannot be the human mind—either in existence or essence. (GPR 182/EPR 186)

Scheler goes on immediately to emphasize that the religious act does not trace through afresh this syllogism, but it does act in conformity with it. As he puts it, we are talking here of a mysterious drama deep in the human person's soul and heart that tests the limits of language. Again he emphasizes the human need to "feel plainly in his heart, and not merely know, how sublimely *indifferent* it is to the sun whether or not it is perceived, thought of or valued by him and his like—by any 'I' at all" (GPR 183/

EPR 187). It is only when we combine the sense of the human's inadequacy to be in any sense a creator of the universe with the necessary connection of world and mind that we can see the need for a creator God-mind not simply as a logical conclusion but as a live, experienced immediate insight. Only then can we move to the final act of this drama in which the religious knowledge of God as mind takes shape. This is the "act of attaching the attribute 'mind' to the holy *ens a se* of which we already feel assured, and to this is joined the experience of the shining of infinite reason—its manifestation—into all rightful activity of finite reason; or the suffusion of the *world's objects and their meaning* by the ideas and values which stand, in their hierarchy, as correlates of the action of infinite reason" (GPR 184–85/EPR 188).

Although it is not an element that Scheler develops at this point in the essay, this last addition is of interest to our concerns, for it means that God's mind is not that of a value-neutral being, but rather a *moral* being. We shall, with Scheler, return to this later, but at this point in the essay he goes on quickly to "immediately transfer" two more formal attributes to God as mind, two attributes inherent in the relationship of the holy *ens a se* to contingent being: *absoluteness* and *infinitude.*

The first is of greatest interest to us because it is, as Scheler points out, tantamount to asserting that God has, as a self-founding mind, absolute freedom: "And only now can the manner of his acting and en-acting or effecting be understood as analogous to volitional acts, or his supreme causality be seen as the mind-like causality of *creative power and freedom*" (GPR 187/EPR 190).

Creation and Realization

Scheler then develops the idea of creation. Because this idea of creation is not only important to his understanding of God but also represents an important development in our understanding of realization, I will present the passage in its entirety:

> Once again, a quite special experience of being underlies the *idea of creation.* Before this idea can enter the mind, the pure fortuitousness of the contingent world-reality must first be grasped in relation to worlds essentially no less possible, worlds as subjected and obedi-

> ent to the general cohesion of essences as is the real world. But the reality of any object is given in the empirical *resistance* which it offers as an intentional object to the (mental) interest or aversion of the experiencing subject. If we had no kind of volitional relationship to the world, we could never have any consciousness of reality. When we encounter a resistance, its point of origin is felt to be a *nucleus of activity,* the nature of which varies according to the kind of resistant. Thus we experience perhaps a nucleus of latent *physical* forces (inanimate objects), of *biophysical* forces (animate objects), of *instinctual* forces (our own bodies) or of *alien volition* (fellowmen).
>
> The principle of the sufficient cause, which postulates a cause (of being rather than not-being) for all contingent existents (real or ideal), leads to the proposition that all real existence is effected in an *activity.* Now, within the whole range of our world-experience we know only one case, one empirical datum, in which a contingent existence is not merely altered, modified or transformed, but actually created by the action of another. That is the form, shape, idea which the originally "creative" human act of will imposes on a given material. And it is only in this one set of circumstances that we may see an ideal thing (the content of the volitional project) "become" real. This crucial perception is quite independent of the question how this happens, *i.e.* all questions of psycho-physical volitional causality. *That* this artefact or that painting is a work of mental volition, posited and carried out by it, is evident, however obscure the paths by which this action of "my" will comes to impinge upon the limbs of my body. For in the process of imagining and creating I see directly that the material more and more closely resembles the content of the project, see the material "growing into" the idea of the project and at the same time know that this is happening "through me." But from that we may clearly see that in so far as there is any question of its *general realness* (as distinct from its mere realness here-and-now, in this or that situation, with these or those properties), the reality of *any contingent real existent* must have been effected by the agency of some kind of *volition.* In other words, a volition must have created any real contingent existent. (GPR 187–88/EPR 190–91)

With this passage Scheler further develops his idea of the nature of realization, and he does so in the context of developing the idea that God is the creator of this real, contingent world. Scheler's connection of mind, volition, and reality in God is of the highest significance not only for an understanding of God and God's relation to the world, but also for our understanding of the fundamental nature of moral action and being. This is because, as we learned in the *Formalism,* the moral values good and evil occur along with the realization of nonmoral values (high or low), making a clear understanding of the nature of realization essential. Yet, as we saw in the last chapter, although the *Formalism* made clear that realization is not simply success in the empirical world, it did not make clear exactly what realization was.[2] Fortunately, as Scheler develops his understanding of the nature of God and God's relationship to the world, we see him simultaneously developing an answer to the question of what realization is. We have already seen Scheler make the general connection between reality and resistance to will, and assert that the only model for apprehending realization was volition. Now, in developing the attribute of the absoluteness of God as mind, he begins to develop this assertion.

Scheler's immediate concern is not ours, however, and so after this passage he moves on to develop the attribute of infinitude. Although his insights are of value, we will not detail them, nor will we detail his attempt to show that the relation between God as mind and human minds is fundamentally misrepresented by pantheism, or his reemphasis of the fact that knowledge of the world alone cannot lead us to God as mind. Since our concern is with the nature of God as it relates to ethics, we will also not detail Scheler's most interesting excursus into a refutation of Kant's *a priorism* and development of his own idea of the way our experience of essences becomes the basis for future experience. Nor will we explore the need for cooperation among us all in the search for knowledge and wisdom, since the foundations are already familiar from the *Formalism* and the development is not crucial to our needs.

What *is* of interest to our study is that when Scheler does return to a consideration of the attributes of the divine mind, after pointing out that one can approach them either by seeking what can

---

[2] Indeed, in the *Formalism* Scheler says very little about realization and the real, and what he does say is limited and qualified. For example, at one point he does connect "practical reality" to resistance to the will, but then in a footnote he states that whether or not the "consciousness of reality" *as such* rests upon resistance to the will is a question to be set aside (GW2 154 n. 3/F 135 n. 25).

be known analogically to us from God's relation to the world as cause, or by looking to the essential nature of the human mind as the basis for an analogy (and surveying quickly several historical examples of both), he returns to the one thing he believes they all missed: the *volitional* nature of God's mind (GPR 213/EPR 217). This time Scheler approaches from the side of the world: "We know the volitional nature of the divine mind from the basic character of the world, which, in conjunction with a series of essential insights, impels us to assume it. The world is not *only* an assemblage of essences in a peculiar interrelation: it also exists *as* this world—in other words, it has as *a whole* the character of concrete, contingent reality" (GPR 213/EPR 218).

Scheler then develops the idea of the "general causal principle" as the basis for all reality, pointing out along the way that such a general principle does not require a God, since an infinite regress of causes is possible, and even a dynamic pantheism could fill the need. Thus we must already know there is an *ens a se,* and that it is mind, to have God as the cause of the world. But given all that has been already established, Scheler believes that the resistance of the world to volition "is in the last resort only comprehensible through a willing of the world by God" (GPR 217/EPR 223).

God Is Love and God Is Good

Yet Scheler quickly points out that our road to the creator God is still not complete. The idea of a creator God requires such a creation be the result of a *freely choosing personal will,* for only such an idea rules out a number of unacceptable possibilities, including a blind and irrational impulse or Aristotle's unmoved mover.

In order to achieve such a free willing, Scheler believes we must recognize that God cannot simply be will. There must also be that which directs the will. Following the analogy with the human mind, Scheler says:

> We see that the most original root of all "mind" in God as in man is *love.* Love alone it is which founds the unity of will and intellect, which but for love would fall dualistically apart.
>
> The first thing which is derived from God's love is his *objective goodness,* and this we must distinguish from its consequence, the

> goodness of his will. God is the *summum bonum,* which when personal is the quality of absolute objective goodness. . . .
>
> However, not only God's love but also God's intellect is set over his volition and directs it, guides it. "In the beginning" was not the *deed,* but the love-guided logos. The intellect is directly set over the will, not as knowledge of all things but as *wisdom in all things.* Yet wisdom is knowing the proper objective hierarchy of value-units and value-qualities. And since we cannot know and grasp the being of anything which we have not originally perceived as a value-unit, the supreme wisdom of God must precede his omniscience. (GPR 219–20/EPR 224–25)

With the attribution of the moral quality of goodness to the nature of God, Scheler finally gets to that constellation of issues focused around the relation of God to morality that will be our chief concern here. It is not surprising that Scheler does finally get to these issues, or that he has been working so hard to show that God is mind, is person. Later, in a section again defending the autonomy of religious knowledge from the metaphysical and contrasting his position with attempts to found religion on extra-religious knowledge, values, and axioms (especially Kant's attempt), he reminds us that

> it is generally wrong to define the good as a content of a previously given *volition*—whether it be God's or that of a practical reason. "Good" is primarily a value-quality, but moral good is a personal quality and any volition—hence the volition which in the hypothesis determines *what* is good and *that* a thing *is* good—must *be* good in the first place in order so to determine. In reference to God, good is thus an *essential predicate* of the divine person *qua person.* (GPR 303/EPR 307)

God is the ultimate moral person as well as the creator of the world, and as such is the best way to a "good" will. As Scheler puts it:

> A (perfect) moral volition without reference to God is an *objective* impossibility. For ideally conceived, the most perfect moral volition is the volition of the person who embodies in the form of personal value (more or less adequately) the evidently highest among values, which is holiness. But the holy person is at the same time he who feels and knows that to the extent of his "holiness" he is manifestly "united" in part—not *realiter,* but by the nature of his inner seat of

> responsible action (hence of his moral deeds)—to the highest good, which as "highest" is itself holy in an infinite and absolute form and is itself a valuate *person.* (GPR 303/EPR 308)

Thus once again we see God, the perfect person, as the best way to an understanding of what it is to be a good person, as well as the "holy person" as the way to God.

A New Problem: God, Reality, and Evil

Scheler has now developed his ideas concerning the nature of both God and realization. He has also created for his ethics serious new problems. One problem arises because, as we developed above, God is both good and the creator of a world that contains evil, and as we will develop below, Scheler's insights present him with a particularly difficult version of this classic problem of evil. This is, however, not the only problem Scheler faces. As we have developed in a number of places, Scheler's ethics depends upon a clear-cut distinction between unrealized values and realized values, since the moral values good and evil occur along with the realization of higher and lower nonmoral values. Yet Scheler's development of the idea of God as creator, and of the *ens a se* as the ground of all that is, places this distinction in great jeopardy. I will begin with this problem first, and in doing so I must retrace some of what we have already covered.

The Use of "Metaphysical" Insights

Before I begin a development of these problems, I must meet a possible objection to my procedure. In what I develop below I will speak of God and the *ens a se* as one being. Given Scheler's insistence on the different intentional access to this single being that religion and metaphysics give us, one must be very careful in doing this. Scheler himself, in the preface to the second (1923) edition of *On the Eternal in Man,* warns that the reader would completely misunderstand the book, especially the "Problems of Religion" section, if he or she were to seek Scheler's metaphysics in it. At the same time, however, Scheler admits: "Of course, here and there certain very formal propositions belonging to metaphysics have been drawn into the argument, but only in so far as required by the formal object *ens a se,* which belongs simultaneously and identically to both metaphysics and religion" (GW5 25/E 30). Later, while speaking of how religion and metaphysics should "come to terms," Scheler says that given their independence there is no obligation they do so, but that each should voluntarily extend a hand to the other. He then adds: "Again, it is true that in ascribing predicates to the *ens a se* neither may contradict the other, but this is a requirement which lies in the *nature* of the *ens* and of the human mind" (GW5 25/E 31).

It is precisely those predicates which are shared that I will draw upon, because, as we shall see below, it is precisely the interrelated insights into the nature of God and the *ens a se* that create so much trouble for Scheler. Thus, in what I am developing below, I am exploring the substantive problems created by his insights into the nature of this single real being that is the object of both metaphysics and religion. Let us now turn to this task.

The Distinction between the Real and the Unreal

Scheler's ethics depends upon a clear-cut distinction between unrealized values and realized values, between the unreal and the real. In the "Problems of Religion" essay we see Scheler beginning to develop what is meant by "reality." But what exactly is something that is unreal but still experienceable (a pure value, for example)? As we saw in chapter 3, Scheler worked hard to show that values were not identical to their bearers, especially the physical bearers called "goods," since conflating values with their bearers had, and continues to have, a serious negative impact on our understanding of values. Yet pure values can be given independent of their bearers, and such a givenness is not subjective, for we have access not only to values, but to their absolute ranking, albeit with difficulty. As Scheler claimed, there is an "objectivity" to values, though this term is quite misleading since values are not objects, just autonomous.

Indeed, Scheler realized quite early that values are quite unique phenomena. As Manfred Frings points out in *The Mind of Max*

Scheler (1997, 23), from the very beginnings of his thought Scheler quite dramatically signaled the unique status of values by insisting that values did not have an independent existence. This is shown clearly by a revealing passage from Scheler's doctoral dissertation of 1887, entitled "Contributions toward Establishing the Relations between Logical and Ethical Principles." As Frings translates the passage: "As to the question: 'What is a value?' I submit the following answer: Insofar as in the question the word 'is' refers to existence (*Existenz*) (and not only to being as mere copula), a value 'is' not at all. The concept of value does not allow more of a definition than does the concept of being."[3]

In this passage Scheler is denying existence and does not rule out entirely some other ontological (or extra-ontological) status to values. (It is significant, however, that he places values on the same level as being, thereby implying a unique status for values.) Yet Scheler does not, at this early point in the development of his thought, help us to make a clear-cut distinction between realized values and unrealized values, a distinction his ethics rests upon.

Now in one way it may seem that the problem can be easily resolved after Scheler adopts the phenomenological approach. Since as a phenomenologist Scheler has argued that values are given as essences (*Wesen*) one might assume that he could make the distinction between the unreal and the real simply by contrasting essence (*Wesen*) and existence (*Dasein*). Yet to do so would be to miss a very important subtlety of Scheler's position at the time of the *Formalism,* namely, that essences have an existence (*Dasein*), as they are given. In fact, for Scheler, every entity has both an essence (*Wesen*) and an existence (*Dasein*). This is attested to by Scheler in another essay that appears in *On The Eternal in Man,* an essay that first appeared in 1917, entitled "The Nature of Philosophy and the Moral Preconditions of Philosophical Knowledge" ("Vom Wesen der Philosophie und der moralischen Bedingen des philosophischen Erkenntnis"). In this essay Scheler states three self-evident insights, the third of which is that every

[3] Max Scheler, "Beiträge zur Feststellung der Beziehungen zwischen den logischen und ethischen Prinzipien" (Ph.D. diss., Jena, 1897 and rpt. 1971 by Franke Verlag of Bern as volume 1 of the *Gesammelte Werke* [now Bonn: Bouvier Verlag]), 98. For the translation see Frings (1997, 23).

entity has both an essence and an existence.[4] Thus one cannot distinguish between unreal and real simply by using the essence-existence distinction. How then does Scheler make this necessary distinction?

He does it by using the ideal-real distinction. Values as given are ideal. As noted in chapter 3, values are given *a priori,* and in the *Formalism* Scheler defines the *a priori* as all *ideal* unities of meaning (GW2 67/F 48). This reference to the ideal is not casual, since in a discussion of the "third self-evident insight" in another essay, placed by Maria Scheler in 1915–16, entitled "The Absolute Sphere and the Positing as Real of the Idea of God" ("Absolutsphäre und Realsetzung der Gottesidee"),[5] Scheler says that "every essence is likewise essence of some existent entity (ideal or real)" and goes on to again use the phrase "every existence (ideal or real)" (ARG 202). It is clear that for Scheler ideal and real are two distinct modes of existence (*Dasein*), and it is *this* difference which he uses to distinguish between unrealized values and realized values.

Yet what, precisely, is the difference between ideal and real existence (*Dasein*)? I ask this question because Scheler's quite dramatic early assertion that values have no independent existence (thus ruling out a Platonic "realism"), and even his development of reality as resistance to the will, does not yet answer the question of what he means by saying that values as given phenomenologically are "ideal unities of meaning."

Now clearly it can be said that for Scheler these ideal entities are "in the mind." Yet his tying of reality to that which gives resistance to will, such that what is created is what is willed, complicates matters because ultimately reality is created by the act of

---

[4] Max Scheler, "Vom Wesen der Philosophie und der moralischen Bedingen des philosophischen Erkenntnis," is reported by Maria Scheler as appearing first in *Summa* (1917, *Heft* 2, *S.* 40ff.) and is reprinted in Scheler, *Vom Ewigen im Menschen.* This passage is in GW5 96. The English translation is "The Nature of Philosophy and the Moral Preconditions of Philosophical Knowledge," in Scheler, *On the Eternal in Man.* This passage is in E 102.

[5] Max Scheler, "Absolutsphäre und Realsetzung der Gottesidee," in *Schriften aus dem Nachlass, Band I* (1915–16; rpt. Bern: Franke Verlag, 1957 [now Bonn: Bouvier Verlag]), 179–253. The English translation is mine. (The dating of this manuscript by Maria Scheler is at GW10 512.) This essay is referred to using the abbreviation ARG.

realization of a willing mind. The problem is not so acute for finite beings, since they can only work on already created reality and modify it. But when we begin to consider the *ens a se* in relation to the world, exactly how do we ultimately distinguish between God as mind (*Geist*) and the world that God realizes through an act of will?

The Problem of Evil

As serious as this problem is, it pales before the classic problem of evil that Scheler's position faced. The problem of evil Scheler faces can be stated simply. If God is creator of this real world, and the moral values good and evil are co-realized with the realization of nonmoral values, how can a good creator God create a world that contains evil? (In Scheler's terms, how can God realize lower values which, given the personal nature of the creator, co-realize in the creator God the moral value "evil"?)

To his credit, Scheler does not attempt to evade this problem. In the "Problems of Religion" essay, after rejecting a number of positions that distort the relationship between God and the creation, Scheler says:

> Since we have not inferred God's existence and essence from the existence and properties of the world, but have concluded, after independent knowledge of God's existence and most formal essence *and* knowledge of the world's existence, that God is the world's prime cause, we may legitimately ask, and must in duty ask, in what way the real world we empirically know is related to *the* world which we might expect as the creation of a supremely good and loving god. Since, indisputably, we would not expect a world made by a creator equipped with the attributes of love and infinite reason to be anything other than a perfectly good and reasonable world, whereas the world we know confronts us at every turn with a stark reality of imperfection, evil and wickedness, we can but draw the inescapable rational conclusion—which is quite independent of revelation—that after the world's creation it was drawn by some free mental cause into a condition basically different from that which it enjoyed immediately upon leaving the creator's hands. The real world known to us is far worse than what accords with its basis. (GPR 225/EPR 230–31)

Scheler's beliefs make the classic problem of evil uniquely difficult for him. To sum up the problem:

1. Scheler has *defined* the moral values good and evil in terms of the *realization* of nonmoral values.
2. God is the creator of the *real* world, a real world that is, as Scheler so eloquently points out, both good and evil.
3. Yet God is all-wise and all-good.

No one has laid out the classic problem of evil so simply or so powerfully as Scheler has. Now there are a number of traditional ways to resolve the problem of evil. For example, one may accept dual *entia a se,* one good, one evil. Second, evil could be traced to human action, for human persons, in their pride, can rebel against God.[6] As I shall now develop, Scheler considers and rejects both of these approaches, and the solution he suggests in their place is not viable.

The Dualism Solution Rejected

The first way of resolving Scheler's problem of evil is quite simple. Although all reality must be rooted in an *ens a se,* an absolute person, it is possible to adopt a dualism. Initially, Scheler does not rule out this position as a possibility. While developing the idea of the mentality of God, Scheler argues that if we look only to the "factual world and its ordering," this possibility is there. Indeed, taken by itself, the "extra-mental world" leads to the assumption of "another underlying principle, one just as fundamental as the first—a blind energy or a substance co-original with God. In other words dualism, as in the religions of the Mani-

[6] I am personally attracted to this idea, along with the idea that "natural evil" is accounted for by the need for true freedom of choice. Put simply, if we as finite, created beings are to have true freedom, God cannot have created a universe of simple absolute causality, nor does God create all there is or control all that happens—true "accidents," often tragic, can and do occur. Furthermore, God cannot intervene in all cases to save us without destroying our essential freedom. Thus there are, I believe, theistic ways to account for evil (lower realized values) both created by persons and occurring "naturally" which would free Scheler's position from the dilemma he faced. The goal of this book is, however, not to develop my beliefs but rather to show the logic of the development of Scheler's, and Scheler rejects these alternative solutions.

chees and the ancient Persians, would not be precluded; on the contrary it would be probable" (GPR 193/EPR 197). But Scheler quickly rejects this possibility as he endorses Augustine's doctrine that knowledge of God as mind is not gained by knowledge of the world—that we do not know God as mind in light of the world, but the world in light of God (GPR 194/EPR 197).

These passages are not the only evidence of Scheler's rejection of dualism. In the *Formalism,* after defining the person as the unity of acts and asserting that each individual person has a separate correlative "world" (GW2 392/F 393), Scheler then raises the question of whether some unity is possible. This is not the question of "a" (*einer*) concrete, real world that is, in principle, accessible to every person as his or her world, but rather the question of "*one identical real world.*" This macrocosm, as Scheler says it is traditionally called, would encompass the individual microcosms of individual persons. The personal counterpart of this would be the idea of an infinite and complete mental person. Thus he concludes that the idea of God (or the *ens a se*) is given along with the unity, identity, and singularity of the world as an "essential connection" (*Wesenszusammenhang*). Or as Scheler puts it: "Therefore, if we posit a single, concrete world it is absurd (though not contradictory) not to posit along with it the idea of a concrete Spirit (*Geistes*)" (GW2 395/F 396).

Rejection of Human Action as the Ultimate Cause of Evil

A second classic answer to the problem of evil is to place evil at the foot of the human person. Created in the image of God, free human persons rebel against God and, in pride and ignorance, cause havoc in and around themselves, corrupting not only themselves but nature as well. There is a great deal of evidence for such a view, but Scheler rejects it, and not simply because of our weakness, or contingency, or finitude, though all of these are plausible reasons for rejecting this approach. Although he does point out that freedom is, essentially, freedom for good and not evil (a fact that in no way keeps us from doing that which produces evil, which makes us evil in the doing), this too is not the core of Scheler's rejection of human being as the root cause of evil in the world. What impresses Scheler most is the depth and the pervasiveness of evil in the world. After asserting that evil is grounded in the wickedness of an evil person, he says:

> For the world-evil is a necessary constituent in the world we empirically know, and is also necessarily *bound to the world's good* by a transparent natural law of *causality*. Indeed, the very ground of all individual evil is this necessary bond between good and evil, even the good and evil of human nature; it is a bond of which we are conscious with an impression of something fatefully *tragic*. The truth that everyone has the virtues of his faults and the faults of his virtues, that the faults and virtues of every person and every people clearly rise and flow from one source of character in each case—that is what makes the *tragic nature of existence*. The phenomenon of the *tragic* is itself a proof that not only pantheism and "theism without the fall" but even assignment of the origin of evil to the world-basis are fallacious. It is the *tragic* necessity lying in the bond of good and evil, good and wickedness, in the world we know, which precludes us from seeking the origin of evil only in human wickedness. This tragic bond is itself the *greatest evil*. It is the constitutionally fragmentary character of everything of positive worth in this world, and to attribute this to the mere "under-development" of the world, to believe it may be overcome by "progress," that is the great puerility of "liberalism" and all its spiritual progeny. As Kant so profoundly remarked, man is indeed "made of timber so crooked that nothing wholly true and straight can ever be carpentered out of him." In general terms, and objectively speaking, the *world-evil* is doubtless the consequence of wickedness (such it can only be, *if* it is mind which controls the world), but it is nevertheless, *antecedent* to human wickedness and man's permanent, great temptation to wickedness in character and conduct. (GPR 229/ EPR 234–35)

It is important to grasp Scheler's point here. He is not simply mouthing the popular idea that we *need* evil in order to understand good. Nor is he claiming that the connection between evil and good is absolutely necessary. What he is saying is that in *this* real world, as we know it, there is this necessary connection at its very core. It is a connection antecedent to the appearance of human persons, and so human persons could not be the cause of it, though it conditions what we are and what we do. Yet at the same time it cannot be rooted in the creator of this world, in the ultimate ground of all existence, in God. Since Scheler has now rejected two classic approaches to solving the problem of evil, what *does* he do?

The Devil Solution

Scheler does suggest an answer to the problem of evil. After admitting in the "Problems of Religion" essay that "the real world known to us is far worse than what accords with its basis" (GPR 225/EPR 231), Scheler then indicates the basic approach he will take: "So the free action of some mind superior to human strength, an action whereby the world has fallen into its present condition, becomes an assured truth of reason. The 'fall' is thus a truth of reason inseparable from theism: it is no mere proposition from revelation" (GPR 225/EPR 231).

Scheler here introduces the idea that since the human person cannot be the cause of evil, there must be a person more powerful than human persons—an evil, demonic, powerful person who is the ultimate cause of the fall, of evil in the world. He continues: "The origin of the *wickedness which is the ultimate basis* of this world's evil and also the cause of direct temptations to human wickedness, can lie neither in the world-basis itself nor, solely, in man. It must reside in a metaphysical zone lying intermediate between the two, in a free insurrection against God instigated by a person having power over the world" (GPR 229/EPR 235).

With the introduction of this new evil person, this "free mental cause" that is a "mind superior to human strength" and capable of a "free insurrection against God," Scheler seems to have solved the problem of evil. The cause of the evil in the world is not God, not the *ens a se* that is the ground of the world. Yet it is a free person powerful enough to rebel against God. At that point, Scheler truly believed he had solved the problem, boasting at one point that "only theism can make sense of evil—without assigning it to the world-basis" (GPR 228/EPR 233).

The Failure of the Devil as the Cause of Evil

Unfortunately, Scheler's solution does not work. The position he has adopted involves basic inconsistency and contradiction. Let me now develop the difficulties Scheler's attempt to solve the problem of evil creates.

In the first place, for this person to successfully undertake a "free insurrection against God," he or she must have powers in some way comparable to God's. He or she must be, in some ways, functionally equal to God. The simplest way for this to be so would be if this person were, at least functionally, a second *ens a se*. But as we saw above, Scheler clearly rejects any such dualism. Thus the free person who undertakes the insurrection against God cannot be a separate *ens a se*.

An appeal to a powerful person created by God who rebels, to a "fallen angel" (now a devil), would seem to be a plausible alternative. Why couldn't a being created by God, a being more powerful than human beings, rebel against God? Indeed, the Christian story of the rebellion of the angel Lucifer against God fits quite nicely into Scheler's position. Since Scheler gives this rebellious being freedom, why can he not freely rebel against God?

Unfortunately, Scheler closes off this possibility as well. As noted above, he rejects the idea that the human person is the cause of the evil in the world because of the depth and pervasiveness of evil. But he also states:

> That man should "fall" exclusively from his own free-will—without temptation by any higher and mightier element of evil above him—is unthinkable for the *god-created* image of God, even if we attribute to him a genuine personal freedom, a genuine freedom of choice. Freedom, being intrinsically a positive good, is *ceteris paribus* freedom for good rather than freedom for evil. The activation of freedom in the sense of a real choice of evil therefore requires a stimulus outside and above man. (GRP 228/EPR 234)

Scheler is here speaking of the human person. What he does not seem to grasp is that despite the greater power of the devil whom he is positing as the cause of evil, this argument applies just as surely to it if it is a "god-created image of God" as it does to us puny humans. What tempted Lucifer to rebel against God? If the human person needs some outside stimulus to choose evil, does not this more powerful being need the same, and where is it to come from? Scheler provides no answer.

Final Comments

Given the positions he has adopted,[7] Scheler cannot account for evil except by either placing evil in the "world-ground" or by adopting a Manichaean dualism. Wishing to do neither, he falls into inconsistencies if not flat contradictions. Since these contradictions are rooted in his understanding of the nature of God and realization, and since these ideas are at the core of his ethics, Scheler had either to modify his understanding of the nature of God or realization or to modify the foundations of his ethics, in a very fundamental way. As we shall develop in the next chapter, it is Scheler's metaphysics and religious views that changed. Let us now turn to these changes.

[7] As noted above, I believe it is possible to provide cogent solutions to the problem of evil in ways that would free Scheler's position from the dilemma he faced. The goal of this book is, however, not to develop my beliefs but rather to show the logic of the development of Scheler's thought, and that his reasons for rejecting alternative solutions are logical and philosophically understandable.

8

From Theism to Panentheism

Introduction

Given the problems Scheler's religious and metaphysical beliefs presented for his ethics, it ought not to have been a surprise when he made basic changes in his position. Furthermore, given the fact that his main concerns were with ethics, not religion or metaphysics, it ought not to have been a surprise that the changes were in his religious and metaphysical views rather than in his ethics. Yet, as we will develop in this chapter, critics were not only surprised by the change; all too many of them abandoned any attempt to understand the change as rooted in philosophical difficulties, opting instead to see it as reflective of personal instability.

Since a key goal of this book is to show that there is a logic to the development of Scheler's thought, and since I believe this psychological approach was often used to negate the need to find such a logic, I will begin this chapter by developing in some detail the pervasiveness of this approach and its dangers. I will then develop the change in position Scheler underwent and show how it allows him to meet the problems that his views of God and the *ens a se* had presented to his ethics. In other words, I will show that the changes made good philosophical sense whether or not you agree with Scheler.

The Psychological Approach to Scheler

It must be admitted that if you had no idea what philosophical problems Scheler's religious and metaphysical views presented to his ethics, the basic change in belief would be perplexing, for after criticizing pantheism in the strongest possible terms in the "Problems of Religion" essay, Scheler abandoned the theism he had been championing and adopted a form of pantheism. Yet all too many critics saw Scheler's change of position not as his response to the philosophical problems he was wrestling with, but rather as symptomatic of some inadequacy of the man himself. Indeed, this judgment became not only a way of explaining (or explaining away) the change in position but a way of dismissing all of the complexity and difficulties of Scheler's thought and its development.

This judgment on Scheler was demonstrated forcefully by Dietrich Von Hildebrand, principally in an article appearing in the journal *Hochland* (1928–29, 70–80) shortly after Scheler's death. The task of the article, he says, is to show Scheler's "spirit" (*Geist*), the "philosophical personality" which Von Hildebrand felt was closely tied to Scheler's work. After sketching Scheler's ability to see into the depths of even the most trivial things and situations, an ability that breathed life into his work, Von Hildebrand then accuses Scheler of a completely uncritical trust in his impressions, an error that laid him open to a dangerous subjectivity. He further accuses Scheler of being blind to his prejudices and of desiring more and more new experience rather than searching for truth and the grounds of his thought. Von Hildebrand presents a man strong in insight but weak in critical discipline, a man easily enmeshed in illusions and contradictions.

There is here a definite inference that, in the case of such an individual, changes in thought are nothing but reflections of inner instability and a lack of discipline. This explanation for the changes Scheler's thought underwent was accepted, echoed, and expanded upon by other writers. Gerhard Lehmann, for example, states in his 1943 survey of German philosophy that Scheler was a phenomenon more of instinct than of thought: he wrote "in the moment, for the moment" and did not allow his books the time to mature (308). And the noted sociologist Howard Becker, in a 1943 essay entitled "Befuddled Germany: A Glimpse of Max Scheler," uses Scheler's changes in thought "not only year by year but almost hour by hour" as a symbol of the intellectual flux and "befuddlement" that prevailed among "even the intellectuals" of Germany at the time. He states that the German mind is, and was, in many instances "chameleon-like" and that failure to recognize this fluidity of German mentality was what led many observers to take Hitler too lightly (207–11).

As noted in chapter 1, we find this image of Scheler adopted even by those who wrote introductions to the early translations of Scheler's work into English. Lewis Coser opens his introduction of the translation of Scheler's *Ressentiment* with the statement that Scheler did not fear contradiction but rather relished it. Coser states that Scheler's intellectual restlessness was symptomatic of the German intellectual life of his time (1972, 5). Hans Meyerhoff, in the introduction to the English edition of Scheler's *Man's Place in Nature,* calls Scheler a Faustian man and says that his personality is a clue to the main currents of his thought (1971, x). Even August Brunner, who in his short foreword to Scheler's *On the Eternal in Man* attempts to focus on Scheler's work, notes that "Scheler was emphatically an intuitive philosopher. It is therefore not surprising that his systematic thinking is rather weak" (Brunner 1960, 9). It is not only the introductions to the early translations of Scheler's work that rest on a psychological approach. For example, Harold Bershady takes this approach in his introduction to a recent anthology of Scheler's works in the Heritage of Sociology Series published by the University of Chicago Press, entitled *Max Scheler: On Feeling, Knowing, and Valuing. Selected Writings.* Indeed, at one point Bershady, after sketching Scheler's life and thought, comments: "From a distance certain patterns become visible that might be obscured by a focus on the details of Scheler's life. Scheler seemed impelled, again and again, symbolically to kill everything he loved and to inflict terrible wounds on himself in the process. At the root of all this, I suspect, lay Scheler's feeling that he had been an accomplice in his father's death" (1992, 35).

It is small wonder, then, that when critics focus on specific changes in Scheler's thought, they use the instabilities of Scheler the person as the explanation for those changes. W. Stark, in his introduction to the English edition of Scheler's *The Nature of Sympathy,* speaks of Scheler's theism and states that the deeper reasons for his "fall away from it" could be revealed only by "a sympathetic study of his life" (1954, xxiv). Stark goes on to emphasize the "pessimism" of Scheler's last period and suggests that his untimely death was the result of the "despair" he felt as he "sank deeper and deeper into materialism, skepticism and atheism" (xxx).

The turn to Scheler's personality and life to explain changes in his thought comes strongly to the fore in understanding the late shift from theism to pantheism for another reason besides Scheler's alleged general lack of discipline. Scheler's shift in position coincides roughly with the reported refusal of the Roman Catholic Church to annul his second marriage. Eckhard Koehle states bluntly that the shift was not the consequence of philosophical progress but rather of a "clash of Scheler the man, not the philosopher, with the legal aspects of the . . . Church" (1941, 9). John Oesterreicher is in agreement with this verdict and states that Scheler, in order to "guard his delusion," had to "divest of their power first the Church, and then God" (1952, 195).

Now if this appeal to Scheler the man as a way to understand his thought and the changes it underwent occurred only in early Scheler scholarship, one might dismiss it as of no great significance. Yet when it infiltrates the introductions to the translations of a thinker, it shows a general acceptance of this approach to Scheler's thought. Nor has this approach disappeared from Scheler scholarship. There have been relatively few book-length studies of Scheler in English (though the number is, thankfully, growing). Two of them take this approach. The first, John Raphael Staude's *Max Scheler: An Intellectual Portrait,* states at the outset that its purpose is "to explain the development of Scheler's social and political ideas" (1967, viii). Staude quickly indicates the approach he will take as he says that, based upon the materials he has collected about Scheler's life, he has "constructed a biographical narrative that is intended to indicate the psychological background of Scheler's intellectual development" (x). He then says:

> What gives the ultimate unity to Scheler's extensive and diverse writing is the stamp of his personality. People who knew him personally, and even those who only heard him lecture, testify to the same fact: his writings were but a pale shadow of his *presence.* Scheler was one of those rare men possessed not only of intellectual brilliance, but also of extreme sensitivity to nuances of emotion. His highly refined sensibility enabled him to weave a spell over his audiences which blinded them to the contradictions and illogicalities of his arguments. (x)

The second book in English that approaches Scheler's thought as inseparable from Scheler the person is by Father John Nota, S.J., and is entitled *Max Scheler: The Man and His Work.* What makes this book so interesting is that in it Father Nota explicitly defends his approach against the charge that the human person's life is irrelevant to his or her philosophy:

> Genuine philosophizing cannot be separated from the life of the philosopher but exists only as *personal* philosophizing, to echo Scheler's emphasis. Putting this point in my own words, I would say that genuine philosophy is not an abstract or dialectical game one plays with concepts or words but is autobiographical; it is a struggle undertaken by a person in which his very existence is at stake, for he tries to achieve a deeper understanding of his relation to his fellow men and women, to the world, and to the Ground of his existence. . . .
>
> Anyone who separates this (Scheler's) philosophy from this life, who puts the philosophy of Scheler in one compartment and Scheler as a person in another, and then believes he has something to say about Scheler's thought may be able to write some pages about a beautiful skeleton, but he will have nothing to say about the intensely alive, profound philosopher with a warm heart to whom I devote my attention in this book—the human philosopher Max Scheler. (1983, 2–3)

There is much in what Father Nota says that is correct. Clearly, philosophy is not a sterile parlor game of logic, and a person's life can profoundly influence both the philosophical problems confronted and the answers to those problems sought and accepted. But that is not the issue here. The problem with the psychological approach to Scheler's philosophy (or anyone else's for that matter) arises not when one uses that life to deepen an understanding of the meaning of the thought, but rather when one uses psychological facts as the sole means of explaining that thought. To know of Scheler's personal turmoil can give added depth and meaning to his thought, but to claim this turmoil as the *sole* reason for the change in thought does not aid us in understanding his thought. Instead, it negates the need to understand the development in his thought as a new step in his "struggle" with the *philosophical* problems he was addressing. It says this change is not to be understood as philosophically meaningful, for it is just a symptom of private turmoil. It is precisely because I so profoundly agree with Father Nota's contention that philosophy and life are intertwined, and that our thought is not a parlor game of logic but rather an integral part of our wrestling with the meaning of life and our place in it, that I reject the reduction of psychologism.

The intimate connection between a person's life and his or her thought makes such a reduction a seductive temptation, as even Father Nota displays. Unlike those I referred to above, Nota by and large resists the temptation to use the personal facts of life in a simplistic fashion as a substitute for philosophical understanding, and his book often contributes to an illumination of Scheler's thought. But even Nota, when he tries to understand Scheler's shift from theism to pantheism, rests too much on the tensions in the circumstances of Scheler's life at that juncture, and not enough on the tensions within Scheler's thought. Again, it is not that Scheler's life is irrelevant to his thought, but rather that we must, finally, be able to understand his thought on its own terms, not just as a symptom of his psychological circumstances. His life may well help to form his thought, but in the end it is the thought that will last through the ages, not the details of his private life. If that life truly informed the thought, the essence of that life will be reflected, and even captured, in the thought. Thus it is the thought that we must, ultimately, understand, and if that thought is philosophically unintelligible, if it is shot through and through with ultimately unreconcilable contradictions and philosophically inexplicable changes, no psychological explanation of the causes will save it as philosophical thought. It is for this reason that I am working to show the logic of the development of Scheler's thought in this book.

The Suddenness of the Change

Although I do not accept the psychological approach to understanding the change in Scheler's thought, there are cogent reasons why some people turned to it. The change of position *was* sudden, at least as far as public evidence was concerned. The preface to the second edition of *On the Eternal in Man,* which still supports the theistic position, bears the dateline "Christmas 1922" (GW5

25/E 31), while a clear statement of at least some aspects of Scheler's new position appeared in 1924 in the essay "Problems of a Sociology of Knowledge" ("Probleme einer Sociologie des Wissens").[1] The speed of the change, particularly in the light of its coincidence with Scheler's personal problems with the Roman Catholic Church, may well have confused people and become, as James Collins puts it, "an enigma which scandalized so many people" (1962, 107). Yet as we developed in the last chapter, there were basic unresolved problems in Scheler's philosophy. Unless we believe with Lewis Coser that Scheler relished contradictions (1972, 5) at the core of his position, changes were necessary, and when they came there ought to have been no great surprise.

Scheler's Comments on the Change

Changes were needed, but why did Scheler make precisely the change he did? The best answer would be his own words explaining the reason for the change. Although, as usual, we do not have as much as we might like, he did make a few revealing comments. In one of the first public references (in December 1923) to the fact that he was moving away from the "system of thought" of the Roman Catholic Church, Scheler specifically states that as to the degree and type of his "removal" from the system, the reader ought to look to "a series of metaphysical discussions, especially those in the second volume of *On the Eternal in Man* which was presently being prepared and whose publication, in due course, would grant precise clarification."[2] This is significant, for as noted

[1] This essay first appeared as Scheler's contribution to "Versuche zur einer Soziologie des Wissens," *Schriften des Forschungsinstitutes in Köln, II,* ed. Max Scheler (München: Verlag Duncker u. Humblot, 1924). The essay is reprinted in volume 8 of the *Gesammelte Werke*. Max Scheler, *Die Wissenformen und die Gesellschaft* (1926; rpt. Bern: Franke Verlag, 1960 [now Bonn: Bouvier Verlag, 1980]), 15–190. The English translation is Max Scheler, *Problems of a Sociology of Knowledge,* translated by Manfred S. Frings (London: Routledge & Kegan Paul, 1980). This essay will be referred to using the abbreviation PSW/PSK.

[2] This passage occurs in a foreword to the essay "Christentum und Gesellschaft" and is datelined "Köln, December 1923" (translation mine) (see GW6 224).

above, this second volume was to be the definitive completion of Scheler's ethics. Since it never appeared we do not have Scheler's own characterization of the difficulties he was wrestling with, but it is clear that they focused on ethical concerns as well as religious and personal concerns.

That Scheler's change in position was related to his ethical concerns is attested to in the preface to the third edition of the *Formalism,* which is datelined "Köln, im December 1926" (GW2 25/F xxxiv). There Scheler, while acknowledging that he has changed his position concerning "primal questions" in metaphysics and philosophy of religion, states that although this was not the place to detail such developments, "it appears to me all the *more necessary,* however, to stress here that the ideas in this work not only remain unaffected by the change in fundamental metaphysical position but rather, to the contrary, *they, for their part, represent some of the grounds and intellectual motives* (*Gründe und geistigen Motive*) *which, in the first place, brought about this change*" (GW2 17/F xxvi) (emphasis Scheler's). He goes on to say that if any changes were to be made in the *Formalism,* they would be in the section on "Microcosm, Macrocosm, and the Idea of God." Then he says: "For it was never my intention to establish in this work a *foundation* of ethics on the basis of some kind of presupposition concerning the nature and existence and the idea and will of God. To me, ethics is today what it has been, an important part of any metaphysics of absolute being; but metaphysics is not important for the foundation of ethics."[3]

It is clear from these passages that ethics was a main focus of concern for Scheler throughout his life. Thus, if there is a conflict or contradiction between his basic ethical beliefs and his basic religious or metaphysical beliefs, it should not be surprising if he changed his metaphysical or religious beliefs rather than his ethical beliefs. This is precisely what happened. Let us now turn to Scheler's new position.

---

[3] See GW2 17/F xxvi. Incidentally, although this seems to contradict Scheler's efforts to provide an adequate philosophical anthropology and metaphysics for his ethics, I believe his point here is that no *single* metaphysics was required, such that if it was inadequate, the ethics would be inadequate (not that no metaphysics at all would be needed).

Panentheism

The core idea of Scheler's new position is simple. In place of his theism, he adopts as a world-basis a single *ens a se* with two attributes, *Geist* ("mind" or "spirit") and *Drang* ("impulse," "drive," or "urge").[4] As we shall see below, God is no longer an existent, real person, but is rather a possible end point of the interaction and interpenetration of these two attributes. This "god" comes into being only in that "point of intersection" between *Geist* and *Drang* which is the human person. I shall now briefly summarize Scheler's conception of *Geist, Drang,* and God in his new position.

Geist and *Drang*

The simplest (if most troubling) statement of Scheler's new position is contained in a short book entitled *Man's Place in Nature* (*Die Stellung des Menschen im Kosmos*).[5] As just noted, Scheler adopts an *ens a se* with two independent attributes, *Geist* and *Drang,* and he emphasizes their independence. *Geist* is not derivable from *Drang,* or vice versa. Scheler asserts of *Geist,* for instance, that "if it is reducible to anything it leads back to the ground of being (*Grund der Dinge*), which is the same ground of which life is also an important manifestation."[6] There is thus an *original* cleavage of being itself into two attributes. Although these

[4] Scheler's terms *Geist* and *Drang,* as he uses them in this new position, present serious difficulties for a translator. For example, to translate *Geist* as "mind" makes it seem too close to the physical, to the brain, and this is misleading, yet to translate it as "spirit" runs the risk of making it too esoteric to capture Scheler's meaning. To translate *Drang* as "urge" makes coming up with an alternative translation for *Trieb* (where "urge" fits well) difficult. To translate *Drang* as "impulse"or "drive," which are better choices, is still not totally free of problems either, for "impulse" or "drive" fits best at higher levels of development. There is no adequate single-word translation of either *Geist* or *Drang,* so I have decided to leave them untranslated to signal just how unique these concepts are in Scheler's new position. I know I risk making them more mysterious to English readers. This was not Scheler's intent, nor is it mine. The reader is forewarned.

[5] *Die Stellung des Menschen im Kosmos* is in volume 9 of the *Gesammelte Werke,* 7–71. The English translation is Scheler, *Man's Place in Nature.* This work will be referred to using the abbreviation SMK/MP.

[6] SMK 31/MP 36. Translation mine.

two attributes of *Geist* and *Drang* are primal, Scheler characterizes them most clearly as they appear in the human person. In human being, *Geist* is essentially what allows the human person to ideate; it is opposed to *Drang,* that force which is the essence of life.

Geist is what distinguishes the human person from the animals. Through *Geist* the human person can grasp the *thusness* (*Sosein selbst*) of what were, before the act of ideation, merely centers of vital reaction and "resistance" ("*Widerstands*"*-und Reaktionszentrum*) (SMK 32/MP 37). This act of ideation is not to be simply identified with intelligence, for animals have intelligence too. An animal has, for instance, a vague grasp of plurality. But the human person alone has numbers, the human person alone separates the class or concept of, say, "threeness" and can operate with the number "three" (SMK 40–41/MP 49–50). This ability to separate essence from existence is, according to Scheler, the basic characteristic of the human *Geist* (SMK 42/MP 51). Through ideation the human person achieves a liberation, freedom, and detachability from the "bondage of life" (SMK 32/MP 37).

The second attribute of the "ground of things" is *Drang.* Although Scheler never gives an exact definition of *Drang,* he characterizes it, to a degree, as he traces the "stages of the *development of psychic powers* and capacities." The lowest form of psychic life is "impulse-feeling," or drive (*Gefühlsdrang*), which is without consciousness, sensation, or representation. This drive or feeling is not truly an urge (*Trieb*), Scheler says, because an urge is always "toward something," it always has a specific direction or goal. This basic impulse-feeling is, however, without such a goal and only has the objectless simple modes of "toward" and "away from" (SMK 13/MP 9). The lowest stage of life, which Scheler calls the vegetative, is characterized by this drive and little else. He then describes the move up the stages of development from the vegetative through the "instinctive" and "associative memory" and finally to the "organically bound practical intelligence" (SMK 13–28/MP 9–30). Despite this development, which shows an increasing differentiation of the basic *Drang* (and even a kind of "objectification" in the case of practical intelligence), all of these stages are bound up with *Drang* in its manifestations as life force and the fulfillment of some "goal" set by life, be it the clearly defined "goals" of practical intelligence or the vague "objectless" drives of the vegetative. All of these manifestations of *Drang* are contrasted by Scheler to that of *Geist,* which, through ideation, frees itself from them.

The Interaction between *Geist* and *Drang*

Even this brief sketch of Scheler's conception of *Geist* and *Drang* is sufficient to show not only that in this new position Scheler's *ens a se* is dualistic but also that the two elements of the dualism are defined antithetically. As with any such dualism, he must answer an important question: is there any interaction between the two elements, and if there is, what type of interaction is it and how can it occur?

Scheler does affirm interaction between *Geist* and *Drang*. The interaction is, in fact, necessary. This is because *Geist,* though it wins freedom from *Drang,* does so at a price, the price of powerlessness. *Geist,* which differentiates the human person from animals, is initially powerless. *Drang,* the initially blind force behind life, supplies the "energy of activity" (*Tätigkeitsenergie*) not only for the higher animals but even for the "highest spiritual level," the "purest acts of thoughts" and the "most tender expressions of good will" of the human person (SMK 13/MP 9). For Scheler, *Geist* begins without power but with vision, whereas *Drang* begins without vision but with power. The human person is the point of intersection where *Drang* and *Geist* interpenetrate, where *Geist* becomes forceful and *Drang becomes* something.

This intersection in the human person is important for another reason over and above its being a synthesis of the two elements of Scheler's new *ens a se.* When the essential insights, freed by *Geist* from the goals and concerns of life forces by the act of ideation, *are* realized, if what becomes is positive, higher value, what becomes is God. In this new position Scheler rejects what he feels is the basic presupposition of theism, a personal God, almighty in its mentality (*Geistigkeit*), and adopts instead this "becoming God." He states that the idea of an all-powerful personal God is a refuge, a haven for weakness unworthy of strong minds. Metaphysics is not an insurance policy for the weak but rather a commitment on the part of strong minds, for it is only through their activity that God *becomes* (SMK 70–71/MP 92–95).

Scheler's Ethics and the New Panentheism

It was, of course, this basic change from theism to a form of pantheistic "becoming God" which raised so much of the furor that surrounded Scheler's change in position. As we developed in the last chapter, however, there were ample philosophical grounds for expecting such a basic change in position. The question now is whether the change in position that Scheler underwent constitutes an improvement over what he left behind. Does Scheler's new understanding of the "ground of things" and of the "becoming God" resolve the dilemmas he earlier faced, and does it thereby supply a more cogent ground for his ethics?

Scheler's earlier position failed as a ground for his ethics because his understanding of God and the *ens a se* led him into dilemmas and contradictions in attempting to resolve the classic problem of evil: how an all-powerful, all-knowing, and all-good God could be the creator of a world so permeated with evil. The core difficulty is that from a moral point of view there was no way to clearly distinguish God from God's creation since all was traced back to a single God (or the *ens a se*) whose essential nature is not differentiated in a way that avoids the problem of evil. This is, of course, a problem for any theism, but given Scheler's ethical beliefs in the moral role of the infinite person and the connection between the moral values of the person and the realization of high and low nonmoral values, it was particularly devastating for Scheler's ethics, especially given the fact that he had ruled out the possibility of two *entia a se* and his own answer (the devil) was untenable.

The question we now face is whether or not Scheler's panentheism provides a better answer to the problem of evil than did his theism. If it does, this will contribute to the evidence that Scheler's change in position was motivated by his ethical concerns and that there is a logic to this development in Scheler's thought. One way to show this is to see if Scheler's new position provides a differentiation in the nature of God (or the *ens a se*) that will allow Scheler to avoid the problem of evil.

It does. Moreover, the distinction that allows Scheler to avoid the problem of evil is not only a distinction within the *ens a se* that obviates the problem of evil. Scheler's distinction between *Geist* and *Drang* is also the first clear-cut distinction he provides between the ideal and the real. Since Scheler uses the ideal-real distinction to distinguish between unrealized and realized values, he not only solves the problem of evil but also provides the foundation for a distinction basic to his ethics. To show all of this I will begin with Scheler's new understanding of the distinction between the ideal and the real.

The Ideal and the Real

The new distinction between the ideal and the real is revealed in one of the most fundamental changes in thought that Scheler underwent. This change is developed in the essay "Problems of a Sociology of Knowledge," in a section entitled "Essence and Concept of a Sociology of Knowledge: Sociology of Culture—Sociology of Reality, and the Laws of the Order of Efficiency of Ideal-Factors and Real-Factors" (PSW 17–51/PSK 31–63). The very title of this section of the essay indicates that Scheler is still using the ideal-real distinction in his new position. Furthermore, it is clear, from passages such as the following, that *Geist* is now part of the ideal realm and *Drang* is part of the real realm. Scheler says that the central task of the essay is the presentation of the "law" referred to in the subtitle above, and "first of all, this law defines the *principal kind of effective interdependence* within whose scope ideal and real factors, the objective spiritual and real conditions of life and their subjective human correlate, i.e. their particular 'spiritual' and 'drive' structures, work out their effects upon the potential movement of social-historical being and activity upon preservation and change" (PSW 20/PSK 36).

The fundamental change that finally allows him to clearly distinguish between the ideal and the real is expressed in the law just referred to. The law is as follows: *Geist* determines, of that which becomes, only the "constitution of its thusness" (*Soseinsbeschaffen-*

heit). *Geist* is a "factor of determination" but not a "factor of realization." In order for the ideal to become real, it must in some way become *united* with interests or drives and thus *indirectly* win power and the possibility of actualization (PSW 21/PSK 37). Ideas that do not find support in the real factors are powerless and pass away. Only by "leading and directing" conditions and events that are "independent of the 'will' of man and *blind* to mind or value" can the human person realize his or her ideas (PSW 40/PSK 54). These real conditions only control which *types* of ideas can be realized, however; they do not specify precisely which ideas will be realized. Scheler uses the following metaphor: "They open and close the sluice gates of the mind in a definite manner and order" (PSW 40/PSK 54; my translation).

The Powerlessness of *Geist*

A most significant change in position is signaled here. Scheler reverses the position he had earlier held. Earlier, *Geist* held ultimate sway. It realized its contents (the ideal project), and the limit concept of pure willing was the condition where there was no "resistance" whatsoever from the material being manipulated. Although the human *Geist* was, as finite, not capable of such pure creation, God, the *ens a se,* was so capable. *Geist* created, and the only determining factor on it was its own nature (or those factors imposed upon it by a stronger *Geist*). Yet now *Geist* is powerless and must get even the power to survive from *Drang.* This is indeed a dramatic reversal of position. Perhaps more importantly for our discussion, the ideal realm—ideas, values, indeed all essences—is now clearly distinguished from the real, including realized values.

Or is it truly a reversal of position? It might be argued that Scheler's "new" position is not really so new after all. Can it not be viewed as simply an extension of an earlier-held idea developed in the "Problems of Religion" essay that the finite (human) mind did not have full creative power and could do no more than modify what had already been created by God (GPR 218/EPR 223–24)? Indeed, Scheler, at a point in the "Problems of Religion" essay where he was developing the limitations of the finite mind, seems to preview the very language of this new position when he talks of the losing battle that even "life" wages against the forces of decay and the law of entropy and suggests an alternative to this "battle with the dead," a battle that will be lost. The alternative he suggests is a "*spiritualization of life*" (*Vergeistigung des Lebens*). Such is achieved through the "donation" by life of its "factor of power" (*Kraftfaktoren*) to the " 'act' of mind, powerless in itself."[7] Is this not really the same doctrine which we are now presenting as new and as a radical reversal?

It is not. Despite the apparent similarity, the new position is significantly different. In the earlier position developed in the "Problems of Religion" essay, although the finite human mind may well have had to rely on techniques similar to those now ascribed to mind in general, in the final analysis the *power* mind used to effect even this process was mental power, the power of the absolute mind, the power of God, the *ens a se*. The powerlessness of mind referred to in this passage from the "Problems of Religion" essay was a relative powerlessness, the powerlessness of a *finite* mind that was, ultimately, dependent upon the infinite mind for its power. The finite mind was not powerless as *mind per se*. It was powerless because it was *finite* mind. There was always the power of the mind of God, of the *ens a se* behind this finite mind. Ultimately it was mind, albeit the absolute mind, that "saw" the ideal, and this absolute mind willed the ideal project into reality. It is this which has been given up in Scheler's new position.

Thus Scheler *has* made a major development in his understanding of the relationship between the ideal and the real. But has he done it without falling into the kind of problems and contradictions we saw in the earlier position? Since both the ideal and the real, both *Geist* and *Drang*, are two aspects of the same *ens a se*, the same "ground of things," can Scheler show their independence any better than he could in his earlier theistic position? Will the distinction between the ideal and the real be, finally, undercut as it was in Scheler's theism?

---

[7] GPR 234/EPR 240. Translation mine.

REALITY, WILL, AND *DRANG*

To see why this does not occur, I will focus on the will. As we saw in the last chapter, Scheler defined reality in terms of its relationship to will. To be real is to be willed, and reality reveals itself in its resistance to will. Since will was a mental act, we were led inexorably back to the primal person, the *ens a se,* as the cause of all reality. The *ens a se* being mind, Scheler was hard put to maintain a meaningful distinction between the ideal and the real, or to solve the problem of evil, and in trying to do so he fell into contradictions of the most basic sort. In his new position Scheler avoids this particular cause of these problems, since reality is no longer ultimately rooted in the act of willing by a *Geist. Geist* and *Drang* are autonomous attributes of the *ens a se,* and Scheler specifically states that reality reveals itself as resistance to *Drang,* not to will. Since will is on the side of *Geist,* not *Drang,* in this dualism, and *Geist* is now powerless, will can no longer be the cause of reality. The distinction between the ideal and the real can now be held consistently and without contradiction at all levels right down to the most primordial manifestations of the *ens a se,* the "ground of things," for the cause of reality now is not *Geist.* The cause of reality is not on the side of the ideal in the ideal-real distinction.

Although Scheler nowhere states this in so many words, his comments on will as he develops his new position clearly show this important shift in position. In another essay developing his new position, entitled "Forms of Knowledge and Culture" ("Die Formen des Wissens und die Bildung"),[8] Scheler says that what we call "free will" in the human person, distinct from drives and instincts, is not a positive power of production and creation but rather of control and release of urges and drives. As he puts it at

[8] Max Scheler, "Die Formen des Wissens und die Bildung," in *Philosophische Weltanschauung* (Bonn: Cohen Verlag, 1925), 48. This essay is reprinted in volume 9 of the *Gesammelte Werke*. Max Scheler, *Späte Schriften* (Bern: Franke Verlag, 1976 [now Bonn: Bouvier Verlag]), 85–119. The English translation, "The Forms of Knowledge and Culture," appears in Max Scheler, *Philosophical Perspectives,* translated by Oscar A. Haac (Boston: Beacon Press, 1958), 13–49. This essay will be referred to using the abbreviation FWB/FKC.

one point: "The act of will, related to action is always primarily a '*non fiat*' (it shall not be done) rather than a '*fiat*' (it shall be done)" (FWB 101/FKC 29).

In another essay, entitled "Idealism-Realism,"[9] Scheler attacks Dilthey because he feels that Dilthey leans toward thinking of a "central conscious 'will' " as the ground of our experience of resistance and thus of reality. Scheler asserts that the resistance is against our "completely involuntary, impulsive life" (*gänzlich unwillkürliches Triebleben*) and not against our "conscious willing," which always finds complete, determined realities (GIR 214/EIR 325).

In Scheler's new position, conscious will does not create but rather modifies reality. It must work through the forces of life; it must control and regulate those drives and impulses which *do* have the power to modify reality. Reality is revealed not as resistance to will, but rather as resistance to life forces, to *Drang.* Thus Scheler does not fall into the problems he faced in the earlier position. *Geist* and *Drang,* the ideal and the real, are separate attributes of the *ens a se;* the distinction is clear-cut and held consistently at all levels by Scheler.

Ethics and the Ideal-Real Distinction

Simply to draw a distinction does not yet show that Scheler is still using it in developing his personalistic ethics. This brings us to another key question concerning Scheler's new position: is this new version of the ideal-real distinction still central to the grounding of his ethics? The answer is yes. This is shown as Scheler develops the relationship between the ideal and the real, now the relationship between *Geist* and *Drang,* especially as he develops his new idea of God.

---

[9] Max Scheler, "Idealismus-Realismus," in *Philosophizer Anzeiger, 2* (Bonn: Cohen Verlag, 1927). This essay is reprinted in Scheler, *Späte Schriften,* 183–241. The English translation, "Idealism-Realism," appears in Scheler, *Selected Philosophical Essays,* 288–356. It will be referred to using the abbreviation GIR/EIR.

God and the *Deitas*

The aspect of Scheler's change in thought that received the most publicity and which caused the furor was his abandonment of personal theism and his adoption of a pantheism. Now the term "pantheism" does in some ways describe the change. Unfortunately, it is misleading if one takes it to mean an identification of God with the world, and this is a common way to understand the term. To understand Scheler's new position in this way is misleading because it overlooks the most important feature of Scheler's new understanding of God.

God is not, in Scheler's new position, identical with the *ens a se* (or the "ground of things," which is Scheler's label in this new position). The *ens a se* is the sum of its two attributes of *Geist* and *Drang*. God only *becomes* insofar as the historical process of the realization of the ideal *Deitas*[10] (the realization of higher values) takes place. It is true that at the ultimate end of such a process God and the *ens a se* might become identical, but this is only a possibility, and until the end of this historical process we cannot speak of such an identity of God and the *ens a se*. The *Deitas* is initially part of the ideal sphere, of *Geist*. It is therefore initially powerless. At one point in *Man's Place in Nature* Scheler speaks almost mythically of the relationship between the "Ground of Being" and the *Deitas:*

> In order to realize its *deitas,* or its inherent plentitude of ideas and values, the Ground of Being was compelled to release the world-creative drive (*Drang*). It was compelled, as it were, to pay the price of this world process in order to realize its own essence in and through this temporal process. And this Being would deserve to be called divine being only to the degree to which it realizes its eternal *deitas* in the processes of world history and in or through man. (SMK 55/MP 70–71)

The interpenetration of *Geist* and *Drang* that realizes the *Deitas* is a process, not a state.

---

[10] Note that I do not translate *Deitas*. This is because I wish to emphasize the unique status the *Deitas* has in Scheler's thought and the fact that it is separate from the traditional idea of God.

THE HUMAN PERSON AND *DEITAS*

The locus of this process of realization is *in* the human person and *through* the human person, for the human person is the point of intersection between the ideal and the real. Thus the realization of values not only remains important to Scheler's ethics in this new position, but it is, if anything, more important than it was in the old. Whereas in the old position Scheler posited a really existing God, in this new position all there is of God to begin with is an ideal possibility, the realization of which depends upon the human person. As Scheler puts it in "Philosopher's Outlook,"[11] the opening essay of *Philosophical Perspectives:* "Man is thus not the imitator of a 'world of ideas' or 'providence' which arose spontaneously, or was already present in God before the creation, but he is *co*-creator, *co*-founder, *co*-executor of an ideal sequence of becoming which becomes within the process of the world and in man himself."[12]

It is thus through the human person that God becomes, that higher values are realized. Not only is the ideal-real distinction still central to Scheler's ethics, but it and human persons now have an increased role in the moral history of the universe, since there is no all-powerful God, no all-powerful *Geist,* behind us.

THE PROBLEM OF EVIL SOLVED

Yet for all of these changes, is Scheler now able to provide a coherent answer to the problem of evil? This was, after all, his theism's most obvious stumbling block.

Again the answer is yes. The reality of the world is now autonomous, free from ideality and *Geist.* God is not initially real, and

---

[11] Max Scheler, "Philosophische Weltanschauung," first appeared in *Münchner Neueste Nachrichten* in 1928. This essay is reprinted in Scheler, *Späte Schriften,* 75–84. The English translation, "Philosopher's Outlook," appears in Scheler, *Philosophical Perspectives,* 1–12. This essay will be referred to using the abbreviation PW/PO. (Incidentally, the reader is warned that the translation of "Philosophische Weltanschauung" as "Philosopher's Outlook" or even "Perspective" is misleading. *Weltanschauung* is much more than simply an "outlook" and is better pointed to by the term "worldview.")

[12] PW 83/PO 12. Translation mine.

is not the creator of the real world we find. Since God is not a real, all-powerful person who creates this real world, Scheler no longer faces the classic problem of evil. He must, however, still provide a viable answer to the question of why this is not the best of all possible worlds, why there is so much evil in the world.

The answer Scheler provides to this question is based upon his identification of *Geist* as a "higher form of being" and *Drang* as a "lower form of being," coupled with the fact that, as we saw above, despite *Geist*'s being a higher order of being, in one way it is less than *Drang,* for it is initially powerless. As Scheler states: "The original order of relations holding between the higher and the lower forms of being and categories of value, on the one hand, and the forces and energies in which these forms are realized, on the other, may be expressed as follows: To begin with, the lowest forms are the most powerful, and the highest the most impotent" (SMK 52/MP 66). He goes on to say that *Geist* and life are related in the same way.

Thus in Scheler's new position the world originally consists of realized lower forms of being and categories of value. Scheler states that the "lower" the form of being, the closer one gets to the most powerful forces manifest in the world, those inorganic centers of force that are "blind" to any idea, form, or meaning (SMK 52/MP 67). Now these lower "forces" are autonomous and not willed, since in this new position realization is no longer defined in terms of willing. Given these necessary differences in Scheler's new position, the world is, at least analogously, initially "evil." (To be precise, the realization of lower values would corealize evil if a person was involved in the realization. Since realization need not involve a person in this new position, the parallel can only be analogous.) Thus, given the fact that a creator God no longer realizes the world and we begin initially with realized lower values, Scheler no longer has to explain how a world created initially as good was corrupted.

Scheler and Schopenhauer

It ought not be too surprising that Scheler can now deal more effectively with the classic problem of evil than he could within theism. Yet has he not now merely adopted the position of Schopenhauer which he had attacked with such devastating effect at the beginning of the "Problems of Evil" essay? Not really. Although he is now much closer to Schopenhauer's position than he was before, there are significant differences. In the first place, Scheler felt that, for Schopenhauer, the blind *Drang* was *itself* evil. In Scheler's new position the analogue is definitely not the case. As just noted above, the realized lower values that initially constitute the world are "evil" (but only analogously), but the *Drang* that is the ultimate source of all power is not. If *Geist* is successful in realizing higher values, *Drang* becomes part of the process of "good," the process of the realization of *Deitas,* rather than merely the realization of lower values, the analogue here of "evil." Thus *Drang* is not essentially evil (or good) but is the power behind the realization of either. In Scheler's last period we are truly embodied spirits, and the body is not essentially evil, even analogously.

Scheler's Optimism

In addition to this most basic of differences, Scheler differs from Schopenhauer in another way as well. Schopenhauer is, ultimately, pessimistic. For him, *Geist* is going to lose; it will eventually be defeated. The best it can do is forestall the end. Scheler disagrees with this prognosis, and his final thought is, I submit, optimistic.[13] Although Scheler does, indeed, sometimes speak of the powers of the "lower forces" with a sad tone,[14] he is speaking of the *present* state of the world, not what might be. *Geist* is not doomed, though it must make use of the power of *Drang* to realize higher values.

To understand how Scheler's new position is ultimately opti-

[13] In this I disagree with those critics such as Werner Stark (1954) and Kurt Lenk (1959), who label Scheler's new position as pessimistic. Stark goes so far as to say: "He sank deeper and deeper into materialism, scepticism and atheism, and it is perhaps not altogether fanciful to suggest that his untimely, all-too-early death was not entirely unconnected with the growing despair that had taken hold of his mind" (1954, xxx).

[14] See, for example, SMK 51–52/MP 65–66.

mistic, one must take very seriously his idea that the empowering of *Geist* is a process and that God is the end of the process, not the beginning. Such a position is far from the pessimism of a Schopenhauer. I do not deny, of course, that Scheler's last years may well have been uncomfortable ones because of his life circumstances, but his new philosophical position is in no way one of despair. Although *Geist* and the higher values of the *Deitas* are initially powerless, this is by no means going to be the case at the end of history, where, it is hoped, *Deitas* will be realized and *Geist* will have interpenetrated with *Drang* in such a way that *Geist* is then all-powerful, and the realized world will have become the best of all possible worlds.

Scheler's rejection of the pessimistic appraisal of *Geist*'s position in the universe is shown in many places in his development of his new position. In the essay "Man and History" ("Mensch und Geschichte"),[15] Scheler sketches five basic types of the human person's conception of him- or herself. In it he is as critical of the idea that *Geist* is simply an epiphenomenon of life forces, or that *Geist* is a disease and life forces are the higher values, as he is of the idea that *Geist* is the powerful ruler of the universe. Scheler is no more interested in the triumph of *Drang* over *Geist,* of the powerful lower forces and values over the powerless higher, than he is of the reverse. It is not the triumph of *Geist* over life (or vice versa) that now interests Scheler, but rather their interpenetration. The human person is, as the title of another essay in this volume suggests, a "Man in an Era of Adjustment" ("Der Mensch im Weltalter des Ausgleiches"),[16] and the goal of this adjustment is not the "superman" (*Übermensch*) but rather the "total man" (*Allmensch*) (MWA 150–51/MEA 101).

Of course, the adjustments Scheler saw as a possibility in modern life are but an introduction to the "total man." We have not

---

[15] "Mensch und Geschichte" first appeared in *Die Neue Rundshau* in 1926. This essay is reprinted in Scheler, *Späte Schriften,* 120–44. The English translation, "Man and History," appears in Scheler, *Philosophical Perspectives,* 65–93. This essay will be referred to using the abbreviation MG/MH.

[16] Max Scheler, "Der Mensch im Weltalter des Ausgleich," first appeared in *Ausgleich als Schicksal und Aufgabe* in 1929. This essay is reprinted in *Späte Schriften,* 145–70. The English translation, "Man in an Era of Adjustment," appears in Scheler, *Philosophical Perspectives,* 94–126. This essay will be referred to using the abbreviation MWA/MEA.

yet established the new "equilibrium" needed to move toward the "total man, i.e., toward the man of *highest tension between spirit* (*Geist*) *and drive* (*Drang*), idea and sensuality, who is *also* the man with an organized, *harmonious integration* of these two forces into *one* form of existence and one kind of action" (MWA 158/MEA 110). What Scheler is attempting to achieve, as he puts it toward the end of this essay, is

> a conception of self, world, and God, which comprises light and darkness, the spirit and the fate-determining, demonic drive for existence and life. This conception roots man, both as a creature of *spirit* (*Geist*) and of *drive* (*Drang*), in the divine source of all things; it accepts the general and total *dependence* of life or nature on spirit, along with the dependence of spirit on life and nature; and it integrates this interdependence into the idea of the source of the world which, as substance, stands above both poles of this contrast, and in which the *reconciliation of spirit and life,* of *idea and power,* takes place, although only in the course of world history and not independently of human action. (MWA 168/MEA 122–23)

Scheler was looking forward, not backward. At the same time, however, unless one has followed the course of the development of his thought, it is possible to miss the optimism of his position. As I noted in chapter 1, Scheler was aware of the difficulties people would have following the development of his thought. He was also aware of the reaction his new position might engender, especially the reaction that might follow his earliest statement of it. He ends the essay *Man's Place in Nature* with a passage I have already drawn from but which is worth repeating now in its entirety:

> I have heard it said that it is not possible for man to endure the idea of an unfinished God, or a God in the process of becoming. My answer is that metaphysics is not an insurance policy for those who are weak and in need of protection. It is something for strong and courageous minds. Thus it is understandable that man reaches the consciousness that he is an ally and co-worker of God only in the process of his own development and growing self-knowledge. The need for safety and protection by an omnipotent being, beyond man and the world, and identical with goodness and wisdom, is too great not to have broken through all barriers of sense and intelligence during the times of man's immaturity. This relationship is

> both childlike and weak. It has detached man from God and it is expressed in the objectifying and evasive relations of contemplation, worship and prayer. In place of this relationship we put the elementary act of a personal commitment to the deity, the self-identification of man with the active spiritual movement of the deity. The final actual "reality" of this Being in itself is not capable of objectification any more than the being of another person. One can take part in its life and spiritual actuality only through participation, through an act of commitment or active identification. Absolute Being does not have the function to protect or to complement man's weakness and needs which always want to make an "object" out of this being.
>
> Yet there is a kind of "support" even for us. This is the support provided by the total process of realizing values in world history in so far as this process has moved forward toward the making of a "God." But we must not wait for theoretical certainties before we commit ourselves. It is the commitment of the person himself that opens up the possibility of "knowing" this Being in itself. (SMK 71/MP 94–95)

These are not the words of a man in despair. Nor are they the words of a man who has abandoned his concern with ethics. Scheler's concern with ethics never waned, and his new position makes eminent sense if it is seen as a new attempt to provide the kind of complementary religious-metaphysical position, the kind of philosophical anthropology, which his version of theism had failed to provide.

New Problems

As is often the case when we solve old problems with a new approach, we create new problems in their stead. Scheler's new position may well make a clear-cut and ethically relevant distinction between the ideal and the real and provide a fresh solution to the problem of evil, but is his *Geist-Drang* dualism viable? This may seem an odd question after all I have done to show how Scheler has been able finally to show a clear-cut distinction between the ideal and the real and to develop an *ens a se,* a ground of things, that does not fall before the problem of evil. Yet his new position faces new—and some critics believe fatal—problems itself. Since these problems are so central to Scheler's new position, I will turn to them, and to their resolution, in the next chapter.

9

The Troubled Relationship between *Geist* and *Drang*

Introduction

As we noted in chapter 1, the apparent lack of philosophical reasons for the change from theism to panentheism was only one element of the enigma created by Scheler's change in position. Despite the fact that I showed in the last chapter why I believe the change is philosophically understandable, the new position displays such apparently serious internal flaws that one must also ask why Scheler would have adopted it. This chapter will develop these problems in Scheler's new position and show how they can be dealt with.

The Problem of the Powerlessness of *Geist*

The most basic of the apparently fatal internal flaws in Scheler's new position can be articulated in two problems. The first problem arises because of Scheler's doctrine of the powerlessness of *Geist*. We have just seen Scheler make a call to commitment on the part of "strong minds" (*Geist*). Only in their activity can God become. The question is, if *Geist* is initially powerless, how is it ever going to be able to become *active,* much less "strong," in the first place? Once the process of interaction between *Geist* and *Drang* has gotten under way, *Geist* is, of course, not powerless anymore, but how was the process ever initiated?

Sections of this chapter appeared in my essay "A New Look at Scheler's Third Period," *Modern Schoolman* 51, no. 2 (1974): 139–58, and are reproduced here with permission.

The Interaction Problem

The second problem has to do with the interaction of *Geist* and *Drang*. Even if the powerlessness problem can be overcome, we are faced with the difficulty Ernst Cassirer raises. Noting that "Life and Spirit" (*Leben und Geist*) are "completely foreign to each other in their nature as well as their origin" (1949, 864), Cassirer raises the issue of how these disparate elements could ever cooperate together at all. He argues that Life must have a "trend toward the Idea" if there is ever to be any interaction between Spirit and Life—in our terms between *Geist* and *Drang* (864–66). It appears to Cassirer that Scheler has so carefully guarded the autonomy of *Geist* and *Drang* that it is difficult to see, even aside from the powerlessness issue, how interaction between them is possible. Nor is Cassirer the only one to raise this issue. In a recent article, Dennis Weiss again raises this problem (while defending the relevance of Scheler to contemporary thought):

> One is left to wonder, though, how two things as distinct as spirit and life can interpenetrate. How can spirit, which Scheler describes as a transpatial and transtemporal realm of reality, guide and direct a psychic process? Further, how can the matter of instinctual energy be transformed into the immaterial activity of spirit? How can a spiritual center of action guide that which is essentially blind and substantial? (Weiss 1998, 244)

Scheler's Emphasis

In order to rescue Scheler's new position from these apparently basic and fatal flaws, we must first recognize that the initial writings we have from Scheler sketching his new position are transitional in nature. They are his attempts to develop and present his new views in such a way as to contrast them as much as possible with his old views, and thus to provide a transition to the later work on philosophical anthropology which he was planning (it never appeared, but we do now have access to fragments). Scheler is, in these initial writings, emphasizing, and perhaps overemphasizing, his new understanding of *Geist* as powerless over against the idea of an all-powerful creator God, a view that had led to the problems of his earlier position. The problem is, however, that Scheler must not only overcome these old problems but he must not introduce fatal new flaws in doing so. How could Scheler not see that by making *Geist* initially powerless he was making it impossible for *Geist* and *Drang* to ever interact, and that he was thus dooming his new position from the start?

The Power of *Geist*

The answer is that, despite the fact that *Geist* is powerless in very important ways in Scheler's panentheism, it is not powerless in all ways. Scheler does not deny to *Geist* all "power." Indeed, he explicitly attributes to *Geist* precisely the kind of power that is needed to initiate interaction between *Geist* and *Drang*. Confusion has arisen because he does not explicitly admit that this kind of "power" is indeed power (*Macht, Kraft*). For Scheler the term "power" designates creative power, and it is creative power that he now wishes to deny to *Geist*. He is so concerned to reject what he calls the "classic thesis" of the original creative power of *Geist* that he emphasizes again and again *Geist*'s powerlessness. As we have developed above in the last chapter, it is this rejection of the creative power of *Geist* that allows Scheler to get out of the problems created by his theism. Seen in this context it is clear why he wishes to reject the creative power of *Geist,* so much so that he is not careful enough to distinguish creative power, which he wishes to reject, from other types of power which *Geist* does still have.

That Scheler does still attribute some kind of power to *Geist* can be shown in a number of passages. One occurs in *Man's Place in Nature* when he rejects what he calls the "negative thesis" that *Geist* only "arises" (*erstehen*) with the repression of instinctual forces. Scheler places Buddha, Schopenhauer, and Freud in the category of those who hold to the negative thesis (SMK 46/MP 57). The crucial weakness of the negative thesis, in whatever form it takes, is, Scheler says, that it has no answer to the basic questions: "What is it that negates in man? What is it that denies the will to live? What is it that represses instincts?" (SMK 48/MP 60–61). It is *Geist,* Scheler asserts, which initiates all of these things (SMK 49/MP 62). In so asserting, he is also indirectly attributing to *Geist* the power to do all of these things.

The power that Scheler gives to *Geist* is evident also when he speaks of willing. A particularly dramatic example occurs in the essay "The Forms of Knowledge and Culture." In a footnote concerning the fact that mental willing is basically a negative, restraining activity, Scheler states that "we do not derive the origin of the world from a 'creation out of nothing,' as does theism, but from the '*non non fiat*' (it shall not be non-existent), through which the divine spirit released the demonic drive in order to realize the idea of the divine which had been only a 'potential.' In order to realize 'himself,' God *had to accept in exchange* the substance of the world and world history" (FWB 148 n. 15/FKC 130–31 n. 15).

In stating that *Geist* originally released *Drang* in order to realize "itself," Scheler is giving to *Geist* a power, albeit a "negative" power—that is to say, a power to release but not to create. Although Scheler usually speaks of this "power" in a way that emphasizes the limited nature of what *Geist* can do, even in so limiting *Geist,* Scheler must admit that there is a positive element to this "negative" power. As he put it in *Man's Place in Nature:*

> There is one thing the spirit cannot do: it cannot generate or cancel the instinctual energy; it cannot enlarge or diminish it. It can only call upon energy complexes which will then act through the organism in order to accomplish what the spirit "wills." But there is something positive, not just in regulating the drives, but also in the goal achieved thereby. It is a process of gaining power and activity for the spirit, inner freedom and autonomy. (SMK 49/MP 62)

Geist is powerless to create, but the ability to "inhibit and release" (*Hemmen und Enthemmen*) the blind force of *Drang is,* clearly, a form of power. To say it is in no way a power would be to use the term "power" in a very odd way. As Martin Buber eloquently puts it: "It may be objected that this is not a positive creative power of its own. But this objection rests upon a confusion of power and force—a confusion which, indeed, Scheler makes many times. . . . [O]ur highest experiences of power are not those of a force which produces a direct change, but those of a capacity to set these forces directly or indirectly in motion" (1961, 188).

Ernst Cassirer similarly suggests that the trouble lies in the fact Scheler had never really clarified the concept of power (1949, 868).

These critics are correct in asserting that *Geist* has power. But the fact that, as Buber puts it, Scheler's "choice of words veils the fact that even in his world's ground the spirit has the power to set the forces in motion" (1961, 188) does not mean that Scheler denies to *Geist* this kind of power. It is not so much that Scheler has not clarified the concept of power as that he uses the term "power" to refer to creative power alone, perhaps because he was overconcerned to deny the classic thesis of the creative power of *Geist.* Though he rejects both this classic thesis and the "negative thesis" equally, Scheler states that the classic thesis is more dangerous because it has prevailed throughout the entire history of Western philosophy (SMK 50/MP 62–63). When one remembers that rejection of this classic thesis that *Geist* has creative power is a crucial element in Scheler's overcoming of the problems that plagued his earlier theism, it is understandable that Scheler overstates the "powerlessness" of *Geist.* It is, however, unfortunate, for it led some to believe that Scheler was, indeed, attempting to deny all power to *Geist,* and this is clearly not the case.

The Interaction between *Geist* and *Drang*

Although saying that *Geist* does indeed have power (albeit "negative" power) does meet the problem of the "powerlessness of mind," it does not get Scheler clear of all difficulties concerning the interaction of *Geist* and *Drang.* There is still the second problem raised above. Scheler must not only give *Geist* power to interact with *Drang* but also show that such interaction is possible. This is still a problem because the two are so different in nature. When Scheler asserts of their interaction that *Geist* "lures the drives with a bait of appropriate images" (SMK 49/MP 62), Cassirer quite rightly inquires how these "blind" life forces could ever *see* these images (1949, 864).

The answer is that, whereas *Drang* was *originally* a "blind" force, by the time we get to its manifestation in human life (*Leben*) it is no longer completely blind and can indeed *see* the images because by the time you get to human being "seeing" is part of the process of life instincts.

Geist below the Human Person

This is not immediately obvious, because once again Scheler's concern to maintain the autonomy of *Geist* and *Drang* produces some rather misleading imbalances in his presentation. The problem this time arises because Scheler's desire to refute the "negative thesis" that *Geist* arises out of suppressed life forces leads him to overemphasize the uniqueness of the human *Geist.* Scheler says, for example, that the human *Geist,* through ideation, introduces a "new principle" into the universe which is not to be accounted for merely as something that "evolves" from "life" (SMK 31/MP 36).

Now *Geist* as manifest in the human person is not reducible to life, and the human *Geist* is a truly new factor in the universe, and so Scheler's statements are appropriate, but they are also misleading if they are taken to mean that *Geist* does not appear in the universe until the human person does. If *Geist* is, indeed, an attribute of the ground of things, it cannot make its appearance only with the human person. The process of interaction between the two primordial attributes of the ground of being, *Geist* and *Drang,* is a temporal one. It is impossible that one of these primordial elements should suddenly appear sometime, and a rather late time at that, within this temporal process. If *Geist is* one of the two primal elements, it must be present from the beginning in some form or other. It *must* have some early manifestations, manifestations other than human *Geist.*

Despite his desire to emphasize the uniqueness of *Geist* in general and human *Geist* in particular, Scheler is not completely unaware of the presence of *Geist* before human being appears. We have already seen him speak of God originally releasing the "demonic urge," though this may have just been a metaphorical image. But further evidence of the manifestation of *Geist,* other than and earlier than human *Geist,* can be shown through a more careful examination of Scheler's conception of *Drang,* which we will now undertake.

As noted above, Scheler never does give a single, clear definition of *Drang.* He speaks variously of *Geist* against *Drang, Geist* against *Leben,* and *Geist* against power (*Macht*). Indeed, in *Man's Place in Nature* he contrasts different manifestations of *Drang.* We can see this at the beginning of Scheler's analysis of the stages of development of psychic powers:

> The lowest form of psychic life is a vital feeling, drive or impulse (*Gefühlsdrang*) devoid of consciousness, sensation and representation. It is the power behind every activity, even behind those on the highest spiritual level, and it provides the energy even for the purest acts of thought and the most tender expressions of good will. As the terms imply, "feeling" and "impulse" are not yet separated. Impulse always has a specific direction, a goal-orientation "toward something," for example, nourishment or sexual satisfaction. A bare movement "toward," as toward light, or "away from," as a state of pleasure or suffering devoid of object, are the only two modes of this primitive feeling. Yet this impulse is quite different from the centers and fields of energy that we associate with the images of inorganic bodies without consciousness. They do not have an inner life in any sense. (SMK 13/MP 9)

Later in this same essay, at a point where he is discussing the relationship between higher and lower forms of being in relation to the energies in which these forms are realized, Scheler says of these "centers of energy" (*Kraftzenten*) that "the most powerful forces are the centers of energy in the inorganic world which represent the most primitive manifestations of this vital impulse (*Drang*). They are 'blind,' as it were, to any idea, form or meaning. According to contemporary physics, it is likely that these centers are not even subject to a strict causal order in their interaction, but only to the accidental order of statistical regularity" (SMK 52/MP 66–67).

This contrast between impulse-feeling (*Gefühlsdrang*) and the inorganic *Kraftzenten* which are the "most primitive manifestation" of *Drang* raises an interesting question. What accounts for the difference? I submit that the difference is attributable to different manifestations of *Geist* or its analogue at levels that Scheler does not explicitly acknowledge. Indeed, *Geist* is present at all levels of being.

I say that Scheler does not *explicitly* acknowledge this because I believe there are many indications in his writings that he at least implicitly accepted the fact that *Geist* is always present. In the "Problems of a Sociology of Knowledge" essay Scheler states that *Geist* is always a "determining factor" and never a "realizing factor" (PSW 21/PSK 37). Now Scheler is contrasting the power of *Geist* to determine with the power of *Drang* to realize, but his choice of terms is revealing. *Geist is* the factor of determination, the form-giving factor, and although there is a world of difference between the human *Geist*'s ability to "ideate" (to see within the "centers of resistance," objects, and essences) and the lower manifestations of determination, there is at all levels of being some sort of determination. Let us look at Scheler's characterization of different levels of being to show this.

At the lowest level are the *Kraftzenten*. Yet even these lowest "centers of powers" are experienced as "centers and fields." There is at least a minimal form of determination to them, even if it is only detectable as a "statistical regularity." When we go up from these lowest levels of the inorganic world to even the lowest form of psychic life, the impulse-feelings (*Gefühlsdrang*), we see a definite increase in determination. These *Gefühlsdrang* may well be "blind to ideas," and we may well still be at a level where "urge" and "feeling" are not yet differentiated and all we have is a movement "toward" or "away," but this is a decided improvement in directedness and coherence over the inorganic centers of energy, which are not even governed by causality. Yet both are manifestations of *Drang*. Furthermore, as noted above, even these lowest levels of inorganic centers of force cannot be totally undetermined. You cannot speak of *a* force, even one noted only through statistical regularity, without differentiating it from the background of total randomness. Determination occurs at every level of being, from the lowest to the highest. Indeed, as Scheler goes up the scale of being he distinguishes the increasingly "higher" levels of being in terms of the type of, and degree of, determination present. This extends right up to human being.

By the time Scheler gets up to the human level, with the "human *Geist*" on one side and *Leben* on the other, we are speaking, when we speak of "life," of a manifestation of *Drang* that is highly developed and coherent, quite far from the totally "blind to ideas" inorganic forces in its determinateness. Let us turn again to Scheler's sketch of the development of psychic life to show this. The lowest stage is, as we have already indicated, the *Gefühlsdrang* stage of the vegetative. The next stage up is the instinctual. Scheler presents as a basic characteristic of the instinctual that it is meaningful (*sinnmässing*) and teleoclitic (*teloklin*) (SMK 18/MP 15). Now although meaningfulness and purposiveness here refer to the rhythms of "living organism" and the "species," we are no longer on the mechanistic level of "tropisms," for example, and we can no longer talk of this activity as mechanistic. Nor is this level of behavior completely "blind." In speaking of the relationship between instinct and sensation, Scheler says:

> It is impossible that instincts are the product of sensory experience. The sensory stimulus only triggers the rhythmically definite sequence of instinctive behavior. It does not determine what this behavior is. Both olfactory and visual stimuli may trigger the same mode of behavior. Therefore it is not necessary to have sensations of the same kind, let alone of the same quality. But the converse holds: *what* an animal can imagine and perceive is controlled by the a priori relation of its instincts to the structure of the environment. The same is true for reproducing memories. They always take place, first, within the meaningful context of dominant tasks set by the instincts (their overdetermination) and, only secondarily, as a result of the frequency of associations, conditioned reflexes and practice. An animal sees and hears what is significant for its instinctive behavior, even in the case of the same stimuli and sensory conditions. (SMK 19–20/MP 18)

As the original German emphasizes more in this last sentence than this translation does, the animal *can* see and hear ("*Das Tier, das sehen und hören kann, sieht und hört*") (SMK 20/MP 18). Furthermore, it is not as mechanistically determined as the vegetative level was.

Scheler continues to work his way up the ladder, but we will not follow him in all of the details. What is significant to us is that, according to Scheler, it is "creative dissociation, not association or synthesis of single pieces," that is the "basic process of psychic evolution" (SMK 21/MP 20). This is because "creative dissociation" tends, for example, to free behavior from instinctual patterns and thus free the individual from the species (SMK 21/MP

20). It allows for the development of "intelligence," not just instinctual response. In other words, as we go up the ladder of psychic development we see a change in the kind of determination that occurs, moving away from a mechanistic, simply reflexive type of causality, with the organism achieving an increasingly "free" self-determination. Even with instinctive behavior, we are talking about a level of psychic life where the primitive *Drang* has already undergone a great deal of "creative dissociation." It is far from the blind "centers of energy" (*Kraftzenten*) level of *Drang,* though compared to the kind of freedom we see the human *Geist* with its ability to ideate achieve, it is, one might say, very "narrow-minded"!

We are now ready to meet the challenge of Cassirer's question of how the "blind" *Drang* can ever see the images *Geist* puts before it. The passage Cassirer reacts to occurs while Scheler is developing how the human *Geist* can gain power from the instinct level of already "developed" *Drang* in order to realize the new "ideas," the essential insights it has gained through ideation. Scheler says: "It is precisely the spirit (*Geist*) that initiates the repression of instincts. It does so in the following manner: Subject to its own ideas and values, the spiritual 'will' withdraws from the opposing vital impulses the images necessary for action. At the same time, it lures the drives with a bait of appropriate images in order to coordinate the vital impulses so that they will execute the project set by the spirit (*Geist*)."[1]

In the light of the fact that Scheler presents the human *Geist* as a totally new element in the universe, it is not surprising that Cassirer asks how the "blind" life force could even "see" the ideas the human *Geist* places before it as bait. Once again the problem lies in the fact that Scheler's concern to contrast his new position with his old one led him to overstate his position. Though human *Geist* is, indeed, a "new principle" insofar as it introduces a very new type of "factor of determination" into the universe, the above analysis makes it clear that *Geist* does not appear only with the appearance of the human being. *Geist,* or at

[1] SMK 49/MP 62. Actually, the German is more descriptive than this English translation, speaking of the drives that are lured as "lurking drives" ("lauernden" Trieben) and the bait "as bait before eyes" ("wie Köder vor Augen").

least its analogue, appears at all levels of being, and so is present before the human *Geist* with its power to ideate, and so its new level of freedom appears. Yet by the time we get to the level of development represented by a life-form that has instincts, "seeing" is part of that life's processes.

Thus "Life" can "see" the ideas that the human *Geist* puts before it because seeing is already part of the process the human *Geist* finds already realized. Scheler's very language in describing how *Geist* initiates the repression of the instinctual drives shows this is the case. Scheler states that the human *Geist* denies instinct the "images necessary for action" ("die zu einer Triebhandlung notwending Vorstellungen") (SMK 49/MP 62). By the time we get to instinct we are already at a stage where "images" and the correlate "seeing of images" are a necessary part of the process. Thus the new human *Geist* is not introducing any essentially new mechanism when it withholds a given set of images and substitutes another. Life was already seeing images at that point and was far from being totally "blind," though until human *Geist* came along it was incapable of seeing true ideas or values.

Defending the Uniqueness of the Human Person

The reader might, at this point, raise a different kind of challenge. We have, in the above, gone beyond the doctrines explicitly developed by Scheler, particularly in our argument that *Geist* appears at levels lower than the human person. Despite the fact that we do this to avoid a serious problem that Scheler's new position seemed to face (and we do so only with textual support), it might be argued that instead of helping Scheler's new position, we have instead subverted it in at least one crucial respect. Has not our contention that *Geist* extends "down" to lower levels of being (combined with the fact that *Drang* extends "up") destroyed the uniqueness of the human person, a uniqueness that Scheler safeguarded when he restricted the appearance of *Geist* to the human person?

This is not the case. The human person *is* unique, and what makes the human person unique is the human *Geist,* which is, indeed, a new kind of "factor of determination" in the universe.

It is so new, in fact, that Scheler is almost justified in calling it a new attribute of being. What is so new and unique about the human *Geist* is its freedom. Whereas intelligence and associative memory (two of the psychic powers at the lower, animal stage) freed the individual from the species, this last step up in "creative dissociation," the appearance of human *Geist,* freed *Geist itself* from the whole of the vital sphere, from "life" itself. In human *Geist* we see, for the first time, *Geist* itself, and in this sense Scheler is correct to assert that *Geist* does not "appear" until we get to human being, or more precisely, to the person.

Not only is *Geist* freed from life by the human person, but, as noted above, as person *Geist* can now transform what were only vital "centers of resistance"—that is to say, entities that were in direct relationship with vital affairs—into "objects." This reverses the relationship to external reality which the animal has. Every action and reaction of the animal proceeds from, and is coordinated with, its instincts and drives, which manifest themselves as psychological conditions. What does not "interest" the animal's drives and instincts is simply not "given." A being with a human *Geist* is not so limited. Its behavior is "motivated" by the "pure thusness" (*puren Sosein*) of a complex of sensations and ideas raised to the status of an object. This object and the behavior it motivates is free, and it may even be diametrically opposed to the goals of the drives and the impulses (SMK 33/MP 38).

We are, as human beings, able to act according to ideal objects. In the animal, *Geist* was able to manifest itself only through "creative dissociation," that is, by the ever more accelerated differentiation of forces and force-complexes into more and more discrete elements. With the human person, *Geist* achieved a quantum leap upward. Human *Geist,* instead of merely blocking the oncoming forces into a new direction or differentiating them into more discrete elements, introduces something truly new, namely ideal objects. *Geist* now has "essences" that can be models for the future development of the cosmos. Scheler comments at one point in "The Forms of Knowledge and Culture" essay that the world had, up to man, evolved "really" (*realiter*), and now man ought to evolve "ideally" (*idealiter*) (FWB 92/FKC 20).

Freedom and Interaction

The assertion of this freedom of the human *Geist* allows the issue of the interaction between *Geist* and *Drang* to be raised again in a new way, however. As noted above, Scheler asserts that human *Geist* initiates the interaction between itself and life by denying to the human instincts the images necessary for their action and then placing before these "lurking drives" the appropriate ideal images like "bait before eyes" (SMK 49/MP 62). We have answered the fears that the lurking drives could not see this bait, but following the metaphor Scheler is using here, a question can still be raised. Why should the drives "take the bait"? Why, deprived of the images necessary for their operation, should they not simply stop operations? Cassirer raises this issue also, and he asserts that there must be some sort of "trend toward the idea" on the part of *Drang* (1949, 866).

In answering this new challenge, we must be careful first to delineate precisely what it amounts to. In one sense Scheler would most certainly agree that the human *Geist* has the freedom to create ideal images which are so far removed from the real images used by the instinctual drives that, if *these* ideal images were placed before the drives, nothing would happen. This is precisely the kind of real powerlessness that the human *Geist* is susceptible to. Human *Geist* can and does get cut off into literally useless abstractions. Yet to say this is not to say that what today is a useless abstraction will always remain so. Nor is it to assert that the ideal images *Geist* places before the drives are always so new as to be totally "unrecognizable." The problem of why the drives should "take the bait" would be a problem only if all the "ideal objects" created by ideation were so totally new as to have no real analogues, or if the drives were so rigid, so "narrow-minded," that *no* deviation from the "images necessary for their operation" was possible.

Neither of these possibilities is the case. In the first place, *Drang* at all levels shows an openness, a pliability, a potential for new and higher-level interactions with *Geist*. This is amply affirmed by the development of the successively higher stages of the psychic life from the vegetative on up. There is, at each level, latent in *Drang* the possibility of newer, higher-level interactions. Scheler at one point even suggests that the concept of sublimation may apply to all natural processes, where the term "sublimation" designates the processes by which energies of the lower sphere of being, in the course of evolution, are made available to higher forms of being and becoming (SMK 53/MP 67–68). Furthermore, he asserts, the process of becoming human would then represent the highest sublimation known to us so far (SMK 53/MP 68). If this is what Cassirer means when he speaks of a "trend toward the idea" in *Drang,* he is quite correct, and Scheler would agree with him.

Despite this openness on the part of *Drang,* one might still fear that the ideal objects introduced by human beings may well be so radically new that *in fact* interaction between *Geist* and *Drang* will be impossible at the human level. Some critics feel that in spite of Scheler's clear intent, the asceticism of ideation does make the gap between the ideal and the real too great. Regarding Scheler's description of the human person as the great naysayer against reality, James Collins says:

> He wanted to make this withdrawal, not in a Buddhistic frame of mind, but with the intention of refashioning the given materials of life according to a better, essential pattern. But he cut himself off so definitively from the experienced being accessible to man that there was no point of insertion left for making his proposed redemptive return.
>
> Scheler's protest against actuality is so complete that there can be no question of regaining contact in a human way. (1962, 129)

As we admitted above, it is true that the human *Geist* can get cut off in useless abstraction, and that some new essences are so new they are unrecognizable by the available drives. Yet as noted above, this would be a problem only if it occurred all the time. This is certainly not the case, and if we reflect upon how the process of ideation works, it should be clear why interaction is not only a real possibility but ought to be more the rule than the exception. In the first place, ideation does not operate in a vacuum. It operates, in fact, upon reality, turning into ideal "objects" the "centers of resistance" (which is another way of saying "what is already real"). In so doing it frees itself and the ideal "essence" from the kind of ecstatic bondage to life in which the animal is trapped, but it does not necessarily free itself or the essence so radically that this "new" ideal object is never realizable. It does, however, allow ideal essences, possibilities latent in *Drang,* to be clearly seen and, if we are wise enough to take advantage of what is already realized (that is to say, of the ongoing drives), allow these new ideal essences themselves to be realized. Since ideation works on what is latent in reality itself, the realization of what is so latent ought not to be surprising.

All of this works only if Scheler accepts the idea that the ideal essences won through ideation are, indeed, latent in *Drang.* Scheler specifically recognizes this in at least one passage. In the essay "The Forms of Knowledge and Culture," he discusses the constitution of the human person. In this discussion he states that human persons are lofty and noble beings who have freed themselves from the subservience to life and purified themselves into *Geist,* a *Geist* whose service "life" enters. Of this process Scheler says:

> We have here an ever new and growing process of "becoming man" in this specific sense, a humanization which is both self-deification and a collaboration in realizing the idea of divinity. It is not waiting for a saviour from the exterior. . . . It is, rather, *self*-deification, and that means also *collaboration* in realizing the idea of the *spiritual* divinity which is "essentially" present in the substrata of the life-force [. . . *der ewig nur "wesende" Idee der geistigen Gottheit im Substrate der Drangs*].[2]

Throughout "world" history, Scheler goes on to say, the human person continually develops "what is incipient in its *essence* [*was es seinen Wesen nach keimhaft ist*], in the sense of Pindar who said: 'Become the one you are' " (FWB 103/FKC 30).

But do we not, in admitting all this, destroy the dualism between *Geist* and *Drang*? Have we not once again undercut the possibility of grounding a viable ethics? The answer is no. The newly won "essences" are not the real "centers of resistance" which the process of ideation works upon. To say that "Godhead" is present as a potential from the start, to say that *Drang* is

[2] FWB 102/FKC 30. Translation mine.

open to an interaction with *Geist* that may lead to the realization of that Godhead, is not to say that it *is* realized, or that this interaction *has* occurred. It is, in fact, to assert that it might *not* occur, that it is only a possibility. *What* will be realized is an open question. Of all the manifestations of *Geist,* human *Geist* is most free. As we drift off into unrealizable abstractions, the break between *Geist* and *Drang can* be made total for the first time. Conversely, we can deny the freeing power of the human *Geist* and fall back to the level of instincts, of "life." The choice is ours. To affirm the potential interaction between the two elements of a dualism is not necessarily to reduce one element to the other but simply to affirm that the dualism is a viable one. To say that any and all ideal essences are possible is not to affirm *which* will be realized.

There is one other concern. In giving to *Drang* a new and most basic role, has Scheler truly kept a balance between *Geist* and *Drang,*, or has he tilted things too far toward the latter? Eugene Kelly, in his book *Structure and Diversity: Studies in the Phenomenology of Max Scheler,* is concerned that Scheler has moved too far toward making *Drang* more basic than *Geist:*

> Perhaps as Scheler left his phenomenological studies, his inclination to attribute the origin of consciousness to spiritual acts grew weaker, and the insistence upon urge, or Drang, grew stronger. In "Idealismus-Realismus" he asserts clearly that consciousness arises out of the drives: "It is resistance, originally experienced ecstatically, that leads to the act of reflection through which the drive-impulse first becomes capable of consciousness." This is a spiritual awakening that does not emanate from spirit, but from the drives.[3]

Now it is clear that Scheler most certainly does give *Drang* equal footing with *Geist* in his new position, and that this downgrades the status of "spirit." But Scheler most certainly does not make *Geist* subordinate to *Drang,* despite the fact that passages such as this one might suggest this. As noted in the last chapter, Scheler's goal is not the "superman" (*Übermensch*), the man in which *Drang* is dominant, but rather the "total man" (*Allmensch*) (MWA 150–51/MEA 101), and the total man is the man "of *highest tension between spirit* (*Geist*) *and drive* (*Drang*), idea and sen-

[3] Kelly 1997, 182. Incidentally, this quote is from Scheler's "Idealismus-Realismus" (GIR 214), with this particular translation by Kelly.

suality, who is *also* the man with an organized, *harmonious integration* of these two forces into *one* form of existence and one kind of action" (MWA 158/MEA 110).

As is often the case with Scheler, the misunderstanding occurs because of the somewhat one-sided and polemical statements he made as he attempted to defend the role of *Drang* in his new position. The passage quoted above which troubles Kelly, for example, appears in a section of the "Idealism-Realism" essay where Scheler is attempting to point out Dilthey's "second basic error"—his belief that "everything given is immanent in consciousness." From Scheler's point of view, Dilthey failed to notice that reality is given in an ecstatic "having of" that is not a "knowledge of" (GIR 214/EIR 324). Thus, Scheler is here dealing with how consciousness of reality arises, and his somewhat enthusiastic defense of *Drang* does seem to suggest that *Geist* arises from *Drang,* yet this is not Scheler's position.[4] The type of dualism Scheler is here proposing requires a delicate balancing act, and we will have to undertake much more detailed investigation and development of his new position to judge just how well a Schelerian dualism maintains that balance, but again I believe he does a better job than it often appears he does.

Geist, Drang, Idealization, and Realization

Scheler himself spent a great many of the last days of his life attempting to flesh out the *Geist-Drang* dualism sketched by the last works available to us in English translation at the present time. Manfred Frings, the editor of Scheler's collected works, has been working for decades to make available to us not only good editions of works already available but also works not yet available, including fragments of the works promised but not completed. I

---

[4] One last comment on Kelly's judgments of Scheler's "metaphysics." Despite the newly enhanced role of *Drang* in Scheler's new position, I must disagree with Kelly's judgment that Scheler has "left his phenomenological studies" here. Although he is not using phenomenological investigations to provide evidence for his new dualism, this is due to the nature of metaphysics. That Scheler develops a new metaphysics in his last period does not mean that he has abandoned phenomenology, though he was never only a phenomenologist (if anyone dealing with practical matters ever could be such).

will not try to draw directly from these works for the present study for two reasons. First of all, my study is focused on Scheler's ethical personalism, and so we need not follow the development of Scheler's new metaphysical insights beyond showing the logic of his adoption of it in place of the unworkable theism he had earlier espoused, and showing it is not so fatally flawed as to be totally unworkable itself. I believe I have done so, and that for Scheler it was his ethics and not metaphysics in and of itself that produced the change. Second, we now have an excellent topical introduction to the totality of Scheler's work in Frings's *The Mind of Max Scheler.* Indeed, in addition to drawing on Scheler's last insights throughout this work, Frings devotes the last chapter to "The Last Vision: The Becoming of God, of World, and the Cosmic Place of Human Existence" (1997, 249–98). Frings's study indicates that Scheler became increasingly aware of the complexity of the relationships between *Geist* and *Drang* and began to develop that relationship.

Given Frings's familiarity with this material, I cannot, however, resist using his work to give you a glimpse of the depth of insight that Scheler was achieving at the very end of his life by recommending this work for serious study. In *Philosophy of Prediction and Capitalism* (1987), a book not intended as an introduction to or survey of Scheler's last thoughts, but drawing upon them, Frings summarizes some of the depth of insight Scheler achieved. Indeed, in a most intriguing passage Frings reflects the subtlety of Scheler's insights while discussing Scheler's critique of the pragmatic theory of truth. While using a "Schelerian analogy," Frings presents the complexity of the dance of *Geist* and *Drang:*

> [The analogy] has, briefly stated, four steps and runs as follows:
>
> 1. Ideas of the mind and the mind itself are powerless, as is the symphony in the mind of the composer only. Unless the symphony, say Beethoven's Fourth, is performed and conducted it has no power to realize itself.
>
> 2. Beethoven's Fourth is dependent upon the performance of the conductor and the orchestra. In this analogy, the conductor has the function of impulsion or the life center, serving as a principle opposite the ideas of the mind. All musical images of the symphony remaining in Beethoven's mind only stay there. They require a life-center to become real. The existence of the images and ideas of the

> symphony is one of "continuous becoming" with conductor and orchestra. The ideas of the symphony are becoming and unbecoming in each phase of the performance, i.e., in the absolute time of pure listening to it. The analogy can also be extended into the area of light. If light does not hit a surface, its waves remain dark. Light realizes itself only with things and surfaces.
>
> 3. But neither the composer nor the conductor alone can account for the realization of the symphony. There must be the orchestra. In the analogy, its players stand for the various drives with their own particular images. On the one hand, they cannot play without a conductor who guides them. On the other, the conductor cannot do without them who play with him.
>
> 4. Finally, the instruments stand for all physical factors necessary for the audibility of the symphony, sound waves, air, even their atomic compositions. Without them, there is no symphony, either.
>
> Hence, the ideas of the symphony are real only by way of their functionalization with their conductor (impulsion), orchestra (drives), and instruments (physical factors). In this analogy, ideas by themselves are not really extant. They are at best in potency to become realized sometime in the future. This holds for mind also whenever its ideas do not find functions with things in life that bring them alive and make them historical. Overstating the argument, we could say: mind's ideas can exist only if they are conjoined with the blood of life. (Frings 1987, 76–77)

Even this short passage suggests that Scheler was beginning to illuminate the complex relationship of both dependence and independence of idea and reality. Scheler's creative work in this, as in so many areas, did not end but was simply interrupted by his untimely death. Although I cannot pursue his last insights in depth in this book, they display, as Frings's work suggests, the kind of complexity one would expect from Scheler and are well worth exploring.[5]

Resolution of the Third Enigma

With this I come to the end of my development of Scheler's change of religious and metaphysical beliefs and my presentation

[5] This is true whether or not you follow Scheler in his rejection of theism. Scheler's illumination of the interaction between the ideal and the real is of value whether it applies to the *ens a se* or just to finite human being.

and defense of his new position. I am now able to resolve the third enigma, the question of why Scheler changed from theism to panentheism and why his new position seemed so flawed. In attempting to forge an ethical personalism adequate to his new views of values, the heart, and the person, Scheler came to a vision of a creator God and reality that presented him with a classic version of the problem of evil. Rather than abandon or change his ethical personalism, he adopted new religious and metaphysical positions, abandoning theism and beginning to forge a panentheism more suitable to his ethical personalism. Thus, when seen in the light of the development of Scheler's thought, the reasons for his change make philosophical sense, whether one agrees with him or not. Furthermore, when one sees the change in the light of its philosophical motives, the apparent flaws can be seen to be rooted in the understandably imbalanced way Scheler presented his new panentheism, and that imbalance can be corrected.

The Completion of Scheler's Ethics: The Unfinished Task

I have now shown that the development of Scheler's work makes sense and that Scheler's panentheism both solves his problem of evil[6] and finally begins to supply a key distinction (between the real and the ideal) necessary for his ethics.[7] Thus the work of Scheler's last period contributes to the completion of his ethics.

Does this mean that the foundations for Scheler's ethics are now complete? The answer is no. There is still much work to be done. Indeed, the core problem Scheler faced at the end of the *Formalism* is, if anything, more pressing than before. To see why, we must backtrack a little. Scheler's search for God, with all of the complex problems and creative solutions this quest entailed, was undertaken to solve the problem of how a finite and limited

[6] Again, I am quite aware of alternative solutions, and as noted above, I personally subscribe to another approach. However, this book is focused on Scheler, not me.

[7] I say "begins to supply" because the ontological status of values, and indeed anything "ideal," remains unclear. I believe that Scheler's last thoughts suggest that his initial insight in his dissertation, that values had as unique a status as "being," may well turn out to be prophetic. But again, this is not an issue we can pursue in the present study.

person could ever morally develop beyond the limits imposed by his or her *ordo amoris.* Yet, despite the fact that Scheler's new panentheism does avoid the problem of evil and does allow new insight into the relationship between the ideal and the real, I would submit that it does not yet provide an answer to the core problem posed at the end of the *Formalism,* the question of how we can turn to persons for moral guidance.

To see why this is still a pressing problem for Scheler's ethical personalism, we must remember that at the end of the *Formalism* Scheler had rejected finite persons as a valid source of moral direction (because of the tragic limitations of finite persons) and had suggested the infinite person of God as a source of moral direction. Yet in Scheler's new panentheism there is no infinite, perfect person, so once again the hope that the tragic limitations to the moral development of finite persons can be overcome seems dashed. Finite human persons are, as Scheler emphasizes again and again in his last position, "on their own."

New Possibilities

The fact that Scheler died before he could show how all of the problems of his ethical personalism could be dealt with does not mean they cannot be resolved. I believe Scheler's work can be completed. As Frings's eloquent work suggests, Scheler's *Nachlass* promises to be as rich in new insights (and new problems) as what has already appeared, and efforts to unearth and develop them will, I expect, be fruitful. Further, as I will show below, it is possible and fruitful to follow up on leads suggested in what we already have.

The fact that Scheler died does not mean that the approach he pioneered need die with him. In the next three chapters I will explore a number of ways both to contribute to the completion of what Scheler started and to defend his ethical personalism from the many attacks that it has received and continues to receive.

4

DEFENDING A SCHELERIAN ETHICAL PERSONALISM

10

Defending the Central Role of the Person in Scheler's Ethics

The New Task

I have now shown the development of Scheler's quest for a new ethical personalism. In doing so I have resolved the three enigmas that have frustrated defenders of Scheler by showing why he failed to develop all of the detailed phenomenological evidence he promised, why he became involved with "religious" investigations as he attempted to complete his ethics, and what the philosophical reasons were for his abandonment of theism. I have also shed light on his insights by putting them into the dynamic context within which they arose, and I have been able to correct some of the misunderstandings that have arisen because of the imbalances in his presentation of his panentheism.

Following the logic of the development of his quest has allowed me to unfold the development of Scheler's thought and to more clearly show what he was pointing to. It has, however, limited me to dealing with Scheler's insights in the order in which they appeared in the dynamic development of his quest. Thus I have dealt with the misunderstandings and negative criticisms of Scheler only when doing so was directly relevant to the clarification of the logic of his quest.

Yet, as I indicated in chapter 1, this book is not intended simply as a historical study, correcting misunderstandings of a dead white

---

Sections of this chapter appeared in my essays "Max Scheler's Practical Ethics and the Model Person," *American Catholic Philosophical Quarterly* 69, no. 1 (1995): 63–81; "A Change of Heart: Scheler's Ordo Amoris, Repentance, and Rebirth," *Listening: Journal of Religion and Culture* 21, no. 3 (1986): 188–96; and "Scheler, Schutz, and Intersubjectivity," *Reflections: Essays in Phenomenology* (Canada) 4 (Summer/Fall 1983): 5–13; they are reproduced here with permission.

European male and his dead position. For all of its incompleteness, Scheler's work does point us to a new approach in ethics that is well worth exploring and developing. It is for this reason that I must now refocus my efforts. It is time to step back and look at Scheler's legacy not simply to better understand it, but to show it as a beginning worthy of the effort needed to complete it.

I must introduce another new focus as well. Although Scheler did show concern for the practical application of his ethical personalism, his main focus was the development of the *foundations* for a new ethical personalism, and indeed it was at this level that most of the problems he attempted to deal with occur. Such work was and is necessary. Yet the ultimate goal of any ethics is not simply to provide such foundations but to construct a complete building upon them. Thus I will work to show that Scheler's ethical personalism can give us a practical ethic, practical direction on what to do and what to be. The task of these last three chapters is to demonstrate that Scheler has truly opened the door to a new ethical personalism.

Given the scope of such a task, I cannot complete Scheler's work or defend it against all attacks in a single book, much less in three chapters. Hence these last three chapters are only a selective indication of such activity. I have chosen three broadly definable areas to develop and defend. First, in this chapter I defend the centrality of the person in Scheler's ethical personalism, both by dealing with two basic problems for Scheler's practical ethics not yet dealt with in our study (the problems of the limits of finite persons and of intersubjectivity) and by meeting a basic attack on the centrality of the person. In the next two chapters I extend my defense of Scheler's ethical personalism by defending the primacy of the heart in value-ception, and the adequacy of Scheler's understanding of the world of values.

I must emphasize, however, that nothing I will do in these last three chapters is complete. In each case all I can do is sketch my development and defense of key elements of a Schelerian ethical personalism. There are many other elements that must be developed and defended. I repeat this caveat so emphatically because I do not want the limited nature of this study to lead to the same kind of misunderstanding that was the fate of Scheler's work. In these last chapters I am attempting to show that completing a Schelerian ethical personalism is possible, not providing a fully worked out practical ethics.

INTRODUCTION TO THIS CHAPTER

As I have demonstrated in this study, Scheler places the person at the center of ethics. For him the person is the highest of values, and the heart of the person—the *ordo amoris* and the feelings of values—are at the center of what we are and do. Yet this centrality of the person in Scheler's ethics creates formidable problems, one of which we must now meet. As noted above, given the depth at which the *ordo amoris* operates, and given the "tragic limitation of finite persons," how can Scheler claim that we ought to turn to persons for moral direction? After all, if finite persons are locked into one level of insight, how can a finite person ever help anyone to see a higher level? Indeed, how can anyone even *see* a higher level? Second, even if it can be shown that it is theoretically possible for a finite person to see a higher level, how exactly is the "change of heart"—the change in the *ordo amoris* needed to see more of the higher values, and see them clearly—possible?

The first task of this chapter is to solve these problems. Fortunately, Scheler's "Problems of Religion" essay contains a fruitful clue which, when combined with other work, suggests that the "tragic limit" may not be as absolute as the *Formalism in Ethics and Non-Formal Ethics of Values* suggests. Furthermore, consideration of a key essay, entitled "Repentance and Rebirth,"[1] suggests how a change of heart is possible.

Yet even with these problems of the limits of finite persons resolved, another basic question must be faced. In order to learn from other persons, I must be able to have some sort of effective contact with them. Thus the question of how we can know other

---

[1] "Repentance and Rebirth" appeared in German as "Reue und Wiedergeburt" in *Vom Ewigen im Menschen* (1921; rpt. Bern: Franke Verlag, 1954), 27–59. The essay first appeared under the title "Zur Apologetik der Reue" in 1917. It was reprinted in volume 5 of the *Gesammelte Werke,* 27–59. The English translation is in Scheler, *On the Eternal in Man,* 35–65. This work will be referred to using the abbreviation RW/RR.

persons is a particularly important one for an ethical personalism. As I will show below, Scheler develops a most creative position on this classic problem of intersubjectivity, but since it is a position that other phenomenologists challenge, I next undertake a defense of Scheler's phenomenology of intersubjectivity.

Finally, in *Guardian of Dialogue: Max Scheler's Phenomenology, Sociology of Knowledge, and Philosophy of Love* (1993), Michael Barber raises the question of whether in Scheler's approach persons are more important than values. Since this is a direct challenge to my contention of the primacy of persons in Scheler, I end this chapter by meeting this challenge.

The Tragic Limits of Finite Persons—Again

My first task is to show that the limits of finite persons Scheler pointed out in the *Formalism* are not as absolute as it seemed when he said there that "it is essentially, not contingently, impossible for one finite (individual or collective) person to represent simultaneously an exemplar of the saint, the genius, and the hero" (GW2 575/F 590). Calling this "*the essential tragic of all finite personal being* and its (essential moral) *imperfection*" (GW2 575/F 590), Scheler also said that "only the hero fully values the hero; only the genius fully values the genius. Who should value both wills when it is impossible to be both perfect hero *and* perfect genius?" (GW2 576/F 591). This limitation seemed devastating, for if we as finite persons are all so tragically limited, how could model persons ever help to open us to higher values?

Although Scheler initially raised the hope that the infinite, personal God might provide a solution to this problem, pursuing that possibility led him into such deep difficulties that attempting to resolve them occupied him for the rest of his life and led to his abandonment of theism, with the problem of the tragic limits of the person still unresolved and more pressing than ever, since at the end we have no existent infinite person to help us.

The Two Ways to God

The clue to a solution to the problem of the tragic limits of finite persons lies in the "Problems of Religion" essay in a section devoted to showing that religion is not rooted in culture. Scheler says that although religion is independent of culture, the study of culture can lead to God. He contrasts two ways to God, direct and indirect. The direct way "consists in a preponderantly sudden or spasmodic manner of coming to the conviction that only in devotion to God and surrender to the divine power can the substance of the person find the full meaning of its existence, its deepest expression, its salvation. Profoundly affecting *personal* experiences are the supreme vehicle of this kind of conversion" (GPR 324/EPR 327–28).

The indirect way is different. The person begins by being interested in the "religious assumptions" operative in some cultural field, and only slowly do these religious assumptions become more than assumptions. Scheler says this indirect path works only because the person can see from the very beginning, if vaguely, that religion is more than an assistance to the exercise of cultural functions (GPR 324/EPR 328).

The Solution to the Problem of the Tragic Limits of Finite Persons

What is interesting about this "educational path" to God, as Scheler calls it, is that as he develops how we can have this "indirect" route to God, to the highest of holy persons, by means of studying the religious values present in culture, he also shows that the tragic limitation may not be as absolute as the passages in the *Formalism* suggested. We see this as Scheler, after indicating that not only the objective ordering of the world of values but even the axiological order of the world is one great signpost to God, makes the following observation:

> Goethe was near the mark with his simple pronouncement: "*Everything which is perfect of its kind also transcends its kind.*" Yes; it breaks through into a *higher* kind of value.
>
> There is in fact a law of *continuity between goods,* though as such it does nothing to alter the discrete and "quantum" character of *values* themselves. By this law the *perfect* embodiment of the goods appropriate to any basic category of values (value-modalities and their subordinate value-qualities) automatically passes over into the

> next higher category, which is modally, or qualitatively, different. (GPR 326/EPR 329–30)

Here Scheler is saying that although the different ranks of values are qualitatively different, as we approach the borders of each by achieving perfection in one rank we naturally pass over into the next highest rank. Scheler illustrates this "law" from a number of ranks, beginning as follows: "Where the exercise of a craft that still lies within the bounds of utilitarian activity achieves a perfection of its kind, it achieves at the same time something *more* than the merely useful—a minor work of art possessing at least an accessory beauty. The useful itself acquires beauty when its utility is perfect" (GPR 326/EPR 330). He then indicates that the assumptions of any positive science must also, if they are true basic assumptions, be essential truths, and that despite the essentially different types of knowledge that positive science and philosophy seek, they "pass over" into each other as they achieve perfection.

What is of significance to us for the problem of the tragic imperfection (which limits us as finite persons in what we can see of the range of model persons we ought to follow) comes out in the next passage:

> And must not a *perfect* hero needs become a genius: an Alexander, Caesar, Napoleon, Frederick the Great, a Prince Eugene—as opposed to "just another hero": a Blücher for example? The higher the spheres of endeavor (as embodying and realizing intentional values), the more they are subjectively of mutual assistance—the more indeed they *require* and enhance each other. . . .
>
> Can one be a perfect "leader of men" other than by being *more* than a leader? Must not the perfect leader be a spiritual figure devoid of personal ambition who as an involuntary exemplar, with no intentions of leadership, attracts a following? Does not the value of such a man appear to lie not in his leadership but in the simple fact that "such a one is in the world"? (GPR 327/EPR 331)

Scheler develops this "law" in order to show how we can reach up to God from every sphere of values, but it has great significance beyond this immediate point. It shows that the tragic separation of individual model persons attested to in the *Formalism* is not absolute. It is possible for us to transcend the separation as we approach perfection in any rank. This is a most important element in making possible moral growth, for it means that finite persons are not inevitably locked into a particular level. A model person (*bon vivant,* "leading spirit," hero, genius, saint) can be a bridge from one level to another. Furthermore, since none of this depends upon the existence of God (indeed, the initial clue appeared in Scheler's consideration of the indirect way *to* God), finite persons can serve as models for moral development despite the pessimism of the passages on the "tragic limitation" in the *Formalism,* and they can do so even if we follow Scheler beyond theism.

The Problem of a Change of Heart

Simply showing that it is possible to move from one level to a higher level is not enough. We must also be able to see *how* the move can occur. If what I see of the hierarchy of values is hedged in by my love and my hate, a move from one level to another requires a basic change in my *ordo amoris.* Yet how can this occur? Given the depth at which love and hate function, how, for example, can I overcome hatred and resentment and see better the true hierarchy of values? How do I change my *ordo amoris*? Nor is this a problem simply for individuals. Since the ethos of a group is determined in the same way, how can a group ever expand its vision of the hierarchy of values?

This is, given the fundamental level on which the change must occur, a most difficult matter to penetrate. Yet it is clear that Scheler not only believes that a change of ethos can occur but that it has occurred and will continue to occur. Indeed, the process of moral development is a historical one that involves and will involve all people and all peoples. As Scheler states in the *Formalism:*

> One can only say that a complete and adequate experience of the cosmos of values and its order of ranks, and, with this, the representation of the moral sense of the world, is *essentially* connected with the *cooperation* of the different forms of ethos which unfold historically according to its laws. It is precisely a correctly understood *absolute ethics* that strictly *requires* these differences—this value-perspectivism of values among peoples and their times and this openness in the formative stages of the ethos. Because moral value-estimations and their systems are more manifold and richer in their

> qualities than the diversity of mere natural dispositions and realities of peoples would allow one reasonably to expect, one must assume an objective realm of values which our experiencing can enter only gradually and according to definite structures of the selection of values. (GW2 307–8/F 303–4)

Furthermore, the change in ethos, and the corresponding change in the objective hierarchy of values we have access to, is not simply a linear process. Again, in the *Formalism,* Scheler notes:

> The most radical form of renewal and growth of the ethos occurs in the movement of *love* and its power, in which "higher" values (with regard to existing ones) are discovered and disclosed. This happens first within the limits of the highest value-modalities, which we mentioned earlier, then within those of the others. Thus it is to the *moral-religious genius* that the realm of values opens up. In such a variation the rules of preferring among old and new values become altered by themselves. Although the rules of preferring among the old values and their mutual objectivity are not necessarily affected, the old realm of values as a whole is nevertheless relativized.[2]

In a footnote to this last passage, Scheler points to the Sermon on the Mount as evidence for a discovery of a new realm of values that relativized an older ethos (GW2 309 n. 1/F 305 n. 83).

The Change of Heart

The more basic question remains, however. Given the deep level of the functioning of love and hate, how are these transformations possible? How as individuals do we change our *ordo amoris* and

[2] Scheler continues: "It is now a matter of blindness or deception to prefer the old values to the new, and it is practically 'evil' to live according to the old values as the highest ones. The virtues of the old ethos now become 'glittering vices.' *But* the rules of preferring among the old values are *not* affected by this. It remains 'better' to retaliate, for instance, or even to seek revenge, than to prefer one's own usefulness (in regard to retaliation) or the common weal to the value of retaliation and revenge—even when these are subordinate in their value to forgiveness as the most valued and therefore the *only* morally 'good' comportment in cases of experienced offenses and guilt. The rules of preferring that belong to an old ethos are not abolished as a new ethos 'grows.' Only a relativizing of the whole of the old ethos occurs" (GW2 309/F 305).

open ourselves to higher values? This question is particularly acute in the light of Scheler's pointing to the moral-religious genius as the key player in important transformations. Few of us are Christs, and so what of us? Even if a moral genius makes the transformation, how can we lesser beings respond? Furthermore, how can the ethos of an entire group change?

Fortunately, Scheler does speak to this question, most clearly in an essay entitled "Repentance and Rebirth" in the volume *On the Eternal in Man.* In it he both shows his belief that a change of heart is possible and explores how it comes about. Scheler begins the essay by denying that repentance is a purely negative and useless act, made useless because it cannot change the past. Though one cannot change what actually happened in the past, the *meaning* of what happened most certainly is not fixed and unchangeable. Nor is repentance simply rooted in a retrospective fear of punishment or a moral "hangover" (RW 29–33/RR 36–39). For Scheler, repentance is a positive act. It is "a form of self-healing of the soul, is in fact its only way of regaining its lost powers" (RW 33/RR 39).

With this statement we see Scheler locating in the act of repentance the possibility of precisely the sort of "change of heart" that is our concern here. Yet how does repentance function to accomplish this feat? As noted above, Scheler begins to lay the foundation for the possibility of a change of heart by pointing out that in repentance what is changed is not the past but rather the meaning the past has in the present:

> Repenting is equivalent to re-appraising part of one's past life and shaping for it a mint-new worth and significance. People tell us that Repentance is a senseless attempt to drive out something "unalterable." But nothing in this life is "unalterable" in the sense of this argument. Even this "senseless" attempt alters the "unalterable" and places the regretted conduct or attitude in a new relation within the totality of one's life, setting it to work in a new direction. People tell us Repentance is absurd, since we enjoyed no freedom and everything had to happen as it did. It is true that no one would be free who could not repent. But only repent—and see how as a result of the act you acquire what in the beginning you unwisely deemed a prerequisite of that act as you saw it—*freedom!* You are now *free* from the flood tide of bygone guilt and

> wickedness that was sweeping you relentlessly away, *free* from that rigid chain of effect, such as subsisted before repentance, which produces ever new guilt from old so that the pressure grows like an avalanche.[3]

After developing the implications of this definition of repentance, Scheler finally begins to wrestle with our question when he considers the difference between repentance of being and repentance of conduct. The latter is simply "rueful introspection," a regretting of what I have done, but repentance of being is deeper. Scheler quotes approvingly Schopenhauer's stressing that the deeper repentance is signaled not in the formula "Alas! what have I done?" but rather in "Alas! what kind of a person I am!" (RW 40/RR 46). But Scheler objects to this last formula because "it is implicitly not possible to repent one's very person in its quintessential Being" (RW 40/RR 46).

Scheler resolves this dilemma by pointing out that although we cannot repent our very person, our "very person in its quintessential Being" *can* change "levels." Thus we do not repent our "very person" but rather that we *were* "such a person as *could* do that deed!" (RW 40/RR 46). This may seem to be an unnecessary splitting of hairs, but it is not. If I had to repent what I *am* in my very being there would be nothing that could *do* the act of repentance. There must be a "self" that can repent. As Scheler puts it:

> The unique impact and significance of the deeper act of repentance—which impels no mere adjustment of outlook or good resolve but a veritable *transformation* of outlook—can be understood only if we take account of the following. The manner in which we

[3] Scheler continues: "It is not repented but only unrepented guilt that holds the power to bind and determine the future. Repentance kills the life-nerve of guilt's action and continuance. It drives motive and deed—the deed with its root—*out* of the living centre of the Self, and thereby enables life to begin, with a spontaneous, virginal beginning, a new course springing forth from the centre of the personality which, by virtue of the act of repentance, is no longer in bonds.

"Thus Repentance effects moral rejuvenation Young forces, as yet guiltless, are dormant in every soul. But they are hampered, indeed smothered, by the tangled growths of oppressive guilt which in the course of time have gathered and thickened within the soul. Tear away the undergrowth, and those forces will rise up of their own accord" (RW 35–36/RR 41–42).

> reflexively experience ourselves has definite *levels* of concentration and self-appraisal, and the change from one level to another is not unreservedly determined by the overall psychic causality which determines psychic processes within any one level. Relatively to the causal pattern which governs the empirical contents on each level, a radical alteration of the very level, or range of levels, whereon the personality currently dwells is a *free act* of our total personal Self. And in the last resort it is to this total Self that all the successive concretions of Self belong as empirical constituents out of which, as this or that circumstance is revealed by memory, we see *the deed* arising. (RW 40/RR 46–47)

It is because I stand now on a higher level that I can see better what I was, and "however necessary the deed appears to us on the level of our existence at that time, however 'understandable' it is, down to its smallest details, in the strict historical sense—once we are confident of having 'placed' that level—there was no *like* necessity for us to *have been* on that level. We could have altered that level. Not only could we have *willed* and *acted* otherwise, we 'could' equally have *been* other than we were" (RW 40–41/RR 47).

Now we come to the sticking point. How do we reach this higher level? Scheler begins by admitting that the awareness of the better things we could have been or done "have their way of bursting through once we know from present experience our capacity for improvement of conduct" (RW 41/RR 47). Yet how do we get to this "present experience" which gives us the higher level to stand upon? Does repentance presuppose repentance? Scheler recognizes this difficulty:

> For it is the peculiar nature of Repentance that in the very act which is so painfully destructive we gain our first complete insight into the badness of our Self and conduct, and that in the same act which seems rationally comprehensible only from the "freer" vantage point of the new plane of existence, this very vantage point is attained. So the act of repentance precedes in a certain sense both its point of departure and its point of arrival, its *terminus a quo* and its *terminus ad quem*. (RW 41/RR 47)

Scheler has little to say about this difficulty, which he calls "the deepest mystery of that vital, deeper act of repentance" (RW 41/RR 48). He states:

> The continuous dynamic of Repentance enables us to glimpse the attainment of an altogether higher, ideal existence—the raising through firm self-revision of the whole plane of our moral existence—and lays open to our gaze, far below us, the whole condition of the old Self. . . . Just as, when climbing a mountain, we see both the summit's approach, and the valley sinking beneath our feet, each picture entering our experience under the control of the one act, so in Repentance the Person mounts, and in mounting sees below it the former constituent Selves. (RW 41–42/RR 47–48)

Despite their brevity, these passages do shed light on our question. In the first place, although Scheler has not said it in so many words, the act of repentance is the work of love. Both the act of repentance and the act of love are movements. It is because the movement of love is occurring that we can now see more clearly the higher values and their objective hierarchy, and also see more clearly the "evil of the old Self." The fact that love and repentance are dynamic activities is an important insight. The mystery of how a change of heart is possible seems most perplexing when we face a dramatic conversion, a seemingly instantaneous change from night to day, but the movement of repentance, the movement of love, need not in its beginnings be such an overwhelmingly obvious and overpowering experience. It is a movement that can, to use Scheler's spatial metaphor, start with a single, small, halting step up the mountain. Yet because it is a movement that initiates new vision and new freedom from the limitations of one's old self, it can result in a dramatic contrast:

> The more Repentance ceases to be mere repentance of conduct and becomes repentance of Being, the more it grasps the *root* of guilt perceived, to pluck it out of the Person and restore the latter's freedom, and the more also it makes the transition from shame over a particular deed to that completeness of "hearty contrition" out of which an indwelling force of regeneration builds up a "new heart" and a "new man." To that extent, then, Repentance even assumes the character of a true *repentance of conversion* and leads finally from good resolutions through a deeper alteration of outlook to *transformation* of outlook—that is, to a positive "rebirth"—wherein, without detriment to its formal and individual identity, the spiritual core of the Person, which is the ultimate root of our moral acts, appears to burn away all remnant of the objects of its former regard and to build itself anew. (RW 42/RR 48)

Although all of this helps to illuminate the nature of the change of heart and the achievement of a new *ordo amoris,* it does not yet answer our core question: What initiates the *first* step up the mountain? What *begins* the change of heart? Scheler's answer to this question at the end of this essay, in the midst of his connecting repentance to contrition, is that the initial impetus comes from outside of us, specifically from God. It is "God's love, constantly knocking at the door of the soul" (RW 58/RR 65), that initiates change.

Whether or not we accept Scheler's Christianity (and he himself went on to reject theism), I believe his basic insight here is sound, if incomplete. In my judgment it *is* the love of another "constantly knocking at the door" that is the initial impetus to our opening ourselves to a change of heart. One warning, though. The term "knocking" might lead one to think that what is needed is a direct personal love immediately present and directed toward us. This is, of course, the most pressing invitation. The fact that others love us, even if we reject their love, thrusting them away in a moment of hurt and pride, can still work upon us and bring us to an opening later. But love need not be aimed directly at us. For example, the fact that others so clearly loved a work of art I did not has, at times, led me to seek what I was missing and in so seeking to begin the process of opening myself to new realms of aesthetic values. Thus even if one does not accept the existence and efficacy of an infinite, personal God, finite persons can open our hearts to new moral levels.

Thus I agree with Scheler that others, both humans and God, play an indispensable part of the initiation of a change of heart. Yet love by another is only half of the story. *We* must still open ourselves to such love. Although such an act of "opening" is at such a basic level that it is unlike the choice between two specific courses of action, it is a form of free "choice" nonetheless, and like all free choice we cannot specify ahead of time all the conditions that will bring it about. The mystery of what initiates a change of heart is, I believe, part of the mystery of the core freedom at the heart of the human person. Scheler does not try to penetrate this mystery, nor could he do so if he tried. We can seek, as Scheler does, to understand the nature and functioning of the *ordo amoris,* of the heart, and the conditions that make a change of heart possible, but we cannot specify the causal conditions for a change of heart. Ultimately, a change of heart is a fundamentally free and deeply personal choice, a choice made possible by the love of others but one that is still a mystery we must live through, not a problem we can solve.

Despite this, it is clear that Scheler's position does allow for genuine moral change and that the problem presented in the *Formalism*—the problem of the tragic limitations of finite persons—is not as refractory as it seemed. There are, of course, many other problems that must be overcome before we will have a practical ethics based on Scheler's approach, but this "limitation" is not an insuperable problem.

Husserl, Scheler, and Intersubjectivity

Scheler's insights into how we can undergo this kind of change of heart again points to the importance of *other* persons. This raises another classic area of concern that Scheler explored in a most creative way—the problem of how we have access to other persons. Yet Scheler's work on the problem of intersubjectivity has been criticized, this time by Husserlian phenomenologists.

Husserl was primarily concerned with showing the foundations of certain knowledge, and his investigations led him ultimately to the espousal of a "transcendental subjectivity." Now both the exact meaning and the import of Husserl's "transcendental subjectivity" are the subject of great interest and great dispute among Husserl's interpreters, but at least some of his followers have criticized Scheler for not providing a "transcendental subjective" grounding for his insights. Indeed, Blosser lists this as one of the reasons for the neglect of Scheler's thought, indicating in his "Historical Introduction" that

> the question of whether Scheler's value theory possesses a sufficient philosophical foundation is also raised . . . by transcendental phenomenology. Like Husserl after his transcendental turn, some of his disciples—especially, perhaps, those of the Mainz school, such as Gerhard Funke and Thomas Seebohm, although others such as J. N. Mohanty also come to mind—have suggested that phenomenology ultimately requires a critical grounding in transcendental

> subjectivity in a sense at least analogous to Kant's. From this perspective too, then, Scheler's critique of Kant is regarded as suffering a critical defect: the lack of a sufficient transcendental ground. (1995, 16)

As Blosser points out, Scheler's phenomenology is also "transcendental" where that term simply points to the fact that the phenomenological given is not empirically contingent. Yet the issue here is not this type of transcendentalism, but rather the idea that all we know is rooted in a "transcendental ego." Scheler rejects such a transcendental ego, and so his approach is, all too often, rejected by Husserlians without sufficient appreciation of what he accomplished.

The General Problem of Intersubjectivity

Intersubjectivity is a thorny subject. It *is* difficult to see how we can know that there are other persons. If, following a standard understanding of Husserl, you believe that the roots of all knowledge are to be found in a subjectivity, a "transcendental ego" that is the only thing left after a final, radical bracketing (epoche), the road back to knowledge of another subjectivity is especially long and difficult.

As we will develop below, Scheler's approach does not face this difficulty, but followers of Husserl such as Alfred Schutz have rejected Scheler's approach. I will focus on Schutz because he is a respected interpreter of Husserl's work in this area, and he thought Scheler's work on intersubjectivity important enough to devote an entire essay to a study of "Scheler's Theory of Intersubjectivity and the General Thesis of the Alter Ego."[4]

Scheler's Phenomenology of Intersubjectivity

I will begin with a brief exposition of some of the relevant features of Scheler's work on intersubjectivity. Scheler took seriously

[4] Alfred Schutz, "Scheler's Theory of Intersubjectivity and the General Thesis of the Alter Ego," *Philosophy and Phenomenological Research* 2 (1942): 323–47.

the question of what he called, in *The Nature of Sympathy,* "the *grounds of the nature, existence and knowledge of the ties of connection between the spirits and souls of men*" (emphasis Scheler's) (GW7 209/ NS 213). In a key essay on the subject, the third section of this study, he attacked the metaphysical and naturalistic attempts to understand intersubjectivity. While dealing with the specific problems of "the perception of other minds," Scheler singled out two theories for special attention: first, the "analogical argument," according to which we infer the presence of other minds on the basis of analogies; and second, the "empathy theory," which is based upon "a process of empathic projection of the self into the physical manifestations evinced by the other" (GW7 232/NS 238). He quickly raised serious questions for both theories. Even simple empirical investigations of animals and young children show behavior that the analogy approach cannot handle. Furthermore, if the analogy theory were correct, the best it could show would *not* be that there is an alien subjectivity before me but rather that *my* subjectivity is also "over there" (GW7 232–35/ NS 238–41). The empathy approach is even worse off, for as Scheler says, "all that the theory seeks to establish is a 'blind' belief, not a self-evident intuition or even a rational postulate" (GW 7 235/NS 241).

Scheler does not simply raise such conventional objections to these theories. He also goes on to examine if there are any phenomenological grounds for what he thinks are the assumptions of such theories. The first such assumption is the idea that "it is always *our own self, merely, that is primarily given to us*" (GW7 238/ NS 244). Scheler allows that such an assumption is quite plausible as long as we stay within the bounds of a "realistic" positing of a substratum of experience such that two substrata cannot enter into one another. But if, as Scheler puts it, we "stick to pure phenomenology," the self-evidence vanishes. Scheler points out that

---

This essay is reprinted in Alfred Schutz, *Collected Papers,* vol. 1, *The Problem of Social Reality* (The Hague: Martinus Nijhoff, 1973), 150–79. Beyond my narrow focus on Schutz, there is a more general comparison relevant to my study: Manfred S. Frings, "Husserl and Scheler: Two Views on Intersubjectivity," *JBSP: The Journal of the British Society for Phenomenology* 9, no. 3 (1978): 143–49.

> nothing is more certain than that we can think the thoughts of others as well as our own, and can feel their feelings (in sympathy) as we do our own. Are we not for ever distinguishing "our own" thoughts from those we have read or which have been told to us? "Our own" feelings from those we merely reproduce, or by which we have been infected (unconsciously, as we later realize)? "Our own" will from that which we merely obey and which is plainly manifest to us at the time as the will of another, just as we distinguish our own true will from that which we are deceived into thinking our own, though it has been suggested to us by someone else, in hypnosis, for instance? Even in these very trivial examples we find a string of "possible" cases of what is supposed, on present assumptions, to be "self-evidently" impossible. (GW7 239/NS 245)

Scheler then points to another possibility: "There is also the case in which an experience is simply given, *without presenting itself either as our own or as another's,* as invariably happens, for example, where we are in doubt as to which of the two it is" (GW7 240/ NS 246).

He sums up his rejection of the two metaphysical theories as follows:

> It is not the case therefore, as these theories suppose, that we have to build up a picture of other people's experiences from the immediately given data furnished by our own, and then to impute these experiences, which have no intrinsic marks of "foreignness" about them, to the physical semblances of other people. What occurs, rather, is an immediate flow of experiences, *undifferentiated as between mine and thine,* which actually contains both our own and others' experiences intermingled and without distinction from one another. Within this flow there is a gradual formation of ever more stable vortices, which slowly attract further elements of the stream into their orbits and thereby become successively and very gradually identified with distinct individuals. (GW7 240/NS 246)

For Scheler we do not start out as sole distinct individuals. Rather, it is by "*the same act of discernment within an as yet undifferentiated whole* that we come to a clear realization *both of what is ours and of what belongs to others*" (GW7 244/NS 250).

Furthermore, even before we are aware of specific others, we are given the "sphere of the Thou." Prior to Scheler's discussion of the problem of "The Perception of Other Minds" in *The Nature of Sympathy,* he has a chapter on "The General Evidence for the Thou." In it he points back to the question he posed earlier (in the *Formalism* [GW2 511/F 521]) to a supposed "epistemological" Robinson Crusoe. The question (to this man who had never had experience of any other human person or trace of him) is whether such a Crusoe could "know anything of the existence of a community or of conscious subjects resembling himself; and whether he could further be aware of 'belonging' to such a community" (GW7 229/NS 234). Scheler's answer is yes, and moreover:

> According to my *Formalismus,* Crusoe's evidence of the existence of a Thou in general and of his own membership of the community is not merely a contingent, observational, inductive "experience," but is certainly *a priori* in both an objective and a subjective sense and has a definite *intuitive basis,* namely a specific and well-defined consciousness of *emptiness* or absence (as compared with the presence of some genuine entity already there), in respect of emotional acts as represented, for instance, by the authentic types of love for other people.[5]

For Scheler there are, as he puts it in the *Formalism,* certain acts where it is "by virtue of their intentional *essence,* and not on the basis of their contingent *objects* or what they empirically have in common, that these acts are factual acts, that is, *social* acts, acts that find their fulfillment only in a possible community" (GW2 511/F 521). Human persons are as essentially social beings as they are individual beings.

By appealing to our immediate experience of other persons, Scheler opened many new insights into the problem of intersubjectivity. I must apologize for not being able to develop them

[5] Scheler continues: "In the case of conative acts one might also refer to the consciousness of 'something lacking' or of 'non-fulfillment' which would invariably and necessarily be felt by our Crusoe when engaged in intellectual or emotional acts which can only constitute an objective unity of meaning *in conjunction with* the possibility of a social *response.* From these necessarily specific and unmistakable blanks, as it were, where his intentional actions miss their mark, he would, in our opinion, derive a most positive intuition and idea of something *present to him as the sphere of the Thou, of which he is merely unacquainted with any particular instance*" (GW7 229–30/NS 235).

here, but I trust that what I have presented will be sufficient to suggest that what Scheler presents us with is worth developing. One might expect his insights to have sparked much interest, but this did not happen.[6] I believe that at least one element in the neglect of Scheler may have come about because of the tendency among classic phenomenologists to view his work in the light of a conventional understanding of Husserl's transcendental phenomenology. We see this clearly in Schutz's reaction to Scheler's work.

The Transcendental Ego and Intersubjectivity

Before I turn to Schutz's specific criticism of Scheler, however, it is important to see why Schutz's understanding of Husserl's transcendental phenomenology became such a roadblock to his understanding of Scheler. To show this I must first sketch the conventional understanding of what Husserl meant by the term "transcendental ego." First of all, Husserl believed that the epoche, which frees us from the naive realism of the natural standpoint and allows us to attend to essences and their modes of givenness in our consciousness, frees the "ego" as well. After the epoche I am no longer experiencing as a mundane ego, but rather as a transcendental ego. Of this transcendental ego Schutz says:

> It is no longer a mind belonging to a body that exists in an objective spatiotemporal Nature being interested in the world, but exclusively the self-identical subject of all its cogitations, their identical focus. That means: All the "intentional objects" of its cogitations are objects only for the ego and by the ego; they are intentional objects for the stream of its cognitive life or, to use Husserl's technical term, they are constituted by its synthetic activities.[7]

---

[6] I am pleased to note that the neglect of Scheler's work in this area is being corrected. See, for example, the creative work of John Crosby already noted (1999) and Rainier R. A. Ibana's "The Stratification of Emotional Life and the Problem of Other Minds According to Max Scheler" (1991).

[7] Alfred Schutz, "William James's Concept of the Stream of Thought Phenomenologically Interpreted," *Philosophy and Phenomenological Research* 1 (June 1941). Reprinted in Alfred Schutz, *Collected Papers,* vol. 3, *Studies in Phenomenological Philosophy* (The Hague: Martinus Nijhoff, 1975), 8.

Such a conception of a transcendental ego does not, in and of itself, make of intersubjectivity an insuperable problem (if we leave aside, for the moment, the issue of "constitution"). It can be taken to be simply a rather dramatic way of indicating that we are, after the reduction, no longer simply in the realm of contingent being, but rather are, already, in an "objective" realm: that, for example, when you and I both grasp the essence of a mathematical equation we as acting subjects are no more "mundane" than the "objective" essences we grasp. But, as Schutz points out concerning Husserl:

> Having performed the transcendental reduction and analyzed the constitutional problems of the consciousness built up by the activities of the transcendental subjectivity, he singles out within the transcendental field what he calls "my own peculiar sphere" by eliminating all the constitutive activities which are immediately or mediately related to the subjectivity of Others. This is done by abstracting from all the "meanings" referring to Others and consequently by withdrawing from surrounding Nature its character of intersubjectivity. Nature is then no longer common to us all. What remains is strictly my private world in the most radical sense. (1973, 165–66)

The problem created by *this* "transcendental reduction" is how to account for the constituting of another ego within "my private world." If you believe that you must perform a reduction that leaves you with nothing but your own ego (your own private stream of consciousness), this is, indeed, a serious problem, and one that Husserl never answered either to his or, for that matter, to Schutz's satisfaction. It is in the light of this problem that Schutz views Scheler's comments on intersubjectivity, as we will now detail.

Schutz's Criticism of Scheler's Phenomenology of Intersubjectivity

As noted above, Schutz took Scheler's work on intersubjectivity seriously enough to devote an entire article to it. The article begins with a relatively detailed presentation of Scheler's ideas, followed by a series of "Critical Observations." Schutz's initial criticism is that Scheler does not provide a "solution of the transcendental constitutional problems." He labels Scheler's position a metaphysical hypothesis, groups it with the metaphysical ideas of Hegel, Bergson, and others, and states that "for the problem of transcendental phenomenology as a science founded on accurate analysis of the transcendental field Scheler's hypothesis does not offer the desired solution" (1973, 165). He also dismisses Scheler's attempts to present evidence for a sphere of the "We" as pregiven to the sphere of the "I" with the following statement: "He supports this theory not by analyses within the transcendental sphere, but by references to empirical facts taken from the psychology of children and primitives" (1973, 165).

The Defense of Scheler's Phenomenology of Intersubjectivity

In the first place, it is not true that Scheler supports his position simply by appeal to "empirical facts." Although Scheler, along with a good number of other phenomenologists, did not follow Husserl in his "transcendental reduction" (and so Scheler's approach does not have the "transcendental problem" sketched above), Scheler *was* a phenomenologist, and it is to phenomenological "givens" that he appeals in providing support for his position. As indicated above, in his development of "The General Evidence for the Thou" Scheler appeals to a definite intuitional basis, a "specific and well-defined consciousness of *emptiness* or absence" (GW7 229–30/NS 235). Indeed, in his discussions of the evidence for the "sphere of the Thou" he does not even mention empirical studies.

It is only when he moves to the problem of the "Perception of Other Minds" that we see Scheler introduce empirical studies, and even then he does not use them as primary evidence. Let me develop this a little. Scheler first points to empirical studies of children and primitives in the section where he is raising questions about the metaphysical theories of analogy and empathy (GW7 233 ff./NS 239 ff.). He does this to show that even conventional empirical studies raise serious questions about such theories: he is meeting such theories initially on their own ground and showing that even there they are highly questionable. But immediately after this he raises the question of whether or not the presuppositions of such theories have phenomenological grounding, and in denying this he points to the phenomenological grounds of our ability to think the thoughts of others (GW7 239/NS 245). Thereafter he does again refer to empirical studies of children and primitive peoples, but he does it not as primary evidence of the givenness of others' thoughts, but rather to illustrate his observation that there is a general tendency among human beings to err more on the side of entertaining the experiences of other people as if they were our own, rather than the tendency toward empathetic imputation of our own experiences to others. Thus, Scheler does not use empirical evidence as a basis for believing either in the sphere of the Thou or that we can and do perceive other minds.

The Possibility of Truly Shared Thoughts

Schutz's criticism is not restricted to a general complaint that Scheler does not help to solve the "transcendental problem," however. He goes on to claim that Scheler does not distinguish between "the naive attitude of living in the acts and thoughts whose objects the others are and the attitude of reflection upon those acts and thoughts" (1973, 170). He objects to Scheler's idea that there are thoughts given without these thoughts being given either as ours or as others': "There is no such thing as an experience 'given' to me that would not indicate which individual stream of consciousness it belongs to. As soon as I turn to the stream of experiences, and this means as soon as I adopt the reflective attitude, this stream is through and through the stream of *my* experiences" (1973, 170). Schutz seems to think we are either in a naive, unreflective stance ecstatically caught up in the world or in a reflection that limits us to ourselves and our own experience.

It is this dichotomy to which I object. Scheler had to undergo a reflective epoche suspending the ordinary assumptions about a realistic substratum to see that there were givens which did not carry "place tags" with them, that we can and do have givens which are not presented either as my own or another's. Now, Scheler does point to this as happening when we are not sure whose thought it is, but it is not simply in confusion that we can note this phenomenon. I have, on occasion, been fortunate enough to enter into a true dialogue in which it made no sense at all to ascribe the ideas discovered to myself or to the other. Indeed, upon reflection, what is most obvious about such dialogue is that what occurs, occurs *between* myself and another. It is a co-acting, a co-discovery, a co-thinking—a *thinking together.* The important point here is that this phenomenon of dialogue is accessible to reflective examination, even reflective phenomenological examination in which I suspend all theses and attend only to what is given. Indeed, the co-ness is one of the things given, despite all my theoretical anticipations that what can be given is only my own stream of experience. At the same time, I am not simply ecstatically caught up in the dialogue but reflecting upon the dialogue, and it is in reflection that its essential structure is revealed.[8] (This is in distinction, for example, from a "crossed monologue," where my thoughts are, indeed, *mine,* and where the other serves only as an occasion for my display of *my* thoughts.)

Now, I suspect that those who are committed to the "transcendental reduction" will accuse me here of still being in a naive stance, for I have not yet undergone the reduction to the sphere of myself and what is in *my* consciousness. Yet if Scheler is correct, that very transcendental reduction may well be based upon a naive and undetected idealistic "realism," a thesis as concealing of some givens as the naive "realism" which Husserl's initial epoche put out of action. Reductions do not always serve to reveal, and a phenomenological reduction *must* always serve to bring things to givenness, not to make us ignore givens in the name of theory.

---

[8] Those familiar with the work of Martin Buber might be disturbed by my assertion that the essential structure of dialogue is revealed in reflection. Buber and others believe that what is given in reflection is thereby objectified. Scheler does not believe this is so. Indeed, for Scheler, we can have access to persons and acts only in non-objectifying acts of reflection, since persons and acts can never be objects, as developed in chapter 5. It is my own belief that Buber's own work on dialogue is itself an excellent example of a non-objectifying phenomenological description, but it is beyond the scope of this study to explore this issue.

Thus I am not so sure who is being naive here, for there are different kinds of naïveté on different levels of awareness.

Until further phenomenological investigations settle the issue of whether or not all must be grounded in a transcendental ego, Scheler's phenomenological approach is as valid an approach as Husserl's. Given my belief in the core of the classic phenomenological approach—what Husserl had called the "principle of all principles," the belief that we can have direct access to the given—once again I call for the further development of the classic phenomenological approach and more detailed phenomenological investigation, from a variety of approaches, in this as in all other areas.

The Question of Whether Persons or Values Are More Important

Scheler's work on illuminating the nature of persons and his creative defense of intersubjectivity do not preclude questions about whether he has, indeed, placed persons as the highest value. Michael Barber's recent book *Guardian of Dialogue: Max Scheler's Phenomenology, Sociology of Knowledge, and Philosophy of Love* presents a creative and sensitive reading of Scheler's work, but Barber also raises in a telling way the question of whether Scheler's material values can dominate the person. After comparing Scheler and Levinas, Barber raises the issue nicely as he says:

> Does the a priori value ranking ultimately subject the Other to the absolutes of Scheler's categorical system? Scheler's separation of the personal value-bearers from the material values makes it possible that those who serve merely as bearers of values could be sacrificed for the values they bear.
>
> His earlier example of human sacrifice should be considered. The sacrifice of virgins and the most beautiful youth actually fulfills Scheler's value ranking since life values, by no means absolute, are inferior to the values of the spiritual and holy. Other than two references to the superstitious underpinnings of this belief in human sacrifices—a form of religious, but not ethical, criticism—Scheler pronounces *no ethical judgment against such human sacrifice!* In addition to the rather strange dualism, criticized by others, that one can

> take someone's life and yet be elevating and affirming their Person, Scheler seems to contradict himself in the following way. Scheler develops a painstaking interpretation of Other, past cultures out of a sense of moral solidarity with them, to offset Wundt's uncomprehending charge that they have felt murder to be praiseworthy. But if Scheler shows such sensitivity to another culture to prevent it from falling prey to demeaning modern categorizations, how can he allow the taking of human lives, even for the best of motives, without a word of ethical protest? Scheler overlooks this inconsistency because his focus on the material ranking of values distracts his attention from what is happening to the bearers of those values. There is a danger that as long as one observes the material value ranking, one can incur no ethical blame, no matter what happens to the bearers of those values, whether they be persons or things. (1993, 162)

Two questions are raised here. The most specific one is why Scheler seems to not condemn human sacrifice, while the more general one is whether he really has placed the person as primary over values. I will deal with the more specific question first.

Scheler and Human Sacrifice

As the italics in the last quote indicates, Barber is troubled by the fact that Scheler does not explicitly condemn human sacrifice, though Barber does recognize that the passages in which Scheler discusses human sacrifice occur in the context of Scheler's attempt to show the meaning of human sacrifice to those who practiced it and to correct what he takes to be a serious insensitivity in William Wundt. Scheler undertakes this task because he believes that his insights into the *ordo amoris* allow us to better understand ethical relativity.

Let me begin by reminding the reader that for Scheler, people, both individually and collectively, have limited and often distorted views of the true ranking of values. Given the different ethos of different cultures, the same act may appear quite differently, and we can understand this only by being able to see from the viewpoint of the different cultural *ordo amoris*. In this case, Scheler was trying to show how human sacrifice did not appear as murder to those who practiced it. The difficulty of any such attempt is, of course, showing such an understanding without at the same time falling into a moral relativity that fails to condemn what is to us a moral outrage. After all, for Scheler there is an absolute ordering of values, and despite our limitations of seeing it there are some basic insights that ought to be accessible to all. Thus, falling into the trap of not condemning what clearly ought to be condemned does seem to suggest a serious weakness in Scheler's approach.

Despite his sympathy for Scheler's insights, Barber clearly believes that Scheler fails to avoid this pitfall. I do not. In the first place, I do not think that Scheler's comments concerning "superstition" ought to be taken simply as a religious criticism. To quote Scheler in a key passage:

> Perhaps Wundt was thinking of the institution of sacrificing humans to gods, i.e., to beings considered absolutely holy. Was such an institution a legitimation of "murder"? Certainly not! It rested on diverse superstitions, e.g., that by sacrificing humans, one could do service to *both* the gods and the sacrificed humans or fulfill the just demands of the gods. In the first place it was the most handsome and noble youths and virgins, as well as the most beloved, who were chosen to be sacrificed. The intention was hardly to annihilate the being of the *person* concerned, or the "let it be annihilated," which belongs essentially to murder. There was rather the contention, implicit in the intention of love and favor, of the *affirmation* of the being of the person. How else could there be a genuine *sacrifice*? (GW2 316/F 312)

Now although Scheler is here attempting to get us to see why human sacrifice was not murder to those who practiced it, his comments about the practice's basis in superstition have a moral as well as religious dimension. Clearly, Scheler's labeling the reasons for the practice "superstitions" indicates that he does not believe such sacrifice does justice either to the gods or to the person being sacrificed.

Despite this indirect evidence that Scheler does disapprove of human sacrifice, it is true that he does not make the strong, explicit condemnation we would expect almost anyone to make. Why not? It must be conceded that Scheler's presentation here, as in so many places, is more truncated and one-sided than it ought to be. Scheler ought to have explicitly stated an "obviously, they fail to do moral justice to the persons being sacrificed," at the very least. As in so many other contexts, his lack of full and balanced presentation breeds misunderstanding.

There is, however, a more basic issue here. Simply condemning a practice does not help us to see why any person could have approved of what is now seen to be so obviously and horribly wrong. Scheler's insights into the functioning of the *ordo amoris* allow us to understand how this occurs. Since the *ordo amoris* of a culture is transformed when love has opened a whole group to new realms of values, the ethos of that culture is transformed as well. The transformed group, just like a transformed person, can then condemn something as horribly wrong and yet understand how a person or a culture might approve of it. In a passage in this section of the *Formalism,* Scheler says:

> In such a variation the rules of preferring among old and new values become altered by themselves. Although the rules of preferring among the old values and their mutual objectivity are not necessarily affected, the old realm of values as a whole is nevertheless relativized. It is now a matter of blindness or deception to prefer the old values to the new, and it is practically "evil" to live according to the old values as the highest ones. The virtues of the old ethos now become "glittering vices." . . . The rules of preferring that belong to an old ethos are not abolished as a new ethos "grows." Only a relativizing of the whole of the old ethos occurs. (GW2 309/F 305)

Now I must admit that in the case of human sacrifice I am grateful that my culture's ethos has moved so far beyond the *ordo amoris* which made human sacrifice possible that our condemnation of it is now so universal that we find it hard to imagine anyone who would approve of such a barbaric act. Yet the process of the moral development of human being is not completed. I have myself lived long enough to see slavery go from a practice still defended by "arguments" to a practice (although sadly still in existence) almost totally condemned by all. Yet because of my awareness of the ongoing nature of moral development, I am also painfully aware of the likelihood that some actions I (or my culture) now find morally acceptable will be looked upon by future generations with the same sense of moral horror we now feel toward human sacrifice. My world's continuing acceptance of warfare comes to mind. It is for this reason that I believe the attempt to understand those still trapped in a more limiting *ordo amoris* is necessary if we are to avoid moral arrogance. Yet such understanding does not imply any approval of what our (relatively) expanded view of the true ranking of values allows us to see as barbaric.

The Primacy of the Person over Values

To show that Scheler does, indeed, condemn human sacrifice does not yet address the more general issue raised by Barber. Are the material values realized more important than the bearers of these values? In Scheler's approach, are persons subordinate to values? I believe there is convincing evidence that the answer to this question is no, but it is not as clear as it might be. Barber suggests that Scheler would have been better off separating his "ethics from his value theory, and to anchor this (intuitive) ethics in the person" (1993, 163–64).

As my present study shows, I believe Scheler was doing just that as he developed his ethical personalism. Furthermore, although one must go beyond the *Formalism* to see this (as Barber suggests [1993, 164]), the primacy of persons over values is apparent even in the *Formalism*. Scheler, for example, begins the section entitled "The Law of the Origin of the Prevailing Ethos—Model Persons": "An ethics which, like the one developed here, locates the highest and ultimate moral meaning of the world in the possible being of (individual and collective) persons of the highest positive value . . ." (GW2 558/F 572). Notice that Scheler does not say "locates the highest value in the person" (which might suggest that values were more basic than persons), but rather "locates the highest and ultimate moral meaning." More importantly, it is the person we must ultimately turn to for moral direction, not a rigid mechanical "table of values." Scheler is truly seeking an ethical personalism, not an ethics of values mechanically imposed on persons.

Yet showing Scheler's intent is not the same as showing that his position can be defended against attack. Is there anything in his understanding of values which would show that persons are not to be ultimately subordinated to an objective ordering of values? After all, even in the quote just presented, Scheler does refer to the "highest positive value." Again we seem to see the possibility that persons ought to be sacrificed (perhaps literally!) to high values.

I believe there are two elements in Scheler's understanding of values that preclude the sacrifice (literally or figuratively) of persons to values. In the first place, the nonformal values are not all alike. From a moral point of view, the most important values that persons bear are the moral values, and as developed above, Scheler makes a basic distinction between the moral values and all nonmoral values. Moral values are realized along with the realization of higher, positive, nonmoral values. Thus to suggest that one might in any way sacrifice the person to realize a high, positive, nonmoral value makes no sense, since it would undercut the realization of moral value by destroying its bearer.

Barber saw a danger: "As long as one observes the material value ranking, one can incur no ethical blame, no matter what happens to the bearers of those values, whether they be persons or things" (1993, 162). Yet this is not possible in the case of persons. To forget that persons, as bearers of moral values, have a primacy over all other considerations is to forget the special place of both the moral values and the persons who bear them.

Second, the fact that Scheler points to a hierarchy of bearers as well as a hierarchy of value ranks again underscores the primacy of the person. It does so not because the person cannot bear the same nonmoral values as things,[9] but simply because persons are not things. Persons have a primacy, both in and of themselves and as bearers of moral values.

The Challenge to the Primacy of the Heart

I have, in this chapter, defended the primacy of the person in Scheler's ethical personalism because I believe that Scheler's in-

[9] As Barber points out (1993, 163), Hurlimann considered and rejected this difference as a way to solve this problem.

sights into the nature of the person are central to all he accomplished. Yet the problems created by the primacy Scheler gave the person are not the only basic challenges to be met. Equally serious criticisms have been lodged against Scheler's giving primacy to the heart in the knowing of values. I will turn to a defense of the primacy of the heart in value-ception in the next chapter.

11

Defending the Central Role of the Heart in Value-Ception

Introduction

This chapter defends Scheler's claim that it is the heart and not the head that gives us values. I return to this issue because Kant's is not the only rationalist position in ethics that challenges Scheler's claim. Even some phenomenologists sensitive to the role of feeling in the seeing of values and appreciative of Scheler's contributions to the phenomenology of values ultimately give reason and not feeling the last word. As examples of such positions I will explore claims by Stephen Strasser and Karol Wojtyla that reason must complete, and sometimes correct, what the heart gives us. For Strasser, feelings may well give us initial access to values, but reason ultimately gives us moral direction. Wojtyla echoes Strasser's concern with the primacy of the heart with cogent questions on how feelings can give us true moral direction, especially in the light of the fact that we often choose against values felt and in the name of values not felt.

Finally, I demonstrate the power of Scheler's insights into the role of the heart in value-ception by using his insights into the *ordo amoris* to meet criticism of Scheler by Dietrich Von Hildebrand. I do so because Von Hildebrand claims that Scheler ignored a distinction key both to the understanding of values and to seeing why people sometimes choose "lower" values, a classic question for an ethics. Von Hildebrand's distinction is between the "subjectively satisfying" and the "intrinsically important," and as I will show, Scheler's understanding of the *ordo amoris,*

Sections of this chapter appeared in my essay "The Primacy of the Heart: Scheler's Challenge to Phenomenology," *Philosophy Today* 29, no. 3 (1985): 223–29, and are reproduced here with permission.

rather than missing this distinction, makes the distinction understandable.

The Primacy of the Heart in Value-Ception

The success of Scheler's ethics depends not only on our ability to show both how it is possible that we can grow morally through finite persons acting as models or exemplars and how it is possible to undergo a change of heart. We must also have adequate access to the hierarchy of values, and Scheler claimed that it is through special acts of feeling, and the heart (the *ordo amoris*), that we have access to values and their hierarchical ranks. These are among the most basic and startling claims made by Scheler, central to his entire enterprise both because of our need to have access to noncontingent, nonformal values and because they are central to his claims about the nature of the person as more than a rational being. It is Scheler's view of the human person as *ens amans* that allows him to regain not only noncontingent, nonformal values but the full richness of the person.

In order to understand the nature of the disagreements some thinkers have with Scheler, it is best to remind ourselves just how startling Scheler's claim is. To do so, let us return again to his own words. As we showed in chapter 4, while defending Pascal's defense of the heart, Scheler asserted that

> there is a type of experiencing whose "objects" are completely inaccessible to reason; reason is as blind to them as ears and hearing are blind to colors. It is a kind of experience that leads us to *genuinely* objective objects and the eternal order among them, i.e., to *values* and the order of ranks among them. And the order and laws contained in this experience are as exact and evident as those of logic and mathematics; that is, there are evident interconnections and oppositions among values and value-attitudes and among the acts of preferring, etc., which are built on them, and on the basis of these a genuine grounding of moral decisions and laws for such decisions is both possible and necessary. (GW2 260/F 255)

As we noted in chapter 4, Scheler's claim is twofold. First, it is *only* through affective intentional acts that we have access to objective values and their hierarchy. Second, such access is not simply a vague, nascent forerunner that must be subsequently clarified by reason. What "feeling" gives us is in itself the basis for moral decision.

Both elements of Scheler's claim have been disputed by phenomenologists appreciative of his contributions. Although the intentional function of feelings is sometimes accepted, and feelings are acknowledged as having a seminal role in our access to values, what is not accepted is the claim that feeling alone gives us access to values, or that what feeling gives us is an adequate basis for moral decision. Instead, it is claimed that feeling must, in some way, be aided by reason. Two phenomenologists in particular have made claims that challenge Scheler's defense of the autonomy and adequacy of feeling in moral matters. Let us now turn to the claims of Stephen Strasser and Karol Wojtyla.

Strasser's Criticism of the Primacy of Feeling

Stephen Strasser, in the *Phenomenology of Feeling* (*Das Gemut*), most certainly pays tribute to the role of feeling and the heart in our access to values. Yet he does not afford feeling, and what it gives us, "ultimacy" (to use Scheler's term) (GW2 267/F 262). For Strasser, "at every moment, even of my mature existence, I am engaged in development—from Bios through Pathos to Logos" (1977, 172). Basically, Strasser rejects the autonomy of what is given in feeling, saying in *his* discussion of Pascal that

> it is indeed not a matter of knowledge being registered in the manner of double-entry book-keeping: once under "heart" and another time under "head." Rational and non-rational moments in no way stand in a relation of irreconcilable opposition; that which distinguishes them does not divide them. . . . Just the opposite: knowledge that is of full value normally occurs through bringing together rational and non-rational moments into a unified world-picture. (1977, 133–34)

Finally, for Strasser it is the rational that is of the highest moment, as we see when he sums up his development of the relationship between the "rational elements" and the "still-not-rational global impression": "In short, rational knowing grows out of the non-rational as its highest necessary totalization, spiritual illumination and completion" (1977, 143).

The True Relationship of the Two Logics

In the first place, Scheler does *not* claim that the logic of the heart *contradicts* the logic of reason. His claim is rather that they are different—that reason is blind to what we are given by the heart. Such difference need not be contradictory. We cannot, for example, reason someone into accepting one rank of values as higher than another, yet such an insight does not contradict the "logic of reason." There is nothing irrational about placing one value or rank of values above another, yet I know of no rational evidence that can be presented for such ranking which carries the kind of evidential force we see presented in the complex feelings Scheler points to as our way to values and their ranks. Thus I believe Strasser's attack upon some readings of Pascal that do claim contradictoriness does not hold against Scheler. Furthermore, Strasser's point that each mode (feeling and reason) can "complement" the other (1977, 134) is not evidence that all that we are given is accessible to both. Indeed, the fact that there is a "complementing" would rather indicate autonomous areas for each.

Wojtyla's Criticism: Feeling and Choice

Karol Wojtyla, in *The Acting Person* (*Osoba I czyn*), raises another problem with feeling as a basis for moral decisions. For Wojtyla, "emotional dynamism introduces a spontaneous turn toward certain values" (1979, 251). Furthermore, such a turn is rooted in nature, since "emotions follow the orientation of nature, which, as we already noted, is expressed by instincts" (251). Thus Wojtyla believes that "the intellect has precedence over emotion, over the emotive spontaneity of the human being, and denotes the power and the ability to be guided in choice and decision by the truth itself about good" (249).

Wojtyla's position rests on the idea that if what we receive through feeling is given in purely passive "spontaneity," then something else must be involved in choosing between values so given, or there could be no true choice. And that something else is reason. As Wojtyla puts it: "The man who in his attitude to values would rely solely on the way his feelings develop is confined to the orbit of what only happens in him and becomes incapable of self-determination" (1979, 233). This is clearly not what happens. As Wojtyla points out: "Indeed, self-determination and the closely related self-governance often require that action be taken in the name of *bare truth* about good, in the name of values that are not felt. It even may require that action be taken against one's actual feelings" (233).

If Wojtyla is correct that feeling merely "happens within us," if feeling is simply passive, then it cannot be the basis of moral decision. This is because, although Scheler and Wojtyla agree that moral choice is between deeds, not values (see GW2 105 and 265/F 87 and 260; and Wojtyla 1979, 137), for Scheler it is the values we have access to that are the basis for such choices. If we can only choose between values given in passive feelings that naturally happen in us, this would restrict the range of choice open to us arbitrarily. And clearly, as Wojtyla's examples show, we are not so trapped in our choices. Thus, Wojtyla's examples of choosing against values felt and in the name of values not felt must be accounted for *within* the affective itself if Scheler's claim for the primacy of the heart is to be sustained.

Furthermore, Wojtyla is not the only one to question whether feelings alone can give us the basis for moral decision. Philip Blosser, in *Scheler's Critique of Kant's Ethics,* while admitting that Scheler had undertaken "brilliant analyses of cases of value-deception," claims that "his theory leaves one with the infelicitous suggestion that any willing that could be called immoral or evil stems from moral deception, that desires and conations never conflict with the felt value of one's own moral disposition, that the felt value of one's personal worth may never be experienced as itself divided against itself, that people are never inclined to do what they knowingly do not wish to do" (1995, 140). Here too we see the adequacy of Scheler's vision of how we see values challenged by a claim that the feeling of values cannot account for the complexity of value conflicts we experience—that Scheler's vision of value-ception is fatally oversimplified and inadequate.

Choosing against Felt Values

To see how Scheler's position can handle these challenges, we must remind ourselves of just how complex Scheler's vision of the world of feelings is. For Scheler, there are distinct *levels* of feeling. As developed in chapter 4, there are at least four emotive levels that must be distinguished. The first is that of feeling states, such as sensible pain. Such nonintentional states are to be distinguished from acts of "feeling of," since acts of "feeling of" are the first level which is truly intentional and gives us values. Then comes the level of acts of "preference" and "placing after," which intend not values but rather the *ranks* of values, their hierarchy. Finally we have the level of acts of love and hate, not cognitive acts at all but rather spontaneous acts (as opposed to reactive; for Scheler "spontaneous" does not mean passive, as it does for Wojtyla). The acts of love and hate are creative acts in that they extend or contract the value realm accessible to a being.

It is this complexity of levels of feeling that allows us to account for the fact that we do take "action against one's actual feeling" and "in the name of values not felt" *without* having to resort to reason. Let us begin with the case where we act against our immediate feelings. The roots of such action still lie entirely within the "logic of the heart" because what we are feeling at any given moment often involves the feelings of several values at once. Therefore, we often do choose a deed to realize a value felt *against* another value felt, and depending upon the state of development of our *ordo amoris,* our loves and hates, sometimes against a lower value which, in terms of intensity of desire, may well be one that is still "felt" more intensely than the higher value we are just beginning to "prefer" as love transforms our older *ordo amoris* and we become open to new orders and ranks of values. This occurs when love is working within me to open me to new higher values but the call of the lower is still strong in my heart. As we developed in chapter 10, Scheler's work on repentance and rebirth shows that moral conversion is not always an instantaneous process.

Thus Wojtyla's example of our taking action against our feelings does not reveal a need for the mediation of reason, since a conflict of values can be an integral element in the value-ception at the root of moral choice.

Choosing Unfelt Values

There is, however, a different but related question raised by Wojtyla that must be met. How can "feeling of values" account for the fact that we sometimes act on the basis of values not felt at all? To see how this is possible we must remind ourselves of another of Scheler's insights into value-ception, his idea of the depth at which the *ordo amoris* operates. For Scheler, what I can see of the range of values depends upon my love and my hate. If I hate, what I see is limited and often distorted. Suppose, for example, that I "hate" a student and yet find that I must judge that student, say in a medal competition, or even simply on a test in a course. It is possible that I may become aware that, given my "attitude" toward this student, I cannot adequately judge the student, or even his or her work. In such a case I may ask to be removed from the judging panel or ask another colleague not so biased as I am to grade the student's paper. In such cases I do not act on my "feeling," for since love is beginning to open the eyes of my heart I sense that what I am being given in my acts of "feeling of" is narrowed and distorted.

The first thing to note here is that I do not come to see this narrowing or distortion by reason. I cannot be argued into seeing that I am so biased toward a person. I must reflectively *feel* this distortion in my intentional "feeling of" and its resulting biasing of my judgment. And what is so annoying about such cases is that even when I am able to grasp the fact that such distortion is keeping me from seeing *truly* a value (in our example, the value of a student or his or her work), it is not easy to overcome such a distortion even when I begin to sense that it is there and love is working to overcome it. Yet there are times when we must act now, and there are even times when we cannot simply ask someone to act for us. Furthermore, if someone does act "for me" I must often "endorse" their so acting. (In my example, I must "stand by" the grade my colleague suggests is fair.)

It is in such situations that we do, as Wojtyla puts it, act "in the name of values not felt"—not felt, that is, by *we* who are blind. But this does not mean that we act in the name of *totally* unfelt values. Though the true values are not felt by us, we act in trust of those who we believe feel more truly. Again, such insight and such decision does not lie in the power of reason but rather in the realm of the heart.

This is seen even more clearly if we move beyond the example of my being biased toward another single person. As Scheler's work on *ressentiment* shows, the problems revealed by such an incident can reach far beyond a single relationship. If, for example, my way of seeing things in general becomes permeated by *ressentiment,* my view of the entire hierarchy of values can become distorted or even reversed. And when I am thus seeing through the distorting glasses of *ressentiment* I cannot grasp such distortion by reason. It is only in an act of affective reflection that I can grasp it, and only a "change of heart" can correct it. Although it is true that in such cases we can sometimes "convince our head" by reasoning, nothing really changes unless our heart is moved—and the roots of such movement are quite independent of our rational skills.

Perhaps the most dramatic (and tragic) examples of the powerlessness of reason to combat this type of moral problem occurs in those cases where the distortion of moral vision is suffered not simply by an individual but rather permeates an entire group—racial prejudice being a notable example. Many people seem to believe that the roots of such prejudice rest in faulty rational judgment and that we can overcome it by showing the mistakes in reasoning (by, for example, showing that members of a given race are not, in fact, inferior). Yet such a purely rational approach fails. It fails because such prejudice *is* rooted in "feeling," often in the feeling of an entire group. Thus if it is to be overcome, it must be overcome by correcting mistakes in the "logic of the heart," not mistakes in reasoning. The problem is a disorder of the heart, not of the head.

Free Choice and the *Ordo Amoris*

There is one final challenge we must meet. If what we see of the objective values and their hierarchy depends upon our loves and hates, does such love and hate simply "happen within us"? If it does, then truly open choice and self-determination would still be lost. This is a most difficult level of experience to penetrate, but I believe the answer is no. As noted above in my discussion of repentance and rebirth, although it is not the same as choosing a deed, on a deeper level we do "choose" to open ourselves to new love and what it brings, or to close ourselves off and nurture our grudges and resentments, our hatreds. But such an "opening" is at so deep a level of our being that it is at best only an analogue to ordinary "choice," and how it occurs is a mystery we live through at the heart of our being. Thus Scheler's position does not rob us of true choice and true self-determination, for although the intentional affective acts that give us access to values and their hierarchy do involve "passive receptivity" (they are, after all, acts of "seeing," just as rational knowing is a "seeing"), they are not simply passive happenings within us, and we do choose to see or not to see.

With this I end my short defense of Scheler's claim that "feeling" gives us an autonomous intentional access to the values (and their hierarchy) that are the bases for moral decisions. I believe that Scheler's work is of great importance because although Wojtyla is correct to point out that simply "feeling" a value is not sufficient grounds for choosing that value, Scheler's pioneering description of the complex levels of the emotive sphere begins to open to us the fact that "feeling" is not *simple.*[1] It is in the light of these explorations that I believe Scheler *has* a plausible basis for his claim that values are given only in "feeling" and that reason plays *no* role in *seeing* the objective values and their hierarchy. Furthermore, what feeling gives us does not need the assistance of reason in order for us to make moral decisions.

[1] One can, of course, follow the terminological path of restricting the word "feeling" to what "happens in us," and, as Robert Solomon does, use the term "emotion" for the intentionally affective (1973, 20–41). I prefer to use the word "feeling" in its full richness, though this is more difficult to do in English than with the root word in German.

The Role of Reason in Ethical Decisions

Although I have just defended Scheler's claim for the primacy of the heart in the seeing of values against key attacks, the dispute between Scheler, Strasser, and Wojtyla highlights a serious incompleteness in Scheler's position. Scheler was so concerned to show that feeling alone gives us *access* to values that he does not give enough emphasis to the role that reason may validly play in moral decisions. I believe there may be a role for reason, and it is a role consistent with Scheler's position. I will now sketch it.

For Scheler, moral values differ from all other values in that good and evil are realized along with the realization of nonmoral values. Good is realized when higher values are realized, evil when lower values are realized. Furthermore, as noted above, for Scheler choosing is a conative act. We choose between deeds, not between values. Thus, strictly speaking, moral choice does not occur on the level of the seeing of values (though we can choose only between values we [or someone else] see). A person is good or evil not simply by "seeing" values, not even by accurately seeing the objective hierarchy of values. It is in willing[2]—in realizing the ideal values known through the intentional acts of feeling—that we co-realize moral values (GW2 47/F 25).

I believe that it is at the level of conative choice of deeds that reason may well play a valid role. Realization is an act of will, and as Scheler develops, willing is not merely wishing, it involves a sense of "being-able-to-do." Now this "being-able-to-do" is not simply a conceived judgment of thought. It is rather "phenomenally given as a special *kind* of conative consciousness" (GW2 144/F 129). But, as Scheler points out, if we experience "not-being-able-to-do" (*Ohnmacht*) we cease willing, and over time, "from the original volitional aims, 'possible' ones are only gradually *filtered,* and within this sphere of what can be done there is again a gradual filtration of what can be realized through this or that kind of acting" (GW2 141/F 126).

[2] I am here dealing with an issue developed by Scheler in the *Formalism,* and so I will not here make any changes that might be needed because of Scheler's shift in his later panentheism from reality being given to will to reality being "given" to *Drang,* since I do not believe the changes are relevant to the issue at hand.

It is here, I believe, that reason may well contribute to our moral decisions, for it provides precisely the kind of discursive, analytic, calculating thought that may well contribute to the organization and judgments of what we can, in *deed,* "be-able-to-do" (even if it is originally *given* only in conative consciousness).

Yet, in so giving to reason a role in the choice of what nonmoral values to realize, that is to say in moral choice, have I not come very close to Strasser's idea that it is Logos which completes what Pathos has begun, or Wojtyla's claim that it is the intellect which chooses? Have I not, in fact, admitted that what feeling gives us is neither complete nor adequate as the basis for moral choice?

I have not, though we can now see the sense in which Strasser and Wojtyla are correct. Moral choice does, or at least may, *involve* reason. But they are incorrect to say that reason completes what feeling starts in the sense that reason *adds* anything to what feeling provides. Rather, at the level of choosing which nonmoral values to realize, reason simply provides technical assistance. But even at this level reason is dependent not only on the values given in feeling, but also upon the sense of "being-able-to-do" given in conative consciousness. Here, too, reason does not add anything to what is given in willing. As Scheler points out, this process of filtering out what can be realized is not creative: "It is first of all *negative* and *selective* within the *span* of *original* volitional contents determined by the contents of specific *value*-qualities" (GW2 141/F 126). Thus reason does play an important role in moral choice, but it is a role secondary to feeling and willing. The primary role is that of feeling, for it is feeling that allows us to see values and their hierarchy, a seeing to which reason is blind.

One final comment. Beyond the possible valid role of reason in moral judgment I have just sketched, we are seeing a number of creative new explorations of the relationship between the head and the heart which, although they still may challenge the primacy of the heart to which Scheler points, do suggest that there is a growing sensitivity to the role of the heart. One such exploration is Andrew Tallon's *Head and Heart: Affection, Cognition, Volition as Triune Consciousness* (1997). I would again suggest that Scheler's insights are not the end of the trail but rather the beginning, and there are many possible ways the relationship between head and heart may be worked out. At the same time, however, I believe that Scheler's insight into the primacy of the heart is still basically correct. To show this I must now defend Scheler against another type of criticism.

Von Hildebrand's Criticism: The Subjectively Satisfying and the Intrinsically Important

We have just defended Scheler's claims for the primacy of the heart against claims that what feeling gives us is not enough to make moral judgments, that reason is also needed. This is not, however, the only area of concern to critics of Scheler's understanding of the primacy of the heart in the knowing of values. Another type of attack is made by Dietrich Von Hildebrand, who developed in *Christian Ethics* (1953) a distinction between the subjectively satisfying and the intrinsically important which he believed was essential to an understanding of why people choose "lower values," a distinction he felt Scheler simply overlooked. If Von Hildebrand is correct, once again Scheler's ethics would be in serious trouble.

To judge how accurate Von Hildebrand's claim is, we must first understand his basic distinction. Von Hildebrand contrasts the subjectively satisfying and the intrinsically important using two examples:

> In the first, let us suppose that someone pays us a compliment. We are perhaps aware that we do not fully deserve it, but it is nevertheless an agreeable and pleasurable experience. It is not a matter neutral and indifferent to us as in the case where someone tells us that his name begins with a T. . . . It presents itself as agreeable and as possessing the character of a *bonum,* in short, as something important.
>
> In the second, let us suppose that we witness a generous action, a man's forgiveness of a grave injury. This again strikes us as distinguishable from the neutral activity of a man dressing himself or lighting a cigarette. Indeed, the act of generous forgiveness shines forth with the mark of importance, with the mark of something noble and precious. . . . We are conscious that this act is something which *ought* to *be,* something *important.*
>
> If we compare these types of importance, we will soon discover

> the essential difference between them. The first, that is, the compliment, is merely *subjectively* important; while the latter, the act of forgiving, is *important in itself.* We are fully conscious that the compliment possesses a character of importance only insofar as it gives us pleasure. Its importance is solely drawn from its relation to our pleasure—as soon as the compliment is divorced from our pleasure, it sinks back into the anonymity of the neutral and indifferent.
>
> In contrast, the generous act of forgiveness presents itself as something intrinsically important. We are clearly conscious that its importance in no way depends on any effect which it produces in us. Its particular importance is not drawn from any relation to our pleasure and satisfaction. It stands before us intrinsically and autonomously important, in no way dependent on any relation to our reaction. . . .
>
> The intrinsic importance with which a generous act of forgiveness is endowed is termed "value" as distinguished from the importance of all those goods which motivate our interest merely because they are agreeable or satisfactory to us. (1953, 34–35)

This distinction is a key way in which Von Hildebrand gets to the essential nature of values, and he believes that Scheler overlooked the significance of this distinction. Furthermore, he believes that Scheler unsuccessfully attempts to account for this difference simply by an appeal to differences in the ranks of the values:

> The difference between the value and the merely subjectively satisfying has sometimes been interpreted as simply a difference in rank. It has been assumed that the difference between the intrinsic importance of justice and the merely subjective importance of something agreeable (for instance, the agreeable quality of a warm bath or a pleasant game of bridge) consists only in the fact that the former ranks higher than the latter. This indeed was the opinion of Max Scheler. (1953, 39–40)

After developing at some length why he believes his distinction is essential, Von Hildebrand returns to his critique of Scheler:

> The reason why Scheler overlooked the essential difference between the value and the subjectively satisfying rests in the fact that he did not clearly separate the question concerning the different points of view of importance in our motivation, from the question concerning the importance which the object possesses indepen-

> dently of any motivation. The fact that no being is completely deprived of all value may divert us from insight into the essential difference between the two points of view. Yet the category of the subjectively satisfying is not directed toward certain things which in themselves would possess no other importance, but toward the point of view under which we *approach* these things. Thus the argument which says that the amusing social affair also has a value, only a lower one, is pointless. In a case where I have to choose between attending the amusing social affair and assisting a man in great moral danger, the conflict is not between the value of assisting this man and the value of attending this party. The conflict is rather between two heterogeneous points of view. In choosing to go to the amusing party, the point of view under which this decision is made is definitely the merely subjectively satisfying. But in the case of the opposite choice in which I decide to assist a sick person, the point of view of my choice is definitely the value. (1953, 43)

Hildebrand believes that Scheler's attempt to appeal to "preferences" fails as well:

> Any attempt to explain the morally wrong attitude as the preference for a good having a lower value to a good possessing a higher one is doomed to fail. In the first place, it is impossible to interpret every action as being rooted in an act of preference. There exist many cases in which an end is chosen by disregarding a value without respect to any preference; for instance, somebody avenges himself in killing his enemy, and in so doing he ignores the high value of the life of a human being. Obviously it would be a completely artificial and wrong interpretation to say that this man prefers the satisfaction of his revenge to the life of his enemy. No conscious comparison, no conscious pondering of two goods, is here in question. Instead there is a simple decision to satisfy his desire for revenge, without in any way bothering about the value of a human life. (1953, 43–44)

For Hildebrand, as he goes on to make clear, the true meaning of preference involves conscious deliberation and choice. Indeed, he believes that

> an ordinary theft is not based on a preference for the value of possessing money over the sacred character of property rights, but is based rather on an indifference toward the point of view of value as such, which conditions an indifference toward the value of prop-

> erty coupled with an unhampered pursuit of something subjectively satisfying. In the case of a conflict in which a man wavers between a temptation toward theft and the voice of conscience exhorting respect for the property of his fellow men and warning against the injustice of theft, there can be no weighing of both possibilities from the same point of view, no comparison by a common denominator, but only an outspoken clash of two different points of view: the two directions of life of which St. Augustine speaks in *De Civitate Dei* (XIV, 3).
>
> Moreover, if it were true that in preferring a lower good to a higher good the choice would be based on a common denominator, namely the point of view of their value, it would be impossible to explain why one could choose the lower instead of the higher. So long as one and the same point of view is really at stake, there must be a reason why that which is inferior from this point of view is nevertheless preferred.
>
> Every time someone approaches two possibilities from one and the same point of view (for instance, where one chooses the lower of two salaries offered for the same kind and amount of work), we try to find out what other point of view could explain such a choice. We take it for granted that one could not choose from the same viewpoint and by the same measure that which is less, if there were not the possibility of approaching this lesser one from another viewpoint or, as we can put it, if another point of view were not responsible for turning the scale. (1953, 44–45)

Now, in the first place, I believe that Von Hildebrand's distinction between the subjectively satisfying and the intrinsically important is a useful one, and so what he says deserves consideration and development. Yet our main concern here must be with his attack on Scheler. If Von Hildebrand's criticism is correct, Scheler has indeed missed a significant way both of seeing the essence of values and of understanding why people choose lower values rather than higher. If this were so, Von Hildebrand's attack would be of grave consequence for our judgment of Scheler's ethics.

The Choice of Lower Values

I do not think Von Hildebrand is correct in his claim that it is impossible to understand morally evil choices on the basis of the different ranks of values and that the distinction between the subjectively satisfying and the intrinsically important is necessary to understand the "choice" of lower values over higher.

To meet Von Hildebrand's challenge, we must remind ourselves that Scheler's understanding of the nature of preference is quite different from that presented in the passage above. For Scheler, preference is a cognitive act, not a conscious choice. Second, for Scheler the understanding of the ultimate roots of the choice of a lower value over a higher one (to be precise, the choice of a deed to realize the lower value rather than a higher value) must ultimately look not to a "consciously chosen" preference of the lower value for the higher but rather to the *ordo amoris,* to the love and hatred that open and close our awareness of the hierarchical ranks of values and the place any particular value has in that hierarchy. We can be aware of values, and choose actions to realize values, only if our loves and hates allow us to see those values and their true place in the hierarchy of values. It is our love and our hatred, our *ordo amoris,* and the immediate preferences of values that are allowed by it that delimit what we see as the highest of values in any given concrete situation and lay the foundations for our choice of actions to realize what we see as the highest of values. Furthermore, as Scheler's work on repentance and rebirth shows, we often are of more than one "point of view" (if the *ordo amoris* can be so crudely characterized).

Thus Scheler is able to account for the choice of a lower value over a higher one not simply by the existence of a hierarchy of values (and even here it is unclear if Von Hildebrand grasps the implications of the fact that Scheler's hierarchy is not linear) but by insight into the *ordo amoris.* Given Von Hildebrand's misunderstanding of Scheler, it is ironic that the very last paragraphs quoted above from his criticism come, crudely to be sure, close to Scheler's insight. If we are to understand a choice of a lower value over a higher one (though salary comparison is a poor choice of an example given the other values in the value complexes we face in choosing between jobs), we must indeed understand the point of view of the person choosing. We must understand what love and hatred allow the person to see of the realm of values. Only then will we also see why that person chose to realize an "objectively" lower value, because only then will we see the limited range of the hierarchy of values which that person's stunted heart allowed, or the inverted values seen through the eyes of *ressentiment,* or the negative values now made attractive through hatred. Only if one grasps the level at which the *ordo amoris* operates and the true complexity of the realm of feelings (and of values) will one finally see how a person can, in the confines constructed by his or her loves and hates, see a value as the highest value when it is, objectively, a very low value, or in the distortion of hatred see a value as high and positive when it is objectively low and negative.

Indeed, far from missing the importance of the distinction between the subjectively satisfying and the intrinsically important as a way of answering the classic question of how people can choose lower values, Scheler's insights into the *ordo amoris* finally give us a way of understanding why people sometimes fall prey to making the subjectively satisfying more important than the intrinsically important, and why they choose lower values.

Let me show this using Von Hildebrand's own examples. One is his contrast of the intrinsic value of life with the subjective satisfaction of revenge. Von Hildebrand claims that one cannot account for the choice by an appeal to the ranking of values, but given the stunted vision of the hierarchy of values of persons under the spell of hatred, it is quite possible for them to place the value of revenge above that of the life of their enemy (note that the very term "enemy" suggests that one no longer sees the enemy as a person). In another example, the pleasure of a party versus saving the life of someone in peril, if I am trapped in an *ordo amoris* that places such selfish pleasures as supreme, I may well see the value of the party to be higher than that of the life of a person in peril (no matter how reprehensible this may seem to those of us not trapped in such a stunted *ordo amoris*). Finally, the thief most certainly is not "ignoring" values when he places the value of the money he steals over that of the property rights of the rightful owner, though his "point of view" is not mine.

As noted above in our discussion of human sacrifice, perhaps the problem we face with recognizing that such acts do reflect an *ordo amoris,* and not simply a difference between the subjectively satisfying and the intrinsically important, is that an *ordo amoris* that would, for example, so radically elevate selfishness is so foreign to our own (or to the ethos of our culture) that we have trouble seeing through the eyes of a person with such a "point of view."

To claim, as Von Hildebrand does, that it is impossible to account for such moral decisions on the basis of the different ranking of values in the hierarchy is to miss entirely the subtlety and power of Scheler's insights. Scheler's work on the orders—and perhaps more importantly here, the disorders—of the heart reached a depth and level that Von Hildebrand does not appreciate, and which, if appreciated, help to supplement and illuminate his insights. Thus, far from being inadequate as a way of understanding the choice of lower values, Scheler's work makes it intelligible.

I could go on pointing to the misunderstanding of the complexity of feeling and the heart (not to mention the world of values) displayed by Von Hildebrand, but it is not my purpose here to show that Scheler is correct and Von Hildebrand is wrong. Indeed, as noted above, I believe that Von Hildebrand's insights have merit, even if they do not reach the deeper levels that Scheler's insights into the *ordo amoris* reveal. Again, what is needed is not a debate about who is correct but rather detailed phenomenological investigations that explore the realms of feelings and values in ways that better reveal their full essential dimensions.

The Values Seen

These attacks on the primacy of the heart are not the only basic challenges to Scheler's insights into values and our access to them. Equally serious challenges have been lodged against Scheler's understanding of values (already a subissue in Von Hildebrand's criticism just considered). Once again, if not met, these challenges would suggest that Scheler's ethical personalism is unworkable. I will turn to this type of challenge in the next chapter.

12

Defending Scheler's Knowledge of Values

Introduction

This chapter will move from attacks focused primarily on Scheler's claims for the primacy of the person and the heart to criticisms that focus more on concerns with the adequacy of Scheler's view of the complex world of values and his understanding of the nature of values. These attacks are significant, for they often lead to claims that Scheler's approach cannot work in practice.

We shall also be considering (both simultaneously and separately) attacks on the adequacy of Scheler's phenomenological approach and the phenomenological approach in general. As noted in chapter 1, it may seem odd that in a book on ethics, and in a chapter on the adequacy of Scheler's grasp of values, I will spend time again defending phenomenology. Yet any ethic that rests so much on values must have an adequate grasp of values. Thus, if Scheler's phenomenological approach is inadequate, then the view of values it gave him may be inadequate as well (not to mention his claims for the special role of the heart in value-ception treated in the last chapter, his view of the person, etc.).

Given the number of attacks on Scheler, I must select representative examples of these types of attack to show how it is possible to defend Scheler against them. And again it is Philip Blosser, in his excellent book *Scheler's Critique of Kant's Ethics* (1995), who raises in a very clear and cogent way a series of attacks on Scheler's grasp of values and their nature. I will begin by meeting these attacks. Then I will deal at length with a suggestion, also raised in Blosser's critique, that Scheler fundamentally misunderstands the

Sections of this chapter appeared in my essay "Aesthetics, Morals, and Max Scheler's Non-Formal Values," *British Journal of Aesthetics* 16, no. 3 (1976): 230–36, and are reproduced here with permission.

relationship between moral and nonmoral values. Blosser's specific objection is that Scheler is wrong to claim that the realization of all nonmoral values has moral significance, suggesting, for example, that the realization of aesthetic values has no necessary moral value. I counter this suggestion by developing the relationship between moral values and aesthetic values afforded by a Schelerian approach. Next, I turn to a criticism of Scheler's grasp of particular values and their proper placement in the hierarchy of values made by Eugene Kelly, in his early study *Max Scheler* (1977), a volume in the Twayne's World Leaders Series. Finally, I confront Parvis Emad's presentation of Heidegger's attack on values in *Heidegger and the Phenomenology of Values* (1981) and end with a defense of Scheler's phenomenological approach against the language-trapped position.

Blosser's Critique of Scheler's Grasp of Values

Although Philip Blosser's recent book is appreciative of much of what Scheler tried to do, it raises both classic and new criticisms of Scheler's ethics. Some of these criticisms have already been met above in passing,[1] but some of the basic criticisms of the workability of Scheler's ethics that are rooted in the adequacy of Scheler's view of the world of values must still be met.

The first and most basic is Blosser's following claim:

> Perhaps the major problem with Scheler's essentialist definition of value is that it fails to specify how values differ from other essences. Subsuming values under the category of "essence" does not in itself accomplish anything more in the way of specifying their nature than subsuming them under the heading of Heideggerian "Being." Scheler says that values are essences. . . . But what distinguishes a *value*-essence from a *thing*-essence? Scheler's term "quality" is not too illuminating on this point. (1995, 82)

As Blosser acknowledges, Scheler's calling values "qualities" occurs at a point where he is trying to show that values are not

[1] In chapter 2 I meet the criticisms of Scheler's understanding of Kant's formalism, and in chapter 11 I meet the criticism that Scheler cannot account for our being "of two hearts."

empirical goods, but the more basic question Blosser raises is how to define values so as to distinguish them from things. Blosser goes on to explore ways of so defining and distinguishing values (using "interest"), but he claims that many of them "have been less than adequate because they have not distinguished clearly the *functional* nature of values, but settled instead for descriptions of various relations between the valuing subject and valued object" (1995, 82). Blosser then indicates that he finds Dooyeweerd's distinction (between how a thing functions in experience and what it is) illuminating (1995, 82).

I object, however, even to defining and distinguishing values in terms of their functionality, for such attempts miss perhaps the most important point that Scheler is trying to make. Values as phenomenologically given are "absolute" in the sense of being independent. They are also quite unique and primal phenomena. Indeed, as noted above, even in his dissertation Scheler placed values on the same level as "Being" in primordiality. Thus all attempts to define values must be rooted, first of all, in the *seeing* of their essences. We cannot define what makes values different from things; rather, we must *see* the essential differences between values and things. Values are values. This sounds tautological, and if we were talking about purely conceptual understanding it would be. Phenomenology is trying to get us to understand, however, that the root of knowledge and of concepts is immediate experience. When you are trying to grasp as primitive a phenomenon as values, if you cannot immediately experience ("see") the essence of values and the essential difference between value and nonvalue essences, you will not see Scheler's understanding of value. You may well attempt to understand values by looking at relationships between values and things, or values and "interests," but you will not *see* the nature of values.

The difficulty here is a typical problem of classic phenomenology. How can I get people to "see" when they cannot see, or to grasp what I am trying to help them grasp? Scheler himself speaks eloquently to this difficulty in the "Problems of Religion" essay in *On the Eternal in Man,* when he defends Otto's descriptions of the holy against Wundt's attack on phenomenology. After quoting Otto's claim that because the holy is "perfectly *sui generis* and irreducible" and that therefore one must help others "see" this by negative description, Scheler says:

> This on the whole negative method of successively peeling away the correlates and contraries that are felt to offer progressive indications to the "phenomenon *demonstrandum,*" with the consequent laying bare of the phenomenon and its presence to the inspecting mind, is the way which leads to the *phenomenological scrutiny of the essence.* The indefinability of the X under investigation (*per genus et differentia specifica*) is a sure sign that in this X we have a genuine elementary essence which underlies ultimate concepts but is itself "inconceivable." For "to conceive" means to reduce the object of a concept in terms of other concepts. It is not surprising that the rationalistic philosopher decries this method as generally fruitless. Unaware of its character as a mind-awakening and guiding procedure (into which indirect thinking in judgments and inferences enters only as a means of leading the mind to the threshold of discovery), he sees only those judgments and inferences and overlooks the sense and nerve of the whole procedure. He then agrees with the finding of Wilhelm Wundt that phenomenology is a wholly profitless affair, since it consists in negative judgments and always ends in a tautology (such as that the holy is simply—the holy).[2]

Unfortunately, as we developed above in chapter 2's presentation of Scheler's phenomenological approach, it is depressingly easy not to "see." If your experience of values is always indirect or laden with theoretical blinders, you will not see values themselves, and no one can be forced to "open" his or her eyes. Thus, to answer this question, all any classic phenomenologist can do is appeal to the phenomenological experience of values themselves and supply the best phenomenological descriptions he or she can

[2] Scheler continues: "Where this priceless verdict is unutterably mistaken is in this: Wundt takes the negative judgments—which in this method are no more than dialectic invitations to redirect the mind's attention closer to the all-important object—to imply theoretical rational definitions of some *thing,* and even the so-called tautology he regards as a theoretical rational definition instead of merely the concluding invitation to look here and now upon the *supraconceptual datum* which can *only* be beheld, to gaze directly upon its *pure* self-given state, now that the husks of approximation have been stripped away. Nobody in his senses could believe, however, that *as* a theoretical rational definition the 'tautology' would be anything but absurd" (GPR 166–67/EPR 170–71).

devise to evoke the experience of the essential nature of values. Nothing can guarantee success, however.

Blosser's Criticism of Scheler's Practical Ethics

This most basic of challenges is not the only one Blosser raises. He also suggests that Scheler's grasp of values is seriously flawed when we come to the practical matter of making moral choices between competing values. While admitting the philosophical level Scheler is working on, Blosser says:

> Surely it is not unfair to ask—or to try to imagine—how an ethics such as his would go about addressing the problem of offering concrete moral guidance.
>
> Let us consider this problem very briefly. Granting that we can distinguish various positive material values such as pleasure, nobility, holiness, and the like, how does this help us to discover what is morally obligatory in the specific circumstances we confront in concrete life-situations? Granting, furthermore, that we can distinguish a priori a ranked hierarchy of values, and that values of a higher rank are preferable a priori to those of a lower rank, this still leaves critical questions. For one thing, it offers no direction for circumstances in which the realization of a lower value (such as famine relief in Africa, which is concerned with the "vital" or "biological" value of human life) might be *more pressing* than that of a higher value (such as building a cathedral in Washington, D.C., which is concerned with the "spiritual" or "religious" value of worship). Many situations call for precisely such decisions. Furthermore, there are plenty of examples one could think of where the "higher" value would obviously not be the morally good choice. Should I rescue the drowning child in the back yard swimming pool, or continue listening to Mozart in my room? The former would realize a "lower," vital value, the latter a "higher" spiritual, aesthetic value. But my duty is obviously to save the child. The question is whether Scheler offers any clear way of showing why this is obvious. I am not sure he does. (1995, 143)

A core difficulty with Blosser's presentation of this practical moral quandary is that it takes into account only one part of the hierarchical ranks of values, the hierarchy of nonmoral values. It leaves out the hierarchical rankings of the bearers of the nonformal values. In both of Blosser's examples—the saving of the lives of the starving Africans and the saving of the life of the drowning child—we are called upon to save not only physical bodies but the bearers of persons as well, and persons are the highest value of all. Thus, once Scheler's understanding of the hierarchical ranking of value bearers is taken into account we have a basis for understanding why saving the lives of the Africans or the child has such a powerful call on us.[3]

This is not the only practical concern Blosser raises, however, for he immediately goes on to say:

> Another difficulty is that Scheler's hierarchy of values offers no guidance as to which specific, positive values *within* a given rank are preferable to others. For example, which "vital" value should the medical profession consider more important in the care of geriatric patients, all things being equal: their physical comfort or longevity? . . . Which value is the "higher," the elimination of physical suffering or the preservation of life? I am not sure Scheler offers any help here either. (1995, 143)

This criticism is more telling, for it is true that Scheler did not develop specific ways to decide within a rank, and it is possible that further investigations may well show that further discrimination may be discerned. For example, are all positive values within a rank equal, or are there degrees of strength of the positive (and negative) within a specific rank?

Yet even if no further discriminations are found, such decisions rarely are made with all things equal. First of all, again we are dealing not just with the biological, "vital" level here, but with persons. Furthermore, the problem with these examples is that they focus only on a contrast between two specific values, while we rarely choose deeds to realize a single value on a single level. The complex interaction of realizable values in various ranks makes decisions difficult, but it also suggests that a sensitivity to the full value complexes before us will, in practice, make choice

[3] Even here, though, there is a complex competition of values. If there were not, cathedrals would never be justifiably built, given the amount of starvation there is in the world. Furthermore, children present a special problem for Scheler, and we will address it below. I am not here claiming a Schelerian ethics will ever make our moral decisions simple, just that it helps to illuminate them better than the oversimplified alternatives we presently have.

between alternatives possible, since one complex will realize more positive, high values, in higher "bearers," than the other.

Blosser goes on to another issue as he says:

> Even in situations presenting clear alternatives between values of *different rank,* one may ask whether what is morally obligatory can be determined adequately by means of Scheler's a priori "laws of preference." For example, what "laws of preference" would help a pregnant woman deliberating over the controversial question of abortion? What a priori "laws of preference" will offer her direction in choosing between the "vital" or "biological" value of carrying the fetus to term and bringing another human life into the world, and any number of other possible "psychological," "utilitarian" or other values that she might weigh against it?[4]

If Scheler were suggesting that one mechanically apply abstract general "laws of preference" to make such a decision, Blosser would be right. Yet, for Scheler the "laws of preference" are not abstract generalizations. Preferences are ultimately rooted in the person's *ordo amoris.* Thus, to say that carrying the fetus to term is simply of vital, biological value is to reflect one such value preference, rooted in a particular *ordo amoris,* that ignores both preferences and values at other levels which another *ordo amoris* would feel and "see." Blosser, is, of course, pointing to a painfully difficult example of a moral dilemma. In the case of abortion we are dealing with a conflict of value complexes on many levels. It is, for example, for many people not just a vital, biological issue but a conflict of the values of the mother and the person-value of the child (or, in the case of the fetus, a "potential person" at the very least). The decision of what to do is both heart- and society-rending. I am not here going to suggest that Scheler's approach will ever make the choice of deeds in the case of such basic conflicts of *ordo amoris* and of values easy. I will suggest, however, that

---

[4] Blosser continues: "Is it sufficient or even helpful to ask *which* value is essentially 'higher,' 'preferable' or essentially more in need of being realized? Is it enough to point out that for *some people,* the value of human life may bear not only a 'biological' value but a 'religious' value? Will that settle the issue? Again, I am not certain Scheler provides much help here. The choice to be made requires moral insight into the nature of the options posed by the situation itself, yet what is morally obligatory seems incapable of being adjudicated on the basis of a priori abstract, essential 'laws of preference' alone" (1995, 143–44).

a careful and open sensitivity to all of the values, all of the complex factors, may well help us both to understand why this type of conflict is so difficult to resolve and, I hope, to see new ways of resolving it. But doing so will not be accomplished by an appeal to the mechanical application of abstract "laws of preference," and Scheler would never suggest that it could be. All that Scheler accomplished points to the fact that the appeal to such laws, or an appeal to simple abstract formulas, is futile. One will resolve such basic value dilemmas only by recognizing the full complexity of the dilemma, not by any approach that oversimplifies the actuality of the value conflicts at the heart of the dilemma.

Scheler, Persons, and Children

Although Blosser does not raise the issue, the position Scheler takes concerning the personhood of children might be taken to imply that a child, or at least a fetus, is not a person and therefore abortion is permitted (on the argument that we have more of an obligation to protect persons than nonpersons). Since we are already discussing abortion, it is probably wise to deal with this issue here as well.

The grounds for claiming that Scheler believes children (or fetuses) are not persons lies in the fact that for him the person is not identical with a biological human being, but is rather defined in terms of the unity of actions. He develops this idea in a key passage in the *Formalism:*

> A second factor involved in the application of the word *person* is this: it is ascribed only to a certain level of development in man. A child manifests egoness, possession of a soul, and consciousness of self, but this does not make him a person in the moral sense. Only a child who has "come of age" is a person in the full sense. But this "*coming of age*" is based on certain phenomena—no matter when it is believed to come about in an individual according to changing positive law, and no matter which varying conditions, true or fictitious, have been established concerning its onset. The basic phenomenon of coming of age consists in the ability to experience insight into the difference between *one's own* and *someone else's* acts, willing, feeling, thinking, an insight which is already given in the

> immediate experiencing of any experience itself (the insight into the difference is not based on the content of the experience). (GW2 471/F 478)

One might take what Scheler says here as a signal that very young children and fetuses are not yet persons and therefore conclude that Scheler's understanding of the nature of person makes abortion (and indeed infanticide) permissible. I do not believe that such a reading is a correct one. The point Scheler is emphasizing in this passage is the requirement for personhood, and he uses children as an example since the idea that children achieve adulthood at a specific point in their development (think of the idea of the "age of reason," or legal age stipulations, etc.) is a common one. Furthermore, since Scheler is focused primarily on developing his insights into the nature of the person, he does not explore all of the implications of his use of children as an example of nonpersons.

Even if one accepts the idea that children, much less fetuses, are not persons, one cannot assume immediately that Scheler approves of abortion. As Manfred Frings develops in *The Mind of Max Scheler,* even if you consider abortion to be the killing of a nonperson,

> according to the order of value-ranks, one must, nevertheless, also say that abortion sacrifices a living entity to lower quantifiable values, such as family-planning, pleasure-sex, or to one-parent family values, etc. Considered in this way, abortion is objectified as a rational choice, defying the evidential preference of the value of life over quantifiable values of lower ranks. In *Formalism,* the fetus is not a person, yet it must be regarded as a life value and its birth be emotively preferred over quantifiable values such as planning. (1997, 49)

Although this argument is quite correct and does cover many of the reasons advanced for abortion, I think there is another element of Scheler's position that is relevant for those still concerned that Scheler denies personhood to children.

First of all, it is true that for Scheler full personhood is not given at or before birth. It is a matter of development. Yet to suggest that we can specify a precise point in human development where personhood first manifests itself is, I suggest, naive. Indeed, I would even suggest that few of us have achieved, or will achieve, fully actualized personhood within this world. With young children it is often clear that whatever personhood they achieve is partial and sporadic at best, yet any mother will tell you that at least some tentative signs of a distinct personality are present from birth, if not before. I am well aware of the studies of development which suggest that the ability to make clear-cut distinctions between one's own and someone else's acts occurs relatively late in childhood. Yet to suggest that there is absolutely no such awareness earlier in childhood, or even in the fetus, is, I believe, questionable. Scheler's admission that personhood develops suggests that it might not be achieved with the crossing of a clear-cut line. Again, his focus and the incompleteness of his presentation leaves the issue open for further study.

Criticism of Scheler's Distinction between Moral and Nonmoral Values

Beyond the criticisms of Scheler's grasp of values ably presented by Blosser, Scheler's basic distinction between the moral values and the nonmoral values has been challenged as well. Again, perhaps the most succinct challenge comes from Blosser in *Scheler's Critique of Kant's Ethics* when he states:

> Even considered together with any possible moral value that may appear in conjunction with them, realizations of non-moral values may still remain refractory to classification as moral. In fact, numerous non-moral values may be identified whose realization in some bearer one would find difficult to avoid classifying as basically "amoral." Take, for instance, the realization of a positive *aesthetic or economic* value. Would we wish to call the realization of such a value, even where it is accompanied by the appearance of a moral value as a byproduct, in every case a "moral" good? I think not. (1995, 85)

Blosser goes on to suggest that we ought to consider the realization of many nonmoral values to co-create not moral values but a whole set of separate "nonmoral goods": "This means that 'moral good' does not appear through the realization of positive nonmoral values (such as the values of 'utility,' 'frugality,' 'eloquence,' 'nobility,' or even 'holiness') but of positive moral values (such as 'faithfulness,' 'remorse,' 'forgiveness,' 'respect,' 'honesty,' 'benevolence,' and the like)'' (1995, 86).

Such a position, Blosser acknowledges, would not be accepted by Scheler. Yet Scheler himself seems to give some credence to Blosser's suggestion when, in the early part of the *Formalism,* Scheler at one point distinguishes ''aesthetic values'' and ''values that belong to the ethical sphere'' (''Werte, die der ethischen Sphäre angehören'') in a way that appears quite similar to Blosser's distinction (GW2 36/F 13–14). Scheler does it, however, at a point where he is focused primarily on distinguishing values from empirical goods rather than on establishing his belief in the separation of the moral values such as ''good'' and ''evil'' (*gut* and *böse*) from all other nonmoral values, a distinction he only introduces in a later section (see GW2 46–48/F 24–25).

Clearly, however, the relationship between moral and nonmoral values must be clarified if we are to meet this basic questioning of it. For there does seem to be a logic to distinguishing not only between moral and nonmoral values, but between those nonmoral values that have a ''moral import'' and those that do not.

The Relationship between Aesthetic and Moral Values

Blosser's use of aesthetic values as one of the examples of values whose realization has no moral impact allows us to use this relationship as a test case. This is a good test area for another reason as well. The relationship between aesthetic values and moral values is a difficult one to grasp, and the debates over it are old. If Scheler is correct, many of the seemingly conflicting positions taken in the debates over the relationship between the moral and the aesthetic can be reconciled. Those who argue that the aesthetic is autonomous are correct; any attempt to reduce aesthetic values to moral values—or any other values for that matter—is wrong. Yet if the realization of an aesthetic value in a particular situation co-realizes, in that situation, a higher positive value, then the moral value ''good'' is simultaneously realized; if it realizes a lower, negative value, ''evil'' is realized. Thus the aesthetic realm is an autonomous realm of nonmoral values, but the realization of these values has moral impact.

As attractive as this rapprochement may seem, so far we have only stated in rather formal terms the relationship between the aesthetic and the moral. Indeed, what we have said may still leave the impression that this is merely another scheme to make art subordinate to ethical considerations in the sense that art must serve ethical purposes (or, conversely, one might also protest that it ties ethics to aesthetics, since to realize the moral values one must realize aesthetic values). Either way, the core objection is that art and ethics are more independent than Scheler allows. No matter how independent Scheler's aesthetic values are asserted to be from the moral values co-realized along with the realization of the positive, higher aesthetic values, there may well be those who will argue that the formal relationships between "nonformal values" we have sketched still do not do justice to the unique autonomy of art or ethics. Blosser, for example, would separate the aesthetic values from moral values entirely and suggest that the realization of aesthetic values co-realizes a nonmoral good.

Before I begin to defend Scheler's position against Blosser, I must admit the idea that aesthetic values are amoral is attractive. At first blush it does seem much more reasonable, for example, to accept the realization of values like courage and honesty as having more to do with morals than would the realization of aesthetic values. We are much more inclined to morally condemn a person for cowardice or dishonesty and morally praise him or her for courage or honesty than we are to morally condemn for an aesthetically bad painting or morally praise for an aesthetically excellent one.

To see why this does not justify Blosser's creation of a new class of "nonmoral goods," we must develop some differences between aesthetic values and both moral and nonmoral values (such as courage and honesty). First of all, aesthetic values differ from moral values in the type of bearers they can have. As Scheler puts it in the *Formalism:* "First, all aesthetic values are in essence values of *objects*. Second, they are values of objects whose posited reality (of any form) has been suspended; such objects are there as '*appearance*' ('Schein')" (GW2 103/F 85–86). In contrast to the aesthetic values, as already noted, the bearers of ethical values are persons who "can never (originally) be given as 'objects.' "

When we contrast the bearers of aesthetic values with the bearers of other nonmoral values, such as courage or honesty, other distinctions appear as well. First of all, values such as honesty are borne not by objects but by persons, just as moral values are. Second, "vital" values such as courage are borne not by persons but by " 'living beings' in general" (GW2 104/F 86).

These distinctions between the types of bearers moral, aesthetic, and other nonmoral values such as honesty or courage have are the reason why the realization of aesthetic values seems less morally significant than the realization of these other values. Aesthetic values are realized in objects, not persons. In contrast, spiritual values such as honesty are borne by persons, just as moral values are. Thus it is natural to think that honesty is closer to the moral values, since both have the same bearer. Furthermore, since "living human beings" are intimately connected with "persons," and all living beings (including living human beings) are the bearers of vital values, if one does not distinguish between "person" and "living human being" one might again think that a vital value such as courage is closer to the moral values than the aesthetic values are, since they would have the same bearer, namely the "living human being." But Scheler does *not* identify the living human being, as a vital being, with the spiritual being, "person." The realization of the vital value of courage (in the live human being) is just as distinct from the resultant realization of the moral value in the person as the realization of a "spiritual" aesthetic value (in an aesthetic object) is from its resultant realization of moral value in this person. Even the realization of the nonmoral spiritual value of honesty is distinct from the co-realization of the moral value "good," despite the fact that both are realized in the person. In each case the realization of moral values occurred along with the realization of the nonmoral values, whether they are vital values such as courage or spiritual values such as honesty or the aesthetic values.

Thus, there is a difference between the aesthetic and the moral, but one must not conflate the vital and the personal in such a way as to claim a greater distance between the aesthetic values and the moral values than between other nonmoral values (for example, the values honesty and courage) and the moral values. For Scheler the difference we sense between aesthetic values and other types of values does not lie in the moral irrelevance of aesthetic values but rather in the fact that the aesthetic values are an autonomous realm of values and are realized in a unique type of bearer.

Finally, regarding Blosser's suggestion that we consider the realization of aesthetic values as co-realizing a "nonmoral good," I see no reason to add to the fact that the realization of a positive nonmoral value is itself a positive value (GW2 100/F 82) by positing a new value, the "nonmoral good," to signal that fact.

One last point. We must not overemphasize the autonomy and uniqueness of art and the aesthetic values. Blosser is correct to insist that we must not make the moral values dependent upon the aesthetic values either. They are not, and for several reasons. In the first place, the aesthetic values are only one set of values that has moral impact when realized. As wrong as it would be to reduce the aesthetic to the moral, it would be equally wrong to subordinate the moral to the aesthetic, and Scheler does not do this. Such subordination is possible by taking the aesthetic values to be the only values worthy of realization, or at any rate the highest values realizable. Such a mistake occurs because finite, human persons cannot grasp the full hierarchy of values and so both individuals and entire societies can take (and have taken) a particular set of values and absolutize them as the basis of the particular morals of that individual or group, what Scheler calls their "ethos." Alfons Deeken, in his study of Scheler, draws on his own experience of Japanese culture to characterize it as an "aesthetic ethos"—that is to say, a culture where the realization of aesthetic values becomes the highest goal (1974, 107–11).[5] The problem with such a culture (and it is unclear whether Japanese culture truly is such a culture) is that it can blind itself to the worth of all but aesthetic values. As high as aesthetic values are, they are neither the only values nor, if Scheler is correct, the

[5] Although Deeken does not develop the idea, I believe his insight into the aesthetic ethos shows the possibility that in such an ethos one might very well morally condemn (or praise) someone on aesthetic grounds. Thus the fact (noted above) that we do not ordinarily condemn someone morally on aesthetic grounds may simply reflect our particular ethos.

highest values, for the values of the "holy and the unholy" are part of a higher rank of nonmoral values than the aesthetic values.

Despite all of this, however, Blosser's suggestion that the realization of aesthetic values be considered totally amoral still seems attractive as a way of resolving at least one serious moral difficulty. The problem occurs when you face a conflict of aesthetic and non-aesthetic, nonmoral values in a work of art. Take, for example, any work of art where the form does realize high, positive, aesthetic values while at the same time the content realizes low, negative, non-aesthetic values. (What you take to be a good example will depend, of course, on your *ordo amoris,* but let us use an example Blosser suggested to me. Take a film that embodies high aesthetic values yet the content is blatantly racist, sexist, or "pornographic" or in any other way realizes low, negative values.) Now it seems that we face a moral quandary in such cases, for how can we praise the aesthetic values while condemning the content? Is it not simpler just to separate the two judgments entirely?

Yes, doing so is simple, and indeed it has been attempted by many people (and not just in the case of works of art; we face similar conflicts between other values as well). One might simply ignore the aesthetic values and condemn all art with such content as co-realizing evil. Or one might simply focus on the aesthetic values and try to totally ignore the content.

Yet our heart tells us that things are not this simple. To say, for example, that I am an artist and do not care how people react to the content (or how they may be affected by it) is to ignore the totality of the value of the content of my work of art. Yet to say that the content of a work of art is the only relevant moral value is also wrong. Scheler's approach allows us to resolve this type of quandary. For Scheler the moral value "good" is realized along with the realization of high, positive values. Once again, as I have done before, I must emphasize the plurality of values we often face. We are rarely if ever in a position where we realize a single value. Most of the time we are dealing with complexes of values, often values in conflict, and often the complex we realize itself still contains conflicting values, some of which are positive and some of which are negative. This does not make for easy judgments, but it is, I believe, true to the actuality of life. In this case we must deal with all of the values, both "formal" aesthetic values and "content" values, when we judge the work of art. Such judgments are not easy given the complexes of sometimes competing values we face. There are, for example, works of art that are morally acceptable due to the high level of aesthetic achievement, despite some level of negativity of content. There are, however, contents so despicable that we not only morally denounce the work of art, despite the high formal aesthetic values it displays, but decry the fact that these high aesthetic values are put to use to display such base contents.

What is so creative about Scheler's position is that he forces us to face all of the values present before us. We cannot simply say that the aesthetic values are the only ones to look at (either by making them the only or highest values or by saying they are totally separate from ethics), nor can we simply look at the contents. Again, Scheler's position does not lead to simple or easy judgments, but it makes us face all of the values present.

With this I end my development of Scheler's understanding of the complex and subtle interaction of the moral and nonmoral values (using aesthetic values as an example). Once again we see that Scheler's approach illuminates a most difficult terrain, not by simplifying the issues but by showing that we can be true to the full range of competing values and their moral import.

Criticism of Scheler's Placement of Particular Values in Particular Ranks

One of Scheler's great contributions to an understanding of the hierarchy of values was his insight that the hierarchy is not linear, that there are distinct ranks of values. At the same time, however, such an approach works only if we can accurately place values in the proper rank. Another line of criticism of Scheler questions whether he was able to do so.

We must, again, pick a typical and significant example. Eugene Kelly, in his early study *Max Scheler,* after raising the question of what exactly Scheler meant when he suggested that the "scale of values" needed to be "worked out further," and discussing the possibility of subdividing the modalities into submodalities (with all the problems such complexity will present), says:

> There seem to be cases in which it is not entirely clear even in which of the four categories a value falls. Scheler holds that the value of the virtue of courage (the courageous) is a vital value, because conditioned by vital impulse (*triebhaft*). Now one might ask whether the value of the virtue of temperance (the temperate) is similarly a vital value, or whether it belongs to the modality of spiritual values. Here the problem of adjudication becomes particularly intense; the question of whether the moment of impulse or similar vital factor belongs to the essence of temperance (a virtue Scheler does not discuss), and if so, whether its value as a human virtue is preferable to that of courage, gives us an example of how complex and slippery are the problems that Scheler has set for himself. The difficulty alone of performing the phenomenological reduction and disengaging the value of the virtue of temperance from its concrete manifestations is enormous, to say nothing of the problem of obtaining insight into its relative worth. (1977, 119)

Kelly is quite correct that there are a host of basic values that must be explored and placed within the hierarchical ranks of values, and that doing so may not always be easy. I myself would, for example, suggest that even in the case of values such as courage, what Scheler has said may well be oversimplified. Clearly, the kind of courage Scheler was talking about is part of the vital sphere, but I would suggest that there are values in the spiritual rank of values that are similar to vital courage. Yet such similarity may well hide differences between vital courage and intellectual courage that are subtle and perhaps essentially significant. It is only after we have explored the full worlds of values with careful, precise phenomenological techniques that we will be able to adequately differentiate such values, much less place them on their proper levels.

Criticism of the "Holy-Unholy" as a Separate Rank of Values

A different type of criticism of Scheler's grasp of values is raised by Parvis Emad in *Heidegger and the Phenomenology of Values* (1981). In this book Emad raises the possibility that Scheler's sins are not only sins of omission, such as missing distinctions (for example, Von Hildebrand's distinction between the subjectively satisfying and the objectively important), or misunderstanding the relationship between moral and nonmoral values (as Blosser suggests), or failing to develop the place of significant values within the hierarchy (as Kelly suggests). In addition, Emad raises the possibility that Scheler posits an entire rank of values that does not exist—namely, the holy-unholy rank of values. Emad does so by appealing to Heidegger's idea that the value "holy" was created by Windelband to round out his interpretation of Kant's works. As Emad develops, Heidegger claims that Windelband interpreted Kant's three *Critiques* as each being devoted to the exploration of a value, with the *Critique of Pure Reason* exploring the value "truth," the *Practical Reason* dealing with the value "good," and the *Judgment* dealing with "beauty." The difficulty with this schema was there seemed to be no single value that Kant's religious work dealt with, and so, in order to round out the schema, as Parvis quotes Heidegger, "the value of the Holy was invented" (Emad 1981, 62).

Now even if Windelband does focus on the value of the holy for schematic reasons, this does not mean that the holy is not a separate value. The question, however, need not be raised only in terms of Windelband's schema. There are many people who would agree with the idea that there is no separate rank for the holy, even if many believe it is a separate value.

Why, then, does Scheler believe the holy-unholy series is in a rank separate from the other spiritual values? Given the wide range of different value pairs that already inhabit the third sphere of spiritual values, why must the holy-unholy pair be given an entirely separate rank in the hierarchy? Why not just leave it on the same level with the other spiritual values? And if there is another, higher, rank, why is it populated only with the holy? Indeed, one can point to people and even entire cultures that accept other spiritual values as their highest value (as we have already seen Deeken suggest when he calls the Japanese culture an "aesthetic ethos" [1974, 107–11]). So why does Scheler place the value "holy" in a new, separate, higher rank?

Scheler does so because he believes that the holy-unholy series is phenomenologically given as a separate rank, and the highest rank, even if many people or even cultures do not see this. Again we must appeal to the *ordo amoris*. Even if the holy and the unholy are the highest rank, it is not surprising that some people or cultures are simply blind to what "objectively" is the highest rank of values, for if Scheler is correct it takes a truly open-hearted grasp of the ranks of values to see that the holy-unholy series is essentially different from the other spiritual values and thus deserves an entirely separate rank. I believe Scheler is correct, but I also believe that showing this requires much fuller phenomenological exploration than Scheler—or for that matter anyone else—has provided.

Heideggerian Criticism of Scheler's Understanding of the Basic Nature of Values

As Emad points out, however, it is not just the creation of a fictitious value or value rank that bothers Heidegger. The key problem is Heidegger's belief that Scheler (along with everyone else) has fundamentally misunderstood what he is trying to point to when he talks of values. Again, Emad quotes Heidegger:

> Along with and under the influence of Nietzsche the learned philosophy of the terminating 19th and beginning 20th centuries turns into a "philosophy" and "phenomenology" of values. Values appear now as things-in-themselves to be arranged in "systems." Despite a tacit rejection of Nietzsche's philosophy, his writings, especially *Zarathustra,* are now examined closely . . . in order to set up an ethics of value "more scientifically" than the "unscientific philosopher-poet Nietzsche" ever could. (Emad 1981, 101)

Emad develops nicely what he believes is so dangerous about this approach to values as he says:

> Since an ethics of values is oriented towards constant presence, it is oblivious of the aboriginal nature of Being which is not present at all. Since an ethics of values promotes reckoning with values, it remains oblivious of the incalculable nature of Being. Devoted to calculative thinking and oblivious of Being, an ethics of values is "metaphysical." The metaphysical character of this ethics calls for its overcoming. (1981, 152)

Now Heidegger and Emad are quite correct that turning values into "things" that could then be "reckoned with" would be a moral disaster. Furthermore, Scheler's limited and incomplete sketch of the hierarchy of values (especially in the *Formalism,* as I noted in chapter 6) might well conjure up visions of a rigidly legalistic practical ethics. But this entire book, especially chapter 6, demonstrates in a variety of ways why Scheler rejects such an understanding or use of values. It is quite sad, given his own position, that Heidegger could have so profoundly mistaken Scheler's position and approach, though given the unsystematic development of Scheler's positions this is, perhaps, not too surprising.

Yet this is still not Heidegger's (and Emad's) main concern. The main concern Emad develops is that Scheler's grasp of values misses and distorts the full dimensions of any value. Emad, using the value "noble," generalizes the idea that Scheler's, and indeed anyone's, grasp of values is necessarily incomplete and distorting in a most basic way:

> To be sure, in certain instances our action is either noble or ignoble. However, no single instance of a noble action thoroughly reflects the inexhaustible state of *Being noble* which renders possible *a* noble action. In short, the nobleness of a noble action immeasurably surpasses what one commonly views as noble. Were this not the case, all noble actions would be identical, which is clearly not the case. This means that nobleness, as a state of Being, is not constantly present in a noble action, the latter is merely a dim reflection of the splendor inherent in the former. Therefore, one may say that the state of Being noble is unobtrusive and holds itself back from being present in a noble action.
>
> Similarly, the state of Being vulgar refrains from being completely present in a vulgar action. Were this ever the case we would never be dismayed by the renewed experience of a vulgar action. All such actions would be identical and thus reprehensible. We merely get a glimpse of the unfathomable and mysterious nature of man when we realize that neither a noble nor a vulgar action exhausts the noble and ignoble resources of his Being.
>
> Instead of pointing in the direction of the states of Being noble and vulgar, Scheler's explication of action in terms of these values diverts the attention from the states of Being noble and vulgar. These states of Being remain unobtrusive, hold back from and refuse to be constantly present in our noble or vulgar actions. It is

due to this refusal and holding back that human action is *free* to be noble or vulgar. The refusal of our states of Being to be constantly present holds the key for grasping the essence of human freedom.

In the same vein, the state of Being holy, *holiness,* by far surpasses the splendor of a deity whose existence is accepted in faith. Similarly, the state of Being unholy, *unholiness,* goes beyond the horrifying defilement evidenced in the experience of the unholy. The divinity of a divine being and the evilness of an evil being equally hold back from and refuse to be exhaustively present in beings which are regarded as holy or unholy. Were this not the case, all deities would be equally holy and all monstrosities equally unholy. This, however, is not the case. . . .

The bifurcation between what *is* and *is not* constantly present in a value must be examined more closely so that we may be fully prepared for taking up the issue of the overcoming of value. (1981, 149–51)

The Defense of Phenomenology

Emad is correct that any single act of nobility does not exhaust the full dimensions of the value "noble," and our grasp of the "holy" is notoriously incomplete. Suggesting that Scheler was not acutely aware of this, given Scheler's sensitivity to the complexity of both the entire world of values and the nuances of individual values, is surprising. His phenomenological investigations of the essence of a value (or anything else for that matter) *are* sensitive to the difficulties of achieving essential knowledge.

Yet to accuse Emad (or Heidegger) of naively misunderstanding phenomenology (even if they have missed the subtlety of Scheler's approach)[6] is to profoundly misunderstand a core point they are attempting to make. It is not simply that Scheler or any other phenomenologist is naive about a hidden bias that causes him to believe he has captured in his descriptions more than he has, a bias that could, at least in theory, be suspended. The profoundly disturbing possibility (raised by the Heidegger presented to us by

[6] For an excellent refutation of Heidegger's criticism of Scheler's understanding of values and the epoche, as well as a general defense of Scheler vis-à-vis Heidegger, see Manfred Frings, "The Background of Max Scheler's 1927 Reading of *Being and Time:* A Critique of a Critique through Ethics" (1992).

Emad) is that there is always more than what the phenomenologist can bring to "givenness"; there is always a metaphysical commitment that is so inextricably bound to the core of phenomenology that no phenomenological investigation can be successful in grasping the essential nature of values, or anything else.[7]

If Heidegger is correct, "phenomenology" is accurately labeled, for it cannot overcome metaphysical commitment, and what it can give us is nothing but the "phenomenon," and never the "noumenon," never the "ding-an-sich," the "thing-in-itself," never the essence of anything.

The difficulty I have with the possibility raised by Emad/Heidegger here (or any of the myriad like positions raised in the last ninety years) can be put in the form of a question. How do they know the nature of the holy, or the vulgar, or being (and how do they know it conceals itself, and when)? Either this being is, in some way, accessible to experience and thus is itself open to a pure, unbiased phenomenological description, or this concealed being (and the "true" nature of the vulgar or the holy) is a metaphysical posit by Emad/Heidegger.

At the same time, however, I am not here accusing Emad/Heidegger of being entirely wrong in their concern with claims to essential knowledge. Indeed, again I believe that more phenomenological investigations will be needed before we can settle claims, especially claims about such a basic and elusive phenomenon as the value "holy." My appeal to more phenomenological study is, of course, rooted in my belief that the classic phenomenological approach as practiced by Scheler and others is valid, and until Heideggerians can provide evidence for their claims, the possibility of classic phenomenology is still alive.

Scheler and Language

Classic phenomenology has, since Scheler's day, been seriously questioned, and not just by Heideggerians. I cannot answer all of

[7] I say raised by Emad's Heidegger because Emad himself does, at least at one point, allow for the possibility of a phenomenology that is not so trapped (1981, 153).

the attacks on phenomenology in general, or even on Scheler's particular version of it. There is, however, one position that constitutes a particularly serious challenge which Scheler anticipated. It is rooted in the now-popular belief that we can never get beyond language, that language defines what we can know, and indeed perhaps even what we can experience. Scheler was a pioneer in recognizing the danger of such a linguistic reductionism. Indeed, he was quite concerned to show that the phenomenological given was free from the constraints of language, free from the limitations of symbols. As we noted in chapter 3, in the essay "The Theory of the Three Facts" Scheler makes the independence from symbols the third of four "essential characteristics" of phenomenological "facts" (LDT 447/TTF 220). As Scheler puts it in the "Phenomenology and the Theory of Cognition" essay: "Something can be *self-given* only if it is no longer given merely through any sort of symbol; in other words, only if it is not 'meant' as the mere 'fulfillment' of a sign which is previously defined in some way or other. In this sense *phenomenological* philosophy is a continual *desymbolization of the world*" (PUE 385/ PTC 143).

Scheler goes on to detail how the natural worldview—and especially the scientific worldview—enmeshes us more and more deeply into the symbolizaton of the world (PUE 385–86/PTC 143–45). Although he is talking of the scientific use of language, what he says is extendable to all such entrapment in symbols. It is quite clear from this passage that Scheler anticipates and works to counter the problems created by a language-trapped stance.

Despite Scheler's pioneering efforts, the task of showing that a phenomenological approach takes us beyond the confines of language is not yet complete. Those of us who wish to defend classic phenomenology against this most basic of attacks must still provide convincing evidence that there is something beyond language, that there is a prelinguistic given. Furthermore, we must complete the equally important task of showing that we can develop a phenomenological method of testing claims to essential knowledge that is itself prelinguistic. Such work is clearly beyond the scope of the present study, and unlike Scheler, who would at this point promise that another study is in the works, I will make no promises, though in fact I have undertaken parts of this task, with key initial elements already published.[8]

Final Comments

With this I have come to the end of my development of the logic of Scheler's quest for an ethical personalism and my development and defense of a Schelerian practical ethics. Since we have ranged far in this book, it is perhaps wise to end by highlighting some key elements of a Schelerian practical ethics that have emerged from this study.

As we have seen, Scheler was quite correct to call his ethics both a "Non-Formal Ethics of Values" and an "Ethical Personalism." The person, the unity of acts, is an essentially dynamic being with an identity that lies solely in the qualitative direction of its pure becoming different. Ethics focuses on the fact that the person is the highest value, with the realization of nonmoral values co-creating the moral values. A complex realm of realizable, noncontingent, nonmoral values, accessible through special acts of "feeling," lies before the person. What a person can see of the hierarchy of values is controlled by his or her *ordo amoris,* and that ordering can change and grow through the workings of the love of others (and the person can open him- or herself to such love). Each person responds to the world of values in his or her own way, as does each group, and as love opens each person (and group) to higher values and clarifies his or her vision of them, new possibilities develop. Indeed, if persons have the ability to share their vision, that part of the hierarchical ranking of values open to us all grows. The best way to see what to be and do is to see the qualitative direction of persons as models or exemplars.

The sketchiness of what I have just said indicates how much work is left at all levels. Max Scheler blazed a trail in many differ-

[8] I have contributed to the attempts to show that language does not limit what we can experience in "Language and the Phenomenological Given" (1982) and, more recently, in "Transcending Language: The Rule of Evocation" (1998). I have also contributed to the development of the phenomenological method as a way of making and testing claims to essential knowledge in "Phenomenology and the Claiming of Essences" (1994–95).

ent areas of investigation, won many insights, and faced and solved many problems while leaving many more. Yet throughout Scheler's odyssey his quest for a new understanding of values, the heart, and the person, and for a new ethical personalism, shines forth. What he accomplished is as exciting in prospect as it is challenging in what it has left undone. Scheler's task, however, was not to complete an ethical personalism but to blaze the trail to it. He was a pioneer who had, in my judgment, an excellent grasp of what needed to be dealt with first, if his quest was ever to be completed. Unfortunately, he died before he could complete even his pioneering efforts. What he left us, however, is not just a set of interesting, if contradictory and incoherent, insights. He left us the discernible outlines of a new approach in ethics. If this book contributes to a better understanding of those outlines, and thus to the possibility of further exploration and development of this new ethical personalism, then its task is accomplished.

BIBLIOGRAPHY

Scheler's Collected Works in German

Scheler's *Gesammelte Werke* were edited initially by Maria Scheler, with Manfred Frings taking over in 1973. They were initially published by Franke Verlag in Bern, but since 1986 they have been published (or reprinted) by Bouvier Verlag in Bonn (which has retained the original publication dates).

Frühe Schriften. Vol. 1, *Gesammelte Werke.* Bonn: Bouvier Verlag, 1971.

Der Formalismus in der Ethik und die Materiale Wertethik: Neuer Versuch der Grundlegung eines Ethischen Personalismus. Vol. 2, *Gesammelte Werke.* Bonn: Bouvier Verlag, 1980.

Vom Umsturz der Werte: Abhandlungen und Aufsätze. Vol. 3, *Gesammelte Werke.* Bonn: Bouvier Verlag, 1972.

Politisch-Pädagogische Schriften. Vol. 4, *Gesammelte Werke.* Bonn: Bouvier Verlag, 1982.

Vom Ewigen im Menschen. Vol. 5, *Gesammelte Werke.* Bonn: Bouvier Verlag, 1954.

Schriften zur Soziologie und Weltanschauungslehre. Vol. 6, *Gesammelte Werke.* Bonn: Bouvier Verlag, 1963.

Wesen und Formen der Sympathie. Vol. 7, *Gesammelte Werke.* Bonn: Bouvier Verlag, 1973.

Die Wissensformen und die Gesellschaft. Vol. 8, *Gesammelte Werke.* Bonn: Bouvier Verlag, 1980.

Späte Schriften. Vol. 9, *Gesammelte Werke.* Bonn: Bouvier Verlag, 1976.

Schriften aus dem Nachlass, I. Zur Ethik und Erkenntnislehre. Vol. 10, *Gesammelte Werke.* Bonn: Bouvier Verlag, 1957.

Schriften aus dem Nachlass, II. Erkenntnislehre und Metaphysik. Vol. 11, *Gesammelte Werke.* Bonn: Bouvier Verlag, 1979.

Schriften aus dem Nachlass, III. Philosophische Anthropologie. Vol. 12, *Gesammelte Werke*. Bonn: Bouvier Verlag, 1987.

Schriften aus dem Nachlass, IV. Philosophie und Geschichte. Vol. 13, *Gesammelte Werke*. Bonn: Bouvier Verlag, 1990.

Schriften aus dem Nachlass, V. Varia I. Vol. 14, *Gesammelte Werke*. Bonn: Bouvier Verlag, 1993.

Schriften aus dem Nachlass, V. Varia II. Vol. 15, *Gesammelte Werke*. Bonn: Bouvier Verlag, 1993.

English Translations of Scheler's Works

"An A Priori Hierarchy of Value-Modalities." In *Readings in Existential Phenomenology,* edited by Nathaniel Morris Lawrence and Daniel Denis O'Connor. Englewood Cliffs, N.J.: Prentice-Hall, 1967.

"Concerning the Meaning of the Feminist Movement." *Philosophical Forum* 9 (1978).

Formalism in Ethics and Non-Formal Ethics of Values: A New Attempt toward the Foundation of an Ethical Personalism. Translated by Manfred S. Frings and Roger L. Funk. Northwestern University Studies in Phenomenology and Existential Philosophy. Evanston: Northwestern University Press, 1973.

"Future of Man." *Monthly Criterion* 7 (1928).

"Humility." *Aletheia* 11 (1981).

"The Idea of Man." *Journal of the British Society for Phenomenology* 9 (1978).

"The Idea of Peace and Pacifism." *Journal of the British Society for Phenomenology* 8 (1976–77).

"Love and Knowledge." In *Max Scheler: On Feeling, Knowing, and Valuing. Selected Writings,* edited by Harold Bershady. Chicago: University of Chicago Press, 1992.

Man's Place in Nature. Translated by Hans Meyerhof. New York: Noonday Press, 1971.

"Max Weber's Exclusion of Philosophy (on the Psychology and Sociology of Nominalist Thought)." In *Max Weber's Science as a Vocation,* edited by Peter Lassman, Irving Velody, and Herminio Martins. London: Unwin Hyman, 1989.

"The Meaning of Suffering." In *Max Scheler: On Feeling, Know-*

ing, and Valuing. Selected Writings, edited by Harold Bershady. Chicago: University of Chicago Press, 1992.

"Metaphysics and Art." In *Max Scheler (1874–1928) Centennial Essays,* edited by Manfred S. Frings. The Hague: Martinus Nijhoff, 1974.

The Nature of Sympathy. London: Routledge & Kegan Paul, 1954.

On the Eternal in Man. Translated by Bernard Noble. Hamden, Conn.: Archon Books by The Shoe String Press, 1972.

"On the Positivistic Philosophy of the History of Knowledge and Its Laws of Three Stages." In *The Sociology of Knowledge: A Reader,* edited by James E. Curtis and John W. Petras. New York: Praeger, 1970.

"On the Tragic." *Cross Currents* 4 (1954).

"On the Tragic." In *Tragedy: Vision and Form,* edited by Robert Willoughby Corrigan. San Francisco: Chandler, 1965.

Person and Self-Value: Three Essays. Edited by Manfred S. Frings. Dordrecht: Martinus Nijhoff, 1987.

Philosophical Perspectives. Translated by Oscar A. Haac. Boston: Beacon Press, 1958.

Problems of a Sociology of Knowledge. Translated by Manfred S. Frings, International Library of Sociology. London: Routledge & Kegan Paul, 1980.

"The Psychology of So-Called Compensation Hysteria and the Real Battle against Illness." *Journal of Phenomenological Psychology* 15 (1984).

"Reality and Resistance: On *Being and Time,* Section 43." In *Listening,* 1977. Reprinted in *Heidegger: The Man and the Thinker,* edited by Thomas Sheehan. Chicago: Precedent, 1981.

Ressentiment. Translated by Lewis B. Coser and William A. Holdheim. Milwaukee: Marquette University Press, 1998.

Selected Philosophical Essays. Translated by David R. Lachterman. Northwestern University Studies in Phenomenology and Existential Philosophy. Evanston: Northwestern University Press, 1973.

"Sociology and the Study and Formulation of Weltanschauung." In *Max Weber's Science as a Vocation,* edited by Peter Lassman, Irving Velody, and Herminio Martins. London: Unwin Hyman, 1989.

"The Thomistic Ethic and the Spirit of Capitalism." *Sociological Analysis* 25, no. 25 (1964).

"Toward a Stratification of the Emotional Life." In *Readings in Existential Phenomenology,* edited by Nathaniel Morris Lawrence and Daniel Denis O'Connor. Englewood Cliffs, N.J.: Prentice-Hall, 1967.

Non-Scheler Works Cited

Barber, Michael D. *Guardian of Dialogue: Max Scheler's Phenomenology, Sociology of Knowledge, and Philosophy of Love*. Lewisburg, Pa.: Bucknell University Press, 1993.

Becker, Howard. "Befuddled Germany: A Glimpse of Max Scheler." *American Sociological Review* 8 (1943): 207–11.

Bershady, Harold, ed. *Max Scheler: On Feeling, Knowing, and Valuing. Selected Writings*. Chicago: University of Chicago Press, 1992.

Blosser, Philip. *Scheler's Critique of Kant's Ethics*. Series in Continental Thought, no. 22. Athens: Ohio University Press, 1995.

Brunner, August. "Foreword." In Scheler, *On the Eternal in Man,* 7–9. Hamden, Conn.: Archon Books by the Shoestring Press, 1972.

Buber, Martin. *Between Man and Man*. Boston: Beacon Press, 1936.

Cassirer, Ernst. *The Philosophy of Ernst Cassirer*. Edited by Paul Schilpp. Evanston, Ill.: Library of Living Philosophers, 1949.

Collins, James. "Roots of Scheler's Evolutionary Pantheism." In *Three Paths in Philosophy*. Chicago: Henry Regency, 1962.

Coser, Lewis A. "Max Scheler: An Introduction." In Scheler, *Ressentiment,* 5–32. New York: Schocken Books by the Free Press, 1972.

Crosby, John F. "The Individuality of Human Persons: A Study in the Ethical Personalism of Max Scheler." *Review of Metaphysics* 52, no. 1 (1999): 21–50.

Deeken, Alfons. *Process and Permanence in Ethics: Max Scheler's Moral Philosophy*. New York: Paulist Press, 1974.

Dunlop, Francis. *Max Scheler*. London: Claridge, 1991.

Dupuy, Maurice. *La philosophie de la religion chez Max Scheler.* Paris: Presses Universitaires de France, 1959.

———. *La philosophie de Max Scheler: Son évolution et son unité.* Paris: Presses Universitaires de France, 1959.

Emad, Parvis. *Heidegger and the Phenomenology of Values: His Critique of Intentionality.* Glen Ellyn, Ill.: Torey Press, 1981.

Frings, Manfred S. "The Background of Max Scheler's 1927 Reading of *Being and Time:* A Critique of a Critique through Ethics." *Philosophy Today* 36, no. 2 (1992): 99–113.

———. "Husserl and Scheler: Two Views on Intersubjectivity." *Journal of the British Society for Phenomenology* 9, no. 3 (1978): 143–49.

———. "Max Scheler." In *Encyclopedia of Phenomenology,* edited by Lester Embree et al., 629–34. Dordrecht: Kluwer, 1997.

———. *Max Scheler: A Concise Introduction into the World of a Great Thinker.* 2nd ed. Milwaukee: Marquette University Press, 1996.

———. *The Mind of Max Scheler: The First Comprehensive Guide Based on the Complete Works.* Marquette Studies in Philosophy, no. 13. Milwaukee: Marquette University Press, 1997.

———. *Philosophy of Prediction and Capitalism.* Dordrecht: Martinus Nijhoff, 1987.

Hartmann, Wilfried. "Max Scheler and the English-Speaking World." *Philosophy Today* 12, no. 1 (1968): 31–41.

———. *Max Scheler: Bibliographie.* Stuttgart: F. Frommann, 1963.

Heath, Peter. "The Idea of a Phenomenological Ethics." In *Phenomenology and Philosophical Understanding,* edited by Edo Pivcevic. London: Cambridge University Press, 1975.

Ibana, Rainier R. A. "The Stratification of Emotional Life and the Problem of Other Minds According to Max Scheler." *International Philosophical Quarterly* 30 (December 1991): 461–71.

Kant, Immanuel. *Critique of Practical Reason and Other Writings in Moral Philosophy.* Translated by Lewis White Beck. Chicago: University of Chicago Press, 1949.

———. *Critique of Pure Reason.* Translated by Norman Kemp Smith. New York: St. Martin's Press, 1965.

———. *The Doctrine of Virtue.* Translated by Mary Gregor. New York: Harper and Row, 1964.

———. *Foundations of the Metaphysics of Morals.* Translated by Lewis White Beck. Indianapolis: Bobbs-Merrill, 1959.

———. *Grundlegung zur Metaphysik der Sitten.* Vol. 4, Preussische Akademie der Wissenschaften. Riga: Johann Friedrich Hartknoch, 1787.

———. *Kritik der praktischen Vernunft.* Vol. 5, Preussische Akademie der Wissenschaften. Riga: Johann Friedrich Hartknoch, 1788.

———. *Kritik der reiner Vernunft.* Vol. 4, Preussische Akademie der Wissenschaften. Riga: Johann Friedrich Hartknoch, 1787.

———. *Metaphysics of Morals.* Translated by Mary Gregor. New York: Cambridge University Press, 1991.

———. *Die Metaphysik der Sitten.* Vol. 6, Preussische Akademie der Wissenschaften. Riga: Johann Friedrich Hartknoch, 1797–98.

Kelly, Eugene. *Max Scheler.* Twayne's World Leaders Series, no. 55. Boston: Twayne, 1977.

———. *Structure and Diversity: Studies in the Phenomenological Philosophy of Max Scheler.* Phaenomenologica, no. 141. Dordrecht: Kluwer Academic, 1997.

Koehle, Eckhard Joseph. *Personality: A Study According to the Philosophies of Value and Spirit of Max Scheler and Nicolai Hartmann.* Arlington, N.J.: Catholic Protectory Press, 1941.

Kohák, Erazim. *The Embers and the Stars: A Philosophical Inquiry into the Moral Sense of Nature.* Chicago: University of Chicago Press, 1984.

Lehmann, Gerhard. *Die Deutsche Philosophie der Gegenwart.* Stuttgart: Kröner Verlag, 1943.

Lenk, Kurt. *Von der Ohnmacht des Geistes: Kritische Darstellung der Spätphilosophie Max Schelers.* Tübingen: Hopfer Verlag, 1959.

Meyerhoff, Hans. "Translator's Introduction." In Scheler, *Man's Place in Nature,* vii–viii. New York: Noonday Press, 1971.

Moosa, Imtiaz. "Formalism of Kant's A Priori versus Scheler's Material A Priori." *International Studies in Philosophy* 27, no. 2 (1995): 32–47.

Nota, John H., S.J. *Max Scheler: The Man and His Work.* Translated by Theodore Plantinga and John H. Nota, S.J. Chicago: Franciscan Herald Press, 1983. Originally published in Dutch as *Max Scheler: De man en zijn werk* by Het Wereldvenster Baarn.

Oesterreicher, John M. *Walls Are Crumbling: Seven Jewish Philosophers Discover Christ.* New York: Devin-Air, 1952.

Owens, Thomas J. *Phenomenology and Intersubjectivity.* The Hague: Martinus Nijhoff, 1970.

Perrin, Ron. *Max Scheler's Concept of the Person: An Ethics of Humanism.* New York: St. Martin's Press, 1991.

Ranly, Ernest W. *Scheler's Phenomenology of Community.* The Hague: Martinus Nijhoff, 1966.

Schutz, Alfred. *Collected Papers.* The Hague: Martinus Nijhoff, 1975.

———. "Scheler's Theory of Intersubjectivity and the General Thesis of the Alter Ego." *Philosophy and Phenomenological Research* 2 (1942): 323–47. Reprinted in Schutz, *Collected Papers,* vol. 1, *The Problem of Social Reality,* 150–79. The Hague: Martinus Nijhoff, 1973.

———. "William James's Concept of the Stream of Thought Phenomenologically Interpreted." *Philosophy and Phenomenological Research* 1 (June 1941). Reprinted in Schutz, *Collected Papers,* vol. 3, *Studies in Phenomenological Philosophy,* 1–14. The Hague: Martinus Nijhoff, 1975.

Sherman, Nancy. "The Place of Emotions in Kantian Morality." In *Identity, Character, and Morality: Essays in Moral Psychology,* edited by Owen Flanagan and Amelie O. Rorty, 149–70. Cambridge: MIT Press, 1990.

Solomon, Robert C. "Emotions and Choice." *Review of Metaphysics* 27, no. 105 (1973): 20–41.

Spader, Peter. "Language and the Phenomenological Given." *Philosophy Today* 26, nos. 3–4 (1982): 254–62.

———. "Phenomenology and the Claiming of Essences." *Husserl Studies* 11, no. 3 (1994–95): 169–99.

———. "Transcending Language: The Rule of Evocation." *The Paideia Project On-Line* (1999): http://www2.bu.edu/wcp/Papers/Lang/LangSpad.htm.

Spiegelberg, Herbert. *The Phenomenological Movement.* 2nd ed. 2 vols. The Hague: Martinus Nijhoff, 1971.

Stark, W. "Editor's Introduction." In Scheler, *The Nature of Sympathy,* ix–xliv. London: Routledge & Kegan Paul, 1954.

Staude, John Raphael. *Max Scheler: An Intellectual Portrait.* New York: Free Press, 1967.

Strasser, Stephen. *Phenomenology of Feeling.* Pittsburgh: Duquesne University Press, 1977.

Tallon, Andrew. *Head and Heart: Affection, Cognition, Volition as Triune Consciousness.* New York: Fordham University Press, 1997.

Von Hildebrand, Dietrich. *Christian Ethics.* New York: David McKay, 1953.

———. "Max Scheler als Personlichkeit." *Hochland* 26, no. 1 (1928–29): 70–80.

Weiss, Dennis M. "Max Scheler and Philosophical Anthropology." *Philosophy Today* 42, no. 3 (1998): 235–49.

Werkmeister, W. H. *Kant: The Architectonic and Development of His Philosophy.* La Salle, Ill.: Open Court, 1980.

Witkop, Philip, ed. *Deutschen Leben der Gegenwart.* Berlin: Wegweister Verlag, 1922.

Wojtyla, Karol. *The Acting Person.* Translated by Andrzej Potocki. Dordrecht: D. Reidel, 1979.

APPENDIX: SECONDARY SOURCES ON SCHELER PUBLISHED BETWEEN 1990 AND 1999

The following is a list of secondary publications from the last decade of the twentieth century. It is presented to demonstrate the continuing interest in Scheler, and not just in the English-speaking world. For other works, see Wilfried Hartmann, *Max Scheler: Bibliographie* (Stuttgart: F. Frommann, 1963). For works since 1963, many of the major studies on Scheler contain general bibliographies, with the works of Manfred S. Frings especially valuable. In addition to printed bibliographies, the internet is becoming an increasingly useful research tool, particularly when searched using computer programs such as *Endnote*. The *Philosopher's Index* is another useful database (your library may have access to this database). I also recommend "Professor Fring's MAX SCHELER Web Site" (presently at http://www.maxscheler.-com) and the website of the Max Scheler Gesellschaft (presently at http://www.max-scheler.de/).

Alemann, Heine von. "Heltmuth Plessner, Max Scheler und die Entstehung der Philosophischen Anthropologie in Köln: Eine Skizze." In Orth and Pfafferott, *Studien zur Philosophie von Max Scheler,* 10–34.

Allodi, Leonardo. "Scheler und die Kritik am Pragmatismus." In Bermes, Henckmann, and Leonardy, *Ursprung des Denkens—Denken des Ursprungs,* 172–83.

Ave-Lallemant, Eberhard. "Die Aktualität von Schelers Politischer Philosophie." In Orth and Pfafferott, *Studien zur Philosophie von Max Scheler,* 116–64.

———. "Die Lebenswerte in der Rangordnung der Werte." In

Pfafferott, *Vom umsturz der Werte in der modernen Gesellschaft,* 81–99.

Baranowska, Maria Malgorzata. "M. Scheler and R. Ingarden on the Concept of Man" (in Polish). *Kwartalnik-Filozoficzny* 26, no. 4 (1998): 47–56.

Barber, Michael D. *Guardian of Dialogue: Max Scheler's Phenomenology, Sociology of Knowledge, and Philosophy of Love.* Lewisburg, Pa.: Bucknell University Press, 1993.

Bermes, Christian. " 'Welt' als Ursprung und Maß des Denkens. Weltkonzepte in Schelers Denken." In Bermes, Henckmann, and Leonardy, *Ursprung des Denkens—Denken des Ursprungs,* 54–67.

Bermes, Christian, Wolfhart Henckmann, and Heinz Leonardy, eds. *Ursprung des Denkens—Denken des Ursprungs: Schelers Philosophie und ihre Anfänge in Jena.* Kritisches Jahrbuck der Philosophie. Würzburg: Königshausen & Neurnann, 1998.

Bershady, Harold J., ed. *Max Scheler: On Feeling, Knowing, and Valuing. Selected Writings.* Heritage of Sociology Series. Chicago: University of Chicago Press, 1992.

Beujic, Branca. "Ethos und geschichtlicher Werdeprozess." In Bermes, Henckmann, and Leonardy, *Ursprung des Denkens—Denken des Ursprungs,* 98–106.

Bianco, Franco. "Die Gegebenheit der Werte. Max Schelers Stellung in der Werturteilsdiskussion der Gegenwart." In Pfafferott, *Vom umsturz der Werte in der modernen Gesellschaft,* 264–80.

Blosser, Philip. "The A Priori in Phenomenology and the Legacy of Logical Empiricism." *Philosophy Today* 34, no. 3 (1990): 195–205.

———. "Is Scheler's Ethic an Ethic of Virtue?" In *Japanese and Western Phenomenology,* edited by Philip Blosser et al., 147–59. The Hague: Kluwer, 1993.

———. *Scheler's Critique of Kant's Ethics.* Series in Continental Thought, no. 22. Athens: Ohio University Press, 1995.

———. "Scheler's Ordo Amoris: Insights and Oversights." In Bermes, Henckmann and Leonardy, *Ursprung des Denkens—Denken des Ursprungs,* 160–71.

———. "Scheler's Theory of Values Reconsidered." In *Phenomenology of Values and Valuing,* edited by James G. Hart. Dordrecht: Kluwer, 1997.

———. "Six Questions Concerning Scheler's Ethics." *Journal of Value Inquiry* 33 (1999): 211–25.

Bosio, Franco. *Invito al pensiero di Max Scheler.* Milano: Mursia, 1995.

———. "Das Motiv des 'Umsturzes der Werte' in der Erkenntnis der Welt und des Menschen in der Philosophie von Max Scheler." In Pfafferott, *Vom umsturz der Werte in der modernen Gesellschaft,* 141–47.

———. "Il significato dell'antropologia filosofica nel pensiero di Max Scheler." *Fenomenologia e Societá* 14, no. 2 (1991): 9–28.

Boudier, Henk Struyker. "The Difference between Man and Animal: Letters of Max Scheler on F J J Buytendijk" (in Dutch). *Bijdragen* 53, no. 3 (1992): 312–22.

Braun, Walter. "Das Problem des 'Interesses' bei den Phanomenologen Husserl und Scheler." *Prima Philosophia* 8, no. 4 (1995): 359–68.

Brujic, Branka. "The World of Work and the Process of Historicity in Max Scheler's Thought." *Filozofska Iztrazivanja* 16, no. 1 (1996): 157–73.

Brümmer, Vincent. *The Model of Love: A Study in Philosophical Theology.* Cambridge: Cambridge University Press, 1993.

Buchheim, Th. "Ähnlichkeit und ihre Bedeutung für die Identität der Person in Max Schelers Wertethik." In Orth and Pfafferott, *Studien zur Philosophie von Max Scheler,* 245–58.

Cremer, Wolfgang. *Person und Technik: die phänomenologische Deutung der Technik in der Philosophie Max Schelers. Wissenschaftliche Schriften im Wissenschaftlichen Verlag Dr. Schulz-Kirchner. Reihe 11, Beiträge zur Philosophie; bd. 105.* Idstein: Schulz-Kirchner Verlag, 1991.

Crespo, Mariano. "Der Phanomenologisch-Ontologische Hintergrund des Personalismus von Max Scheler: Eine Antwort auf das Referat von John F. Crosby." In *Menschenwurde: Metaphysik und Ethik,* edited by Mariano Crespo. Heidelberg: Carl Winter Univ, 1998.

Crosby, John F. "The Individuality of Human Persons: A Study in the Ethical Personalism of Max Scheler." *Review of Metaphysics* 52, no. 1 (1999): 21–50.

———. "Zum Personalismus Max Schelers." In *Menschenwurde:*

Metaphysik und Ethik, edited by Mariano Crespo. Heidelberg: Carl Winter University, 1998.

Cusinato, Guido. "Absolute Rangordnung und Relativität der Werte im Denken Max Schelers." In Pfafferott, *Vom umsturz der Werte in der modernen Gesellschaft,* 62–80.

———. "Die Historisierung des Apriori und der Funktionalisierungsbegriff im Denken Max Schelers." In *Cognitio humana: Dynamik des Wissens und der Werte (Deutscher Kongress für Philosophie).* Leipzig, 1996.

———. "Methode oder Techne? Ethik und Realitat in der 'phänomenologischen' Reduktion Schelers." In Bermes, Henckmann, and Leonardy, *Ursprung des Denkens—Denken des Ursprungs,* 83–97.

Da Re, Antonio. "Die Tyrannei der Werte: Carl Schmitt und die phänomenologische Ethik." In Pfafferott, *Vom umsturz der Werte in der modernen Gesellschaft,* 238–50.

Därmann, Iris. "Die Unmöglichkeit der Gabe. Zur Kritik von Schelers Wertbegrif in Ausgang von Nietzsche, Heidegger, und Derrida." In Bermes, Henckmann, and Leonardy, *Ursprung des Denkens—Denken des Ursprungs,* 137–48.

Dhar, Benulal. "The Phenomenology of Value-Experience: Some Reflections on Scheler and Hartmann." *Indian Philosophical Quarterly* 26, no. 2 (1999): 183–97.

Dunlop, Francis. *Max Scheler.* Thinkers of Our Time Series. London: Claridge Press, 1991.

Fedoryka, Kateryna. "Dietrich von Hildebrand on Max Scheler as Philosopher and Personality: Toward an Understanding of Phenomenology Method." *Aletheia* 6 (1994): 321–39.

Frings, Manfred S. "The Background of Max Scheler's 1927 Reading of *Being and Time:* A Critique of a Critique through Ethics." *Philosophy Today* 36, no. 2 (1992): 99–113.

———. "Begrüßungsansprache zum II. Internationalen Kolloquium der Max-Scheler-Gesellschaft." In Pfafferott, *Vom umsturz der Werte in der modernen Gesellschaft,* 1–6.

———. "Capitalism and Ethics. The World Era of Adjustment and the Call of the Hour." In Orth and Pfafferott, *Studien zur Philosophie von Max Scheler,* 96–115.

———. "Max Scheler." In *The Encyclopedia of Phenomenology,* edited by Lester Embree et al., 629–34. Dordrecht: Kluwer Academic Publishing, 1997.

———. *Max Scheler: A Concise Introduction into the World of a Great Thinker.* 2nd ed. Milwaukee: Marquette University Press, 1996.

———. "Max Scheler: A Novel Look at the Origin of Evil." *Philosophy and Theology: Marquette University Quarterly* 6, no. 3 (1992): 201–11.

———. *Max Scheler. Von der Ganzheit des Menschen: Ausgewahlte Schriften: Liebe, Ethik, Erkenntnis, Leiden, Zukunft, Realitat, Soziologie, Philosophie.* Bonn: Bouvier, 1991.

———. *The Mind of Max Scheler: The First Comprehensive Guide Based on the Complete Works.* Marquette Studies in Philosophy, no. 13. Milwaukee: Marquette University Press, 1997.

Gabel, Michael. "Ausgleich und Verzicht. Schelers 'später' Gedanke des Ausgleichs im Licht seines phänomenologischen Ansatzes." In Orth and Pfafferott, *Studien zur Philosophie von Max Scheler,* 204–39.

———. "Das Heilige in Schelers Systematik der Wertrangordnung." In Pfafferott, *Vom umsturz der Werte in der modernen Gesellschaft,* 113–28.

———. *Intentionalität des Geistes: der phänomenologische Denkansatz bei Max Scheler: Untersuchung zum Verständnis der Intentionalität in Max Scheler "Der Formalismus in der Ethik und die materiale Wertethik"* [1. Aufl.]. ed, Erfurter theologische Studien; bd. 61. Leipzig: Benno Verlag, 1991.

———. "Die logischen und ethischen Prinzipien bei Scheler in ihren Verhältnis zur Religionsphilosophie." In Bermes, Henckmann, and Leonardy, *Ursprung des Denkens—Denken des Ursprungs,* 68–82.

Glauser, Richard. "Ressentiment et valeurs morales: Max Scheler, critique de Nietzsche." *Revue de Théologie et de Philosophie* 128, no. 3 (1996): 209–28.

Gooch, Augusta O. "Value Hierarchies in Scheler and Von Hildebrand." *Southwest Philosophical Studies* 15 (1993): 19–27.

Gorevan, Patrick. "Heidegger and Scheler—A Dialogue." *Journal of the British Society for Phenomenology* 24, no. 3 (1993): 276–82.

———. "Scheler's Response to Schopenhauer." *Schopenhauer-Jahrbuch* 77 (1996): 167–79.

Hammer, F. "Glauben an den Menschen. Helmuth Plessners Religionskritik im Vergleich mit Max Schelers Religionsphilosophie." *Dilthey-Jahrbuch* 7 (1990–91).

Henckmann, Wolfhart. "Die Anfänge von Schelers Philosophie in Jena." In Bermes, Henckmann, and Leonardy, *Ursprung des Denkens—Denken des Ursprungs,* 11–34.

———. "Das Intentionalitätsproblem bei Scheler." *Brentano-Studien* 3 (1990–91): 203–28.

———. *Max Scheler. Beck'scheReihe; BsR 543. Denker.* München: Verlag C.H. Beck, 1998.

———. "M. Scheler: Phänomenologie der Werte." In *Philosophen des 20. Jahrhunderts,* edited by M. Fleischer, 94–116. Darmstadt, 1992.

———. "Schelers Begriff der Philosophie in der Zeit des 'Umsturzes der Werte.' " In Pfafferott, *Vom umsturz der Werte in der modernen Gesellschaft,* 20–33.

———. "Der Systemanspruch von Schelers Philosophie." In Orth and Pfafferott, *Studien zur Philosophie von Max Scheler,* 271–312.

Ibana, Rainier R. A. "Max Scheler's Analysis of Illusions, Idols, and Ideologies." *Philosophy Today* (1990): 312–20.

———. "The Stratification of Emotional Life and the Problem of Other Minds According to Max Scheler." *International Philosophical Quarterly* (1991): 461–71.

Janssen, Paul. "Feeling/Knowledge—Values/Being." *Filozofska Iztrazivanja* 16, no. 1 (1996): 115–28.

———. "Fühlen/Erkennen—Werte/Sein. Von verschiedenen Möglichkeiten, die Eigenart von Wissen zu bestimmen." In Pfafferott, *Vom umsturz der Werte in der modernen Gesellschaft,* 281–96.

———. "Nachtrag zur Verabschiedung der philosophischen Anthropologie—am Beispiel Schelers." In *Perspektiven Der Philosophie,* edited by Rudolph Berlinger. Amsterdam: Rodopi, 1997.

———. "Über einige Schwierigkeiten einer zeitgemäßen philosophischen Anthropologie—am Beispiel Schelers." In *Jahrbücher d. Staatlichen Universität Wolgograd,* 281–96. Moscow: Bouvier Verlag, 1995.

———. "Die Verwandlung der phänomenologischen Reduktion im Werke Max Schelers und das Realitätsproblem." In Orth and Pfafferott, *Studien zur Philosophie von Max Scheler,* 281–96.

Joisten, Karen. "Ressentiment: Nietzsche's and Scheler's Contribution to the Basic Condition of Man's Being." *Synthesis Philosophica* 11, no. 1 (1996): 65–77.

Kaehler, Klaus E. "Selbsterkenntnis, Selbsttäuschung und das Subjektive der Werte." In Orth and Pfafferott, *Studien zur Philosophie von Max Scheler,* 314–21.

Kalinowski, Georges. *Expérience et phénoménologie: Husserl, Ingarden, Scheler, Collection Les Grandes leçons de philosophie.* Paris: Editions Universitaires, 1992.

———. *La phénoménologie de l'homme chez Husserl, Ingarden et Scheler, Collection Les Grandes leçons de philosophie.* Paris: Editions Universitaires, 1991.

Kaufmann, Peter. *Gemüt und Gefühl als Komplement der Vernunft: eine Auseinandersetzung mit der Tradition und der phänomenologischen Ethik, besonders Max Schelers.* Forum interdisziplinäre Ethik, bd. 3. Frankfurt am Main: P. Lang, 1992.

Kelly, Eugene. "Der Begriff des Schicksals in Schelers Denken." In Bermes, Henckmann, and Leonardy, *Ursprung des Denkens—Denken des Ursprungs,* 149–59.

———. "Essences." *Aletheia* 6 (1994): 100–115.

———. "Revisiting Max Scheler's Formalism in Ethics: Virtue-Based Ethics and Moral Rules in the Non-Formal Ethics of Value." *Journal of Value Inquiry* 31, no. 3 (1997): 381–97.

———. *Structure and Diversity: Studies in the Phenomenological Philosophy of Max Scheler.* Phaenomenologica, no. 141. Dordrecht; Boston: Kluwer Academic, 1997.

Kiss, Endre. "Max Schelers 'Umsturz der Werte' als Kritik der Europäischen Moderne." In Pfafferott, *Vom umsturz der Werte in der modernen Gesellschaft,* 129–40.

Kodalle, Klaus M. "'Verzeihung' als Grundbegriff der Ethik: Schelers Anregungen." In Bermes, Henckmann, and Leonardy, *Ursprung des Denkens—Denken des Ursprungs,* 107–20.

Kovacs, George. "Death and the Search for Ultimate Meaning in Max Scheler: A Further Contribution to URAM Scheler Studies ('Uram' 3: 135–43)." *Ultimate Reality and Meaning* 22, no. 3 (1999): 208–22.

Krahl, A., and M. Schifferdecker. "Max Scheler und Kurt Schneider. Wissenschaftlicher Einfluß und persönliche Begegnung." *Fortschritte der Neurologie u. Psychiatrie* 66 (1998): 94–100.

Lacoste, Jean-Yves. "Du Phenomene de la Valeur au Discours de la Norme." *Frieberger Zeitschrift für Philosophie und Theologie* 44, nos. 1–2 (1997): 87–103.

Lambertino, Antonio. "Scheler und die Psychoanalytische Freudsche Theorie." In Pfafferott, *Vom umsturz der Werte in der modernen Gesellschaft,* 148–64.

Lembeck, Karl-Heinz. " 'Deutscher Weltberuf'? Natorps und Schelers Kriegsphilosophie." In Pfafferott, *Vom umsturz der Werte in der modernen Gesellschaft,* 220–37.

Lenoci, Michele. *Autocoscienza, valori, storicità: Studi su Meinong, Scheler, Heidegger.* Filosofia, no. 54. Milano: Franco Angeli, 1992.

Leonardy, Heinz. " 'Es ist schwer, ein Mensch zu sein': Zur Anthropologie des späten Scheler." In Orth and Pfafferott, *Studien zur Philosophie von Max Scheler,* 71–94.

Leroux, Henri. "Fonction Hermeneutique de la Notion de Umsturz der Werte en Sociologie et en Anthropologie." In Pfafferott, *Vom umsturz der Werte in der modernen Gesellschaft,* 165–79.

———. "Sur quelques aspects de la reception de Max Scheler en France." In Orth and Pfafferott, *Studien zur Philosophie von Max Scheler,* 332–56.

Liu, Hsiao-feng. *Personwerdung: Eine theologische Untersuchung zu Max Schelers Phänomenologie der "Person-Gefühle" mit besonderer Berücksichtigung seiner Kritik an der Moderne.* Basler und Berner Studien zur historischen und systematischen Theologie, bd. 64. Bern: P. Lang, 1996.

———. "Scheler's Christian Thought and the Phenomenology of Values." In *Christian Thought in the Twentieth Century,* edited by Hsiao-feng Liu. Hong Kong: Joint Publishing House, 1990.

Macann, Christopher E. "Towards a Genetics Ethics." *Journal of the British Society for Phenomenology* 29, no. 1 (1998): 75–94.

———. "Zu einer genetischen Ethik: Eine interpretative Transformation von Schelers Wertethik." In Orth and Pfafferott, *Studien zur Philosophie von Max Scheler,* 203–19.

Mall, Ram Adbar. "Schelers Idee einer werdenden Anthropologie und Geschichtsteleologie." In Orth and Pfafferott, *Studien zur Philosophie von Max Scheler,* 35–69.

Massimilla, Edoardo. "Ernst Robert Curtius: La critica a Weber e l'influenza di Scheler." *Giornale Critico della Filosofia Italiana* 18, no. 2 (1998): 241–63.

Melle, Ullrich. "Schelersche Motive in Husserls Freiburger Ethik." In Pfafferott, *Vom umsturz der Werte in der modernen Gesellschaft,* 203–19.

Michalski, Mark. *Fremdwahrnehmung und Mitsein: Zur Grundlegung der Sozialphilosophie im Denken Max Schelers und Martin Heideggers.* Abhandlungen zur Philosophie, Psychologie und Pädagogok, bd. 244. Bonn: Bouvier, 1997.

Mikoshiba, Y. "Ueber den Begriff der Weltoffentheit bei Max Scheler" (in Japanese). In *Shisosi-wo-yomu,* edited by Hideo Mineshima. Tokyo: Hokujushuppan, 1995.

Moosa, Imtiaz. "Are Values Independent Entities? Scheler's Discussion of the Relation between Values and Persons." *Journal of the British Society for Phenomenology* 24, no. 3 (1993): 265–75.

———. "A Critical Examination of Scheler's Justification of the Existence of Values." *Journal of Value Inquiry* (1991): 23–41.

———. "Formalism of Kant's A Priori versus Scheler's Material A Priori." *International Studies in Philosophy* 27, no. 2 (1995): 33–47.

Nusser, Karl-Heinz. "Wissenschaft, Weltanschauung, und Charisma bei Max Scheler und Max Weber." In Pfafferott, *Vom umsturz der Werte in der modernen Gesellschaft,* 251–63.

Olmo, Javier. "El amor al projimo en la etica fenomenologica de los valores." *Diálogo Filosófica nel 500 Europeo* 6, no. 2 (1990): 195–212.

Orth, Ernst Wolfgang. "Lebensformen und Werte." In Orth and Pfafferott, *Studien zur Philosophie von Max Scheler,* 297–305.

Orth, Ernst Wolfgang, and Gerhard Pfafferott, eds. *Studien zur Philosophie von Max Scheler.* Phänomenologische Forschungen, bd. 28–29. Freiburg/München: Karl Alber, 1994.

Ortiz-Ortiz, Rafael. "Scheler and Hartmann: In the Threshold of Axiological Ontology" (in Spanish). *Fronesis: Revista de Filosofía Jurídica, Social y Política* 3, no. 2 (1996): 1–66.

Pazanin, Ante. "Relevance of Max Scheler's Philosophy and Values: Introductory." *Filozofska Iztrazivanja* 16, no. 1 (1996): 87–92.

Perrin, Ron. *Max Scheler's Concept of the Person: An Ethics of Humanism.* New York: St. Martin's Press, 1991.

Petropulos, William. *The Person as "Imago Dei": Augustine and Max Scheler in Eric Voegelin's "Herrschaftslehre" and "The Political Religions."* Occasional papers. Eric-Voegelin-Archiv. Ludwig-Maximilians-Universitat, Munchen; 4. 1997.

Pfafferott, Gerhard. "Präferenzwandel und sittliche Wertordnung." In Pfafferott, *Vom umsturz der Werte in der modernen Gesellschaft,* 100–112.

———. "Vorwort Studien zur Philosophie von Max Scheler. Internationales Max-Scheler-Kolloquium 'Der Mensch im Weltalter des Ausgleichs.' " In Orth and Pfafferott, *Studien zur Philosophie von Max Scheler,* 7–8.

———, ed. *Vom umsturz der Werte in der modernen Gesellschaft.* Bonn: Bouvier Verlag, 1997.

Pigalev, Alexandre. "Wertewandel, Phänomenologie der Liebe, und die Frage nach dem fremden Ich im Denken Max Schelers." In Pfafferott, *Vom umsturz der Werte in der modernen Gesellschaft,* 53–61.

Platter, G. "Max Schelers Lehre von Politik und Moral." *Forum der Forschung* 1 (1995).

Pöggeler, Otto. "Ressentiment and Virtue in Max Scheler's Thought." *Filozofska Iztrazivanja* 16, no. 1 (1996): 129–39.

———. "Ressentiment und Tugend bei Max Scheler." In Pfafferott, *Vom umsturz der Werte in der modernen Gesellschaft,* 7–19.

Poree, Jerome. "Normativite et Verification immanentes des Valeurs chez Max Scheler." *Frieberger Zeitschrift für Philosophie und Theologie* 44, nos. 1–2 (1997): 104–16.

Pressler, Charles A., and Fabio B. Dasilva. *Sociology and Interpretation: From Weber to Habermas.* Albany: SUNY Press, 1996.

Pyka, Marek. "Hume and Scheler: At the Base of the Controversy between Naturalism and Ethical Emotional Intuitionism." *Kwartalnik Filozoficzny* 24, no. 2 (1996): 51–60.

Ramirez, Salvador Verges. "La persona es un 'valor por si misma,' segun Max Scheler." *Pensamiento* 55 (1999): 245–67.

Ramos, Antonio Pintor. "Schelers Einfluß auf das Denken der spanischsprachigen Welt." In Orth and Pfafferott, *Studien zur Philosophie von Max Scheler,* 314–31.

Sander, Angelika. "Asceticism and the Confirmation of the World." *Filozofska Iztrazivanja* 16, no. 1 (1996): 141–56.

———. "Askese und Weltbejahung: Zum Problem des Dualismus in der Anthropologie und Metaphysik Max Schelers." In Pfafferott, *Vom umsturz der Werte in der modernen Gesellschaft,* 34–52.

———. *Mensch, Subjekt, Person: die Dezentrierung des Subjekts in der Philosophie Max Schelers.* Abhandlungen zur Philosophie, Psychologie und Pädagogik, bd. 240. Bonn: Bouvier, 1996.

Schalow, Frank. "The Anomaly of World: From Scheler to Heidegger." *Man and World* 24, no. 1 (1991): 75–87.

———. "Religious Transcendence: Scheler's Forgotten Quest." *Philosophy and Theology: Marquette University Quarterly* 4, no. 4 (1990): 351–64.

Schneider, Gabriele. " 'Vorbilder' in Max Schelers wertfundiertem Ethikkonzept." In Pfafferott, *Vom umsturz der Werte in der modernen Gesellschaft,* 180–200.

Seifert, Josef. "Schelers Denken des absoluten Ursprungs. Zum Verhältnis zwischen Schelers Metaphysik und Religionsphilosophie zum ontologischen Gottesbeweis." In Bermes, Henckmann, and Leonardy, *Ursprung des Denkens—Denken des Ursprungs,* 34–53.

Sepp, Hans Rainer. "Denkt Scheler über den Gegensatz von Relativismus und Universalismus hinaus?" *Studien zur Interkulturellen Philosophie* 5 (1996): 95–104.

———. "Das Werk Max Schelers in der gegenwartigen Edition und Diskussion." *Philosophische Rundschau* 42, no. 2 (1995): 110–28.

Spader, Peter H. "Max Scheler's Practical Ethics and the Model Person." *American Catholic Philosophical Quarterly* 69, no. 1 (1995): 63–81.

———. "Scheler's Criticism of the Emptiness of Kant's Formal Ethics." In Bermes, Henckmann, and Leonardy, *Ursprung des Denkens—Denken des Ursprungs,* 121–36.

Stikkers, Kenneth W. "Technologies of the World, Technologies of the Self: A Schelerian Critique of Dewey and Hickman." *Journal of Speculative Philosophy* 10, no. 1 (1996): 62–73.

Tallon, Andrew. *Head and Heart: Affection, Cognition, Volition as Triune Consciousness.* New York: Fordham University Press, 1997.

Theisen, Marion. *Max Schelers Metapsychologie als Grundlage für einen integrativen anthropologischen Ansatz: eine Synthese der ver-*

schiedenen Paradigmen. In *Psychologie und Psychosomatik,* European University Studies. Series 20, Philosophy; vol. 413. Frankfurt am Main: P. Lang, 1994.

Thiemer, Elfi. *Solidarität begreifen: Karl Marx, Max Scheler, Aristoteles, Talcott Parsons: 4 Wege zum Verständnis eines menschlichen Miteinander.* European University Studies. Series 31, Political Science; vol. 306. Frankfurt am Main: P. Lang, 1996.

Vacek, Edward. "Contemporary Ethics and Scheler's Phenomenology of Community." *Philosophy Today* 35, no. 2 (1991): 161–74.

Van Hooft, Stan. "Scheler on Sharing Emotions." *Philosophy Today* 38, no. 1 (1994): 18–28.

Veauthier, Frank W. "Social Apriori of Responsibility in Scheler's Phenomenology" (in Serbo-Croatian). *Filozofska Iztrazivanja* (1990): 209–26.

Verducci, Daniela. "L'analogia depotenziata. Ovvero: elementi di metafisica fenomenologica nella filosofia di Max Scheler." In *Studi di filosofia transcendentale,* edited by V. Melchiorre, 215–58. Milano, 1993.

———. "Meraviglia e disincanto nel pensiero di Max Scheler." In *Interpretazione e meraviglia. XIV Colloquio sulla interpretazione 1993,* edited by G. Galli, 53–64. Pisa, 1994.

———. "Scheler—Duns Scoto: Volontarismo e interpretazione del moderno." In *Via Scoti. Methodologica ad mentem Joannis Duns Scoti. Atti del Congresso Scotistico Internazionale, Roma 1993,* 1127–44. Roma, 1995.

Vergés, Salvador. *El hombre, su valor en Max Scheler.* 1st ed., *Biblioteca universitaria de filosofía.* Barcelona, 1993.

Waldenfels, Bernhard. "Value Qualities or Experience Requests?" *Filozofska Iztrazivanja* 16, no. 1 (1996): 93–99.

———. "Wertqualitäten oder Erfahrungsansprüche?" In Orth and Pfafferott, *Studien zur Philosophie von Max Scheler,* 306–13.

Weiss, Dennis M. "Max Scheler and Philosophical Anthropology." *Philosophy Today* 42, no. 3 (1998): 235–49.

Zhok, Andrea. *Intersoggettività e fondamento in Max Scheler. Pubblicazioni della Facoltà di lettere e filosofia dell'Università degli studi di Milano; 172.* Firenze: La nuova Italia, 1997.

PERMISSIONS

I would like to thank the following publishers for granting me permission to use all or part of the following articles I had previously published:

British Journal of Aesthetics for "Aesthetics, Morals, and Max Scheler's Non-Formal Values." *British Journal of Aesthetics* 16, no. 3 (1976): 230–36.

JBSP: Journal of the British Society for Phenomenology for "Scheler's Phenomenological Given." *JBSP: Journal of the British Society for Phenomenology* 9, no. 3 (1978): 150–57.

Karl Alber for "Scheler's Ethics vs. the Ethics of Success." In *Person und Wert: Scheler's "Formalismus" Perspektiven und Wirkungen,* edited by Christian Bermes, Wolfhart Henckmann, and Heinz Leonardy, 192–203. Freiburg/München: Verlag Karl Alber, 2000.

Kritisches Jahrbuch der Philosophie for "Scheler's Criticism of the Emptiness of Kant's Formal Ethics." In *Kritisches Jahrbuch der Philosophie Band 3: Denken des Ursprungs-Ursprung des Denkens: Schelers Philosophie und ihre Anfänge in Jena,* 121–36. Wurzburg: Königshausen & Neuman, 1998.

Listening: Journal of Religion and Culture for "A Change of Heart: Scheler's Ordo Amoris, Repentance and Rebirth." *Listening: Journal of Religion and Culture* 21, no. 3 (1986): 188–96.

Modern Schoolman for "A New Look at Scheler's Third Period." *Modern Schoolman* 51, no. 2 (1974): 139–58.

The Ontario Institute for Studies in Education for "Scheler, Schutz, and Intersubjectivity." *Reflections: Essays in Phenomenology* (Canada) 4 (Summer/Fall 1983): 5–13.

Philosophy Today for "The Primacy of the Heart: Scheler's Challenge to Phenomenology." *Philosophy Today* 29 (Fall 1985): 223–29.

I would like to give special thanks to Robert Woods, the editor of the *American Catholic Philosophical Quarterly,* for transferring copyright back to me for the following articles:

"Max Scheler's Practical Ethics and the Model Person." *American Catholic Philosophical Quarterly* 69, no. 1 (1995): 63–81.

"Person, Acts and Meaning: Max Scheler's Insight." *New Scholasticism* 59, no. 2 (1985): 200–212.

I would also like to thank the following publishers for permission to quote from the following sources:

Beacon Press for *Man's Place in Nature* by Max Scheler, Copyright © 1961 by Beacon Press; originally published in German under the title *Die Stellung des Menschen im Kosmos,* Copyright © 1928 by A. Franke A.G., Bern. Reprinted by permission of Beacon Press, Boston.

HarperCollins and SCM Press Ltd. for Max Scheler, *On the Eternal in Man.* Copyright © 1960 SCM Press Ltd. Reprinted 1972 by arrangement with Harper and Row Publishers in an unaltered and unabridged edition as an Archon Book by the Shoe String Press, Inc.

Marquette University Press for Max Scheler, *Ressentiment,* in the Marquette Studies in Philosophy IV, Andrew Tallon, editor. Milwaukee, Wis.: Marquette University Press, 1994. Printed with permission of Marquette University Press.

Northwestern University Press for Max Scheler, *Formalism in Ethics and Non-Formal Ethics of Values: A New Attempt toward the Foundation of an Ethical Personalism.* Translated by Manfred S. Frings and Roger L. Funk. Northwestern University Studies in Phenomenology and Existential Philosophy, John Wild, editor. Evanston, Ill.: Northwestern University Press, 1973. Copyright © 1973 by Northwestern University Press.

Northwestern University Press for Max Scheler, *Selected Philosophical Essays.* Translated by David R. Lachterman, Northwestern University Studies in Phenomenology and Existential Philosophy, John Wild, editor. Evanston, Ill.: Northwestern University Press, 1973. Copyright © 1973 by Northwestern University Press.

Ohio University Press for Philip Blosser, *Scheler's Critique of Kant's Ethics*. Series in Continental Thought, no. 22. Athens: Ohio University Press, 1995. Reprinted with permission of Ohio University Press.

Pearson Higher Education for Immanuel Kant, *Foundations of the Metaphysics of Morals*. Translated by Lewis White Beck. Indianapolis: Bobbs-Merrill, 1959.

Routledge (Taylor and Francis ITPS) for Max Scheler, *The Nature of Sympathy*. London: Routledge & Kegan Paul, 1954.

INDEX